Disability Studies Today

Disability Studies Today

Edited by
Colin Barnes, Mike Oliver and Len Barton

polity

Copyright © this collection Polity Press 2002

First published in 2002 by Polity Press in association
with Blackwell Publishers Ltd, a Blackwell Publishing Company.

Editorial office:
Polity Press
65 Bridge Street
Cambridge CB2 1UR, UK

Marketing and production:
Blackwell Publishers Ltd
108 Cowley Road
Oxford OX4 1JF, UK

Published in the USA by
Blackwell Publishers Inc.
350 Main Street
Malden, MA 02148, USA

A catalogue record for this book is available from the British Library.

Library of Congress Cataloging-in-Publication Data

Disability studies today / edited by Colin Barnes, Mike Oliver, and Len Barton.
   p. cm.
   Includes bibliographical references and index.
      ISBN 0-7456-2656-4 (hc)–ISBN 0-7456-2657-2 (pb)
      1. Disability studies. 2. Sociology of disability. 3. People with disabilities
   I. Barnes, Colin. II. Oliver, Mike. III. Barton, Len.
HV1568.2 D595 2002
305.9'0816—dc21

                                                                    2002001668

Typeset in 10 on 12 pt Sabon
by Kolam Information Services Pvt Ltd., Pondicherry, India

Printed in Great Britain by MPG Books, Bodmin, Cornwall
This book is printed on acid-free paper.

Contents

vi   *Contents*

Contributors

Paul Abberley is Tutor/Counsellor for the Open University, Milton Keynes, working in South Devon, England.

Gary L. Albrecht is Professor of Public Health, Disability and Human Development at the University of Illinois at Chicago, United States of America.

Colin Barnes is Professor of Disability Studies at the Centre for Disability Studies, Department of Sociology and Social Policy, University of Leeds, England.

Len Barton is Professor of Inclusive Education at the Institute of Education, University of London, England.

Peter Beresford is Professor of Social Policy and Director of the Centre for Citizen Participation at Brunel University, England.

Anne Borsay is Reader in the Department of History at the University of Wales, Lampeter, Ceredigion, United Kingdom.

Harlan Hahn gained his Ph.D. in Political Science in 1964, M.S. in Rehabilitation in 1983, and has published over a hundred journal articles and seven books in the United States of America.

Chris Holden is a lecturer in Social Policy at Brunel University, England, with research interests in the political economy of the welfare state and globalization.

Bill Hughes is Head of the Division of Sociology and Social Policy, Glasgow Caledonian University, Glasgow, Scotland.

Phil Lee is Head of the Centre for Studies in the Social Sciences at Edge Hill College (Associate College of the University of Lancaster), Ormskirk, England.

Geof Mercer is Senior Lecturer in the Department of Sociology and Social Policy, University of Leeds, England.

Mike Oliver is Professor of Disability Studies in the School of Social Sciences at the University of Greenwich, England.

Marcia H. Rioux is Professor and Chair of the School of Health Policy and Management at York University, Toronto, Canada.

John Swain is Professor of Disability and Inclusion in the School of Health, Social Work and Education at the University of Northumbria in Newcastle, England.

Carol Thomas is Senior Lecturer in Applied Social Science in the Department of Applied Social Science at the University of Lancaster, England.

Ayesha Vernon is Senior Lecturer and Senior Research Fellow in Disability Studies in the School of Health, Social Work and Education at the University of Northumbria in Newcastle, England.

1

Introduction

Colin Barnes, Mike Oliver and Len Barton

Over recent years there has been an unprecedented upsurge of interest in the general area of disability amongst social scientists in universities and colleges across the world. There are now 'disability studies' courses and specialist journals in the United States and Canada (Albrecht et al., 2001), Britain (Barton and Oliver 1997), and Australia and New Zealand (Sullivan and Muntford 1998). There are also networks of scholars studying disability in the Nordic countries (Tideman 1999) and throughout Europe (van Oorschot and Hvinden 2001). This has been accompanied by an increasingly expansive literature from a variety of perspectives. Recent examples include cultural studies (Mitchell and Snyder 2001), development studies (Stone 1999), geography (Gleeson 1999), history (Longmore and Umansky 2001), philosophy (Wendell 1996), social policy (Drake 1999), social psychology (Marks 1999) and sociology (Barnes et al., 1999). Perhaps inevitably, with this heightened interest a number of important challenges and debates have emerged which raise a number of important questions for all those interested in this newly emergent and increasingly important field of enquiry.

This Reader aims to provide an introduction to, and an overview of, these concerns and controversies. Although the field is increasingly inter-disciplinary in nature, the emphasis is predominantly a sociological one, as it is our contention that sociological theories and insights, whether intentionally or otherwise, have and can continue to play a crucial role in the development of disability studies. Although the focus is primarily on theoretical innovation and advancement, the arguments presented here have important political and policy implications for both disabled and non-disabled people.

Disability studies, like ethnic, women's, and gay and lesbian studies, has developed from a position of engagement and activism rather than one of detachment. Thus, as editors, we have sought contributors who could write from such a position. This is because it is our firm conviction that this enhances, rather than detracts from, the quality of their contributions, and that the dialogue within these chapters will provide yet further stimulus for the future development of disability studies.

Background

The increased interest in disability in the academy should not be surprising, given that there is now a growing recognition that it raises a number of important theoretical and empirical questions at both the individual and the structural level that are not easily answered with reference to established wisdom. Disability is both a common personal experience and a global phenomenon, with widespread economic, cultural and political implications for society as a whole. People with accredited impairments have existed since the dawn of time, and have had a presence in all societies.

Recent estimates suggest that there are around 8.2 million disabled people in Britain, 50 million in the European Union and 500 million worldwide. Moreover, these figures are set to rise dramatically over the coming decades, both in the rich, 'developed' nations of the minority world and in the poorer, 'developing' countries of the majority world (IDF 1998). In rich and poor countries alike, disabled people are amongst the poorest of the poor (Coleridge 1993: Stone 1999: WHO 2001), which raises a number of issues for politicians and policy makers at all levels and in all states.

Since its politicization in the 1960s by disability activists and disability organizations across the world, disability has become an increasingly important issue for politicians and policy makers at both the national and the international levels. Many national governments now have some form of anti-discrimination law or policy to secure the equal rights of disabled people. Early examples include Britain's 1970 Chronically Sick and Disabled Person's Act and the American 1973 Rehabilitation Act. Although relatively ineffective, both promoted improved environmental access and the development of more comprehensive services for disabled people. The latter included the historic Section 504 which prohibited discrimination against disabled people in federally funded programmes.

Government responsibility for securing equal rights for disabled people was formally recognized at the international level by the United Nations in 1981, the UN's International Year of Disabled People. The following year the UN General Assembly adopted by consensus a 'World Programme of Action Concerning Disabled Persons', outlining a global strategy on the prevention of disability and the realization of the full potential of disabled people. The next ten years were designated 'The UN Decade of Disabled Persons'. Between 1990 and 1993 member states in close collaboration with international disabled peoples' organizations developed 'The Standard Rules on the Equalization of Opportunities for Persons with Disabilities'. There are twenty-two Standard Rules covering medical and community-based services and facilities. The Rules were formally adopted by the UN in 1993 (WHO, 2001).

The coming of disability studies

Prior to the 1980s, one or two notable exceptions aside, academic interest in disability was confined almost exclusively to conventional, individualistic medical explanations, and even where others had become involved, they tended to reproduce disability uncritically within these frameworks. A classic exemplar is found in the work of the influential American functionalist sociologist Talcott Parsons (1951), which centred on medicine as a mechanism of social integration and control. Since then various 'illness' perspectives have predominated in American sociology in particular. Initially, Parsons's (1951) interpretation of sickness as a social status and the rights and responsibilities associated with the 'sick role' exerted a considerable influence within sociology throughout the world. Subsequently, this work was supplemented by various interactionist and interpretive perspectives.

For Parsons sickness, whether short or long term, is a deviation from the norm. Consequently the sociological analysis of the social responses to disability became largely the preserve of sociologists interested in the reaction to and management of ascribed social deviance. One notable example is Erving Goffman's (1968) account of the interactions between the 'normal' and 'abnormal' entitled *Stigma*. During the following decade particular attention was paid to the social construction of 'mental illness'. Examples include Thomas Scheff (1966) and D. L. Rosenhan (1975). Around the same time a psychoanalyst, Thomas Szasz (1961), had denied the very existence of mental illness, the validity of psychiatry as a legitimate medical discipline, and the rehabilitation potential of psychiatric hospitals. For Szasz, the term 'mental illness' was a substitute for a multitude of problems of living. The idea that mental illness and other forms of ascribed social deviance are little more than social constructs generated by an increasingly dominant, moralistic social order was given a further boost by the writings of the French philosopher Michel Foucault (1975, 1979). Foucault's work was particularly influential on the development of postmodern thinking in a variety of fields, including disability studies, during the 1990s, as we shall see in several of the contributions to this book.

However, within sociology interest in the general area of 'disability' increased during the late 1960s and 1970s with the publication in the United States of Robert Scott's *The Making of Blind Men* (1969) and Gary Albrecht's edited collection *The Sociology of Physical Disability and Rehabilitation* (1976) and in Britain of Mildred Blaxter's *The Meaning of Disability* (1976) and Peter Townsend's *Poverty in the United Kingdom* (1979). But whilst each of these studies drew attention to the various economic and social consequences of the ascription of a conventional 'disabled' identity, none made any serious attempt to question its ideological underpinnings: what has variously been called the 'individual', 'medical' or 'personal tragedy' model of disability. In sum, while this work recognized the significance of economic, social and cultural factors in the production of disability, the causes of the widespread economic and social deprivation encountered by disabled people were located within the individual and their impairment. The theoretical insights that had been applied to the concept of mental illness were never extended to address other impairments, particularly 'physical disability'.

The challenge to orthodox views came not from within the academy but from disabled people themselves. Although the origins of political activism amongst people with accredited impairments can be traced back to the nineteenth century (Campbell and Oliver 1996; Longmore and Umansky 2001), it escalated significantly during the 1960s and 1970s. Inspired by the political and social upheavals of the period, disabled people began to organize collectively in increasingly large numbers to protest against their incarceration in residential institutions, their poverty and the discrimination they encountered. The pattern is demonstrated across the United States, Canada and various countries throughout Europe. Notable early examples include the American Independent Living Movement and the Swedish Self Advocacy Movement, as well as the formation of The Disablement Income Group (DIG) and the Union of the Physically Impaired Against Segregation (UPIAS) in Britain (Campbell and Oliver 1996).

But the British experience is especially important, since it generated a radical and controversial new approach to theory and practice now generally referred to as 'the social model of disability'. Here the activities of grass roots organizations controlled and run by disabled people, such as the UPIAS and the Liberation Network of People with Disabilities, are especially important. These and similar organizations provided the fertile ground in which disabled activists could explore and reconfigure the whole notion of disability. These 'organic intellectuals' (Gramsci 1971) produced an impressive body of work, the impact of which is only now being fully appreciated. Key texts include Paul Hunt's edited collection of disabled people's narratives entitled *Stigma: The Experience of Disability* (1966), UPIAS's *Fundamental Principles of Disability* (1976), Vic Finkelstein's *Attitudes and Disabled People* (1980), Alan Sutherland's *Disabled We Stand* (1981), Mike Oliver's *Social Work with Disabled People* (1983) and *The Politics of Disablement* (1990).

Drawing implicitly, if not explicitly, on both personal experience and sociological insights, this literature constitutes a direct challenge to conventional thinking and practice on disability. For example, although not a sociologist, Paul Hunt, a resident in a residential home for 'physically disabled people' during the 1950s and 1960s, 'read a lot to supplement his curtailed education' and was 'especially interested in the social and psychological aspects of disablement' (Hunt 1966: 144). Moreover, Finkelstein's early work is heavily influenced by the writings of Karl Marx and Friedrich Engels (see Feuer 1969). As noted earlier, traditional approaches centred almost exclusively on individual limitations, whether real or imagined, as the principal cause of the multiple deprivations encountered by disabled people. By contrast, the social interpretation of disability argues that people with accredited or perceived impairments, regardless of cause, are disabled by society's failure to accommodate their needs.

This approach does not deny the significance of impairment in disabled people's lives, but concentrates instead on the various barriers, economic, political and social, constructed on top of impairment. Thus 'disability' is not a product of individual failings, but is socially created; explanations of its changing character are found in the organization and structures of society. Rather than identifying disability as an individual limitation, the social model identifies society as the problem, and looks to fundamental political and cultural changes to generate solutions.

Disability studies and the academy

None the less, although the emergence of the social model of disability provided the 'big idea' (Hasler 1993) for the mobilization of disabled people across the UK during the 1980s and 1990s, it was slow to find acceptance in sociology departments in British universities. This is especially surprising given sociology's traditional focus on social inequality and divisions associated with social class, gender and race. Studies of disability have been typically situated within the context of medical sociology and the sociology of health and illness courses where interactionist and phenomenological perspectives have prevailed. These have documented the impact and meaning of the onset of specific acute and chronic illness. This has been accompanied by a largely atheoretical tradition of socio-medical research driven by practical medical and health service concerns. The outcome is an extensive literature that chronicles the extent and nature of chronic illness, its consequences for daily living, and its impact on social relationships, the sense of self and identity (Williams 1997).

Consequently, despite the sociological insights of social model thinking, Britain's first disability studies course was not developed within a sociology department or even within a conventional university setting. It was conceived and produced by an interdisciplinary team at the Open University (OU) in 1975. A key figure in the development of this course was a disabled South African clinical psychologist, Vic Finkelstein; he was also an anti-apartheid and disability activist, and a founder member of the UPIAS. The OU provided an appropriate setting for this new course, as its emergence signalled a radical new approach to university education. It began operations in 1971, and had no formal entry qualifications apart from being over 18, resident in the UK, and competent in English. Pioneering a variety of multi-media teaching strategies and distance learning techniques, the OU provided unprecedented opportunities for all those disadvantaged by Britain's education system, including disabled people.

The course attracted more than 1,200 students in its first year. These included professionals, voluntary workers and disabled people from all over the country. Entitled 'The Handicapped Person in the Community', its stated aim was to help students improve their 'professional and social skills in order to assist handicapped people to achieve *maximum autonomy*' (Finkelstein 1997: 41; emphasis added). From the outset the course was criticized for its 'sociological bias' (Finkelstein 1997: 46). It was updated twice before its abolition in 1994, and each time more and more disabled people were involved in the production of course materials. The final version of the programme was re-titled 'The Disabling Society', to reflect its wider content. Over the years the OU team generated a wealth of material, which provided the basis for the development of a whole host of disability studies courses and professional training schemes at both the undergraduate and postgraduate levels in mainstream colleges and universities across the UK. Notable examples include *Handicap in a Social World* edited by Anne Brechin and Penny Liddiard (1981) and *Disabling Barriers – Enabling Environments* edited by John Swain, Vic Finkelstein, Sally French and Mike Oliver (1993).

By way of contrast, disability was introduced on to the mainstream academic agenda in the United States and Canada in the 1970s. Again the link between disability activism and the academy was instrumental in this process. Disability rights advocates and academics concerned with disability issues came together at numerous conferences and discovered that they shared similar concerns. Several were both advocates and academics, 'much like the participants in numerous civil rights movements'. A major catalyst in bringing these two groups together was the 1977 'White House Conference on Handicapped Individuals', which attracted over 3,000 delegates. In the same year the first disability studies course was offered. It was in the area of medical sociology, and focused on the experience of living with a 'disability, a critical life experience which many persons avoid recognising' (Pfeiffer and Yoshida 1995: 476). The main tutor was a disabled person. In 1981 a disabled sociologist and the chairperson of the Medical Sociology Section of the American Sociology Association, Irving K. Zola, founded the *Disability Studies Quarterly* and co-founded the American-based Society for Disability Studies. In the same year twelve disability studies courses were being taught in American institutions. By 1986 the number had risen to 23 (Pfeiffer and Yoshida 1995).

As in the UK, these early activities generated a small but significant body of work. Examples include Frank Bowe's *Handicapping America* (1978) and Zola's *Missing Pieces: A Chronicle of Living with a Disability* (1982). These and other studies drew attention to the disabling tendencies of American rehabilitation programmes as well as in American society. However, this literature, along with American approaches generally, failed to recognize the significance of the distinction between impairment and disability that characterized the British social model approach. In keeping with the traditions of American pragmatism, the arguments for civil rights for disabled people were linked with a minority group approach, rather than providing a comprehensive theoretical explanation for disability and the exclusion of disabled people from the mainstream of everyday life. Moreover, it has recently been suggested that socio-political interpretations of disability have hitherto had relatively little impact on American sociology (Gordon and Rosenblum 2001).

However, over the last few years, a contrary and more radical perspective has emerged, championed by a small but vocal band of predominantly disabled scholars, many of whom are based in the humanities and cultural studies fields, in universities in North America and Australasia. This has led to a growing demand for the development of a more critical, interdisciplinary field of enquiry more in keeping with the socio-political position associated with the social model approach (Rioux and Bach 1994; Davis 1995; Meekoshe and Dowse 1997; Linton 1998; Albrecht et al. 2001). These initiatives provide increasingly common ground between academics and researchers in the disability studies field, and signify a growing interest in the social-political approach pioneered by British writers. All of which has stimulated lively debates about the best ways forward for the future development of the social model of disability and the relations between disability activists and academics. It is these debates which form the starting point for the collection of papers that follow.

What is disability studies, and how is it reflected in this book?

In many ways this collection charts the changing nature of disability studies: that is the transition from a relatively straightforward demand by disabled people for a shift in emphasis away from the individual and on to the structural and cultural forces that shape their lives into an increasingly complex body of knowledge. For the originators of the OU course, disability studies concerned the 'study of disabled people's lifestyles and aspirations' (Finkelstein 1997: 37). As a consequence, the content of the OU course, and the few others that were developed from it in Britain during the 1980s, was concerned primarily with social policy concerns and the practicalities of coming to terms with a disabled lifestyle in a world designed almost exclusively for non-disabled living. The establishment in 1986 of the first international journal devoted exclusively to disability issues, *Disability, Handicap and Society*, renamed *Disability and Society* in 1993, by two of the co-editors of this book, Len Barton and Mike Oliver, provided an appropriate forum for the further development of a truly comprehensive 'disability theory'.

This was forthcoming in 1990 with the publication of Oliver's *The Politics of Disablement*. Drawing on a variety of influences including personal experience, the writings of disabled people such as Finkelstein and Hunt, and the sociological insights of Marx, Auguste Comte (Lenzer 1975) and Antonio Gramsci (1971) amongst others, the book provides a theoretical explanation of the materialist and ideological foundations upon which contemporary responses to disability are based. Generally associated with the social model of disability, this book has had a considerable influence both within and without universities and colleges across the world.

As well as providing a much-needed theoretical dimension to the disability studies agenda, the book generated considerable debate amongst both activists and academics alike, not least concerning the role of non-disabled academics and previous studies of the experience of impairment. Other concerns have been expressed regarding the social model's apparent neglect of the experience of impairment, the body, and questions of difference in relation to gender, ethnicity, sexuality and social class. Equally important is the contention that the largely materialist interpretation of history generally associated with social model writings is overly simplistic. This is said to undermine the importance of cultural factors in the oppression of disabled people and to over-emphasize the roles of paid work and the disabled people's movement in the struggle for equality. More recently, questions have been raised regarding the social model's Anglo-American leanings and its potential inapplicability within a majority world context in terms of both policy and politics. All of which raises further issues regarding the social model's use value as a meaningful theoretical base upon which to conduct socio-logical research. It is these issues and concerns that underlie the chapters for this book.

In chapter 2 Gary Albrecht argues that the development of disability studies should be examined and understood in context. He discusses how American pragmatism and sociology influenced its development in the United States and directly or indirectly addresses a number of important questions. These include the contention that those involved in disability studies share a common discourse, that leaders and spokespeople in the field represent all disabled people, and that only disabled people can effectively understand disability and contribute to the development of the discipline. Other concerns include whether disability studies share a common history and intellectual tradition across countries and through-out history, and whether a disability studies perspective can generate an agreed agenda for health and welfare policy.

In response Albrecht argues that pragmatism had a profound influence on American thinking, social policy and world-view. When combined with the early development of American sociology – notably including survey research and the interactionism of the Chicago school – it pro-vided a broad framework and methodology for addressing disability issues. He also shows how the American Independent Living Movement exerted political pressure in the American context, and shaped disability studies as a field. He concludes by suggesting that disability studies in the

United States have been characterized by a historical insensibility and a disconcerting insularity. He maintains that a respectful dialogue between scholars, policy makers and activists might address these concerns.

A similar theme emerges in the third chapter, by Carol Thomas. She focuses on the reconceptualization of disability by mainly British writers. In her review of the emergence of disability studies as an academic discipline, she centres on various developments surrounding the social model. She maintains that in the early stages the flesh that was added to the bones of the model had a materialist cast. Here the roots of the socially engendered restrictions on activity experienced by people with impairments are sought in the social relations of the capitalist system of commodity production. Contemporary exclusion is located in the operation of socially created 'social barriers'. More recently, she argues, and as disability studies has gathered strength, other theoretical perspectives, much influenced by social constructionist thought, have also made their presence felt in disability studies.

The social model itself has been criticized and vigorously defended. Ensuing debates about disability have demanded an engagement with the significance of culture in the creation of disability and with the matter of impairment itself. The intersection of disability with other forms of oppression – gender, race, sexual orientation and to a lesser extent social class and age – has been placed on the agenda by disabled feminists and those who are of a more postmodernist persuasion. This has demanded that the lived experiences of categories of disabled people (men, women, straight, gay, and impairment-specific groups such as people with 'learning difficulties' or 'mental health' system users and survivors) be better understood, and, in a postmodernist sense, that these categories are themselves deconstructed because they are essentialist and discursively constructed.

She argues that debates within disability studies and between disability studies writers and those in other disciplines, and especially medical sociologists, are engines for the formulation of an even more sophisticated materialist sociology of disability. For Thomas this must encompass the further recognition and theorization of the psycho-emotional dimensions of disability: namely, those disablist practices that undermine the psychological and emotional well-being of people with impairments – what disabled activists have referred to as 'internalised oppression' (Rieser 1990).

Bill Hughes takes up the question of impairment in the fourth chapter. He argues that the sociology of the body offers an opportunity for drawing disability studies into mainstream sociology, but suggests that it has so far failed to do so. He maintains that the problem for the latter is that the accusations of disablism are warranted, since it has ignored the question of disability. Conversely, the problem for disability studies is that it has all but cut itself off from the possibility of developing a meaningful sociology of impairment. In tracing the development of orthodox, 'medical' sociological approaches to the study of the body, he maintains that, despite the partial advances offered by labelling theory and Goffman's study *Stigma* (1968), sociology has reinforced the physician's view that disability is a sickness. It is the antithesis of the conception of disability as a corporeal essence provided by disability studies, as it emerged from the social model of disability, that makes sociology a truly valuable frame of reference for reflections on disability. However, the social model pushed the study of impairment to the fringes of disability studies, and it is only recently that it and the sociology of the body have combined to try to map out the case for a sociology of impairment.

Drawing on research that examines the multiple oppression encountered by disabled women from minority ethnic communities, Ayesha Vernon and John Swain remind us in chapter 5 that disabled people will not judge disability theory by its contribution to academic or research discourses, but ultimately by its role in initiating social change. It is in these terms that they argue that a consideration of social divisions needs to inform the development of disability theory. Again feminist and postmodern insights are pertinent: in particular, the recognition of the contradiction that women are simultaneously united through the imbalance of power relations between women and men in the economic and social structures of society, but divided through multiple social divisions. They argue that similar contradictions are relevant to an understanding of the oppression experienced by disabled people. They maintain that the challenges of addressing the contradictions between commonality and diversity are critical to the future development of disability theory. In order to theorize and promote the development of a meaningful inclusive society, the relationships between disability, ethnicity, sexuality, age and gender must be critically examined.

In the following chapter Anne Borsay draws our attention to the point that history is a missing piece of the jigsaw in disability studies. She argues that whilst the field has expanded from its origins in social theory and social policy to include politics, culture, leisure and the media, historical perspectives across the entire range of disabled people's experiences are virtually non-existent. This, she contends, is due to the incompatibilities between sociology and history. Hence, an evaluation of the historical models developed by social scientists is used to launch a social history of disability in which materialism and culturalism are complementary rather than mutually exclusive. A comprehensive historical survey is not attempted. Instead, attention is centred on the interface between physical impairment, charity and medicine in the late nineteenth and early twentieth centuries. Demonstrating the usefulness of historical sources, moral and medical surveillance procedures and the ensuing resistance strategies are examined. The chapter concludes by exploring the place of the past in shaping present responses to, and the identities of, disabled people.

In chapter 7 Paul Abberley argues that if we are to explain disability as a form of social oppression, then we must develop an understanding of what society might look like if people with impairments are not to be disabled. This is necessary if we are to develop effective policies to combat social exclusion. To achieve this, he considers how two forms of classical social theory, one conservative and the other radical, address the relationship between work and social inclusion. He maintains that, despite their differences, they are similar in the sense that both imply the inevitability of social exclusion of some people with impairments in any possible society. He draws upon feminist approaches to provide a vision of a more inclusive society in which work is not regarded as the defining characteristic of full social inclusion. The practical application of such a view is the advocacy of a dual strategy that takes account of those who can work and valorizes the non-working lives for those who are unable to. This he relates to the economic and social upheavals of contemporary European society.

The next chapter by Phil Lee charts the development of political activity around the issue of disability, primarily, but not exclusively, within the United Kingdom over the last two decades. He shows that whilst the disabled people's movement has made considerable progress, not least in advancing the social model of disability and placing civil rights for disabled people firmly on the political agenda, real political gains have been quite limited. Furthermore, translating the social model into practical administrative procedures is likely to remain problematic. This is largely because the social fabric of the last third of the twentieth century has been transformed with the coming of postmodernity and the ensuing lurch to the right of Britain's political institutions. Lee suggests that rather than intensify the shift toward inclusivity, this has resulted in heightened social divisions. He continues with an assessment of whether there are grounds for optimism in four key areas: the environment, the world of work, anti-discrimination legislation and wider social policy developments. The chapter concludes with the contention that there are a number of political paradoxes that envelop the future politics of disability and the disabled people's movement that are likely to inhibit, rather than enhance, the prospect of further substantial political gains.

We stay in the realm of politics in chapter 9, by the American writer and disability activist Harlan Hahn. His analysis examines several different concepts that have previously been adopted as a basis for improving the status of disabled people, and explores innovative ideas and proposals that might achieve this objective in coming years. Although an effort is made to include comparative data, this investigation focuses primarily on a case study of changes in disability laws and programmes in the United States. The first section contains a brief history of disability policy, including the problems created by judicial resistance to anti-discrimination statutes such as the 1990 Americans with Disabilities Act. An attempt is made to assess the strengths and weaknesses of proposals that stem from the emerging social model for research and advocacy on behalf of disabled people. The second section assesses the threats to the lives of disabled citizens posed by plans such as rationing health care, assisted suicide and other medical interventions founded, in part, on quasi-utilitarian constructs and on cost–value analysis. The final part investigates several possible innovations implied by the principle of empowerment. In particular, emphasis is given to the possibility of enhancing the strength of disabled citizens through permanent, systemic and institutional change in the policy-making process.

The tenth chapter, by Chris Holden and Peter Beresford, addresses the issues raised by a globalized political economy and ensuing debates within the discipline of social policy concerning the impact of changes in the world market on the welfare state. They take up the claim that there has been little attempt to relate the emergent discourses on globalization and post-industrial capitalism to those of the disabled peoples' movement and disability theorists. They contend that globalization impacts powerfully on the lives of disabled people, with reference to various globalized responses to disability and disabled people and their organizations. They postulate that, in turn, this holds out the potential for the generation of a meaningful challenge to the narrowly conceived economistic way in which globalization has often been presented and understood.

The chapter begins with a brief summary of some of the economic changes which have been associated with globalization and the different positions which have been taken on the significance of these within the political economy literature. These are juxtaposed with earlier economic developments and their implications for disability policy globally. The discussion then addresses the impact of globalization upon welfare policy, and considers the significance of these debates for disabled people and the welfare state. The authors argue that just as the last century witnessed the generation of a meaningful political analysis of the role of industrial capitalism in the creation of disability, so this must now be extended to take account of the impact of globalization and post-industrial capitalism. It must address both national and international inequalities, as well as notions of welfare and welfare policy development.

The theme of globalization continues in the next chapter in which Marcia Rioux discusses the relationship between disability and the concept of human rights within an international context. She argues that the way governments allocate their resources reflects their interpretation of citizenship, the notion of rights and the role of the state. She suggests that the protection of social rights must be considered as a minimum standard of life and an entitlement that is fundamental to contemporary notions of social justice. She draws an important distinction between social and economic globalization. She draws our attention to the fact that the former is not so much a new idea but one that needs to be pursued with renewed vigour and clarity in the face of the latter. She argues that disabled people have never been included in the mainstream of social rights. Traditionally their issues have been relegated to social development, to charity, to dispensation, or to the determination of their assumed best interests. But economic liberalization and globalization have highlighted the extent to which some people are excluded. The denial of liberties and the restriction of participation in society, those fundamental freedoms that governments promise their citizens in democracies, must also be protected for those with inpairments.

Chapter 12 by Geof Mercer considers the reformulation of disability-related research since the coming of the social model of disability. He provides a broad overview of the growing critique of established ways of researching disability in the latter half of the twentieth century from disabled people and their organizations. The starting point is the re-focusing of studies of disability away from the ways in which individual limitations contribute to the exclusion of disabled people from everyday social activities, and towards the ways in which environmental and cultural barriers effectively disable people with impairments. He shows how the coming of the social model stimulated the nurturing of a new research paradigm that is informed by similar emancipatory intentions. A review of key issues pertaining to its development is provided with particular reference to the British literature.

The discussion is located within competing paradigms of social inquiry. Drawing on the work of critical theorists, Mercer explores the emancipatory claims of this new approach to researching disability issues. In contrast to the more recent, overly pessimistic suggestion that emancipatory disability research might prove to be nothing more or less than an 'impossible dream' (Oliver 1999) he argues that disability researchers are engaged in the advancement of both theory and practice. He concludes by suggesting that in order to sustain this momentum, disability researchers must devote far more attention to established methodological considerations and concerns.

In the concluding chapter we begin by arguing that, given the increasing interest in disability studies within the academy, it is essential that academics maintain strong links with disabled people and their organizations. We examine the ways in which these interactions are currently being developed. We argue that further interaction is essential if we are to cultivate a more comprehensive understanding of the process and experience of disability and the ongoing exclusion of disabled people from the mainstream of everyday life. Finally, we examine some of the encroaching economic and political forces that are likely to influence the shaping of this hitherto mutually beneficial interface.

REFERENCES

Albrecht, G. L. (ed.) 1976: *The Sociology of Physical Disability and Rehabilitation*. Pittsburgh: University of Pittsburgh Press.
Albrecht, G. L., Seelman, K. and Bury, M. (eds) 2001: *Handbook of Disability Studies*. London: Sage.
Barnes, C., Mercer, G. and Shakespeare, T. 1999: *Exploring Disability: A Sociological Introduction*. Cambridge: Polity.
Barton, L. and Oliver, M. (eds) 1997: *Disability Studies: Past, Present and Future*. Leeds: Disability Press.
Blaxter, M. 1976: *The Meaning of Disability*. London: Heinemann.
Bowe, F. 1978: *Handicapping America*. New York: Harper & Row.
Brechin, A., Liddiard, P. with Swain, J. 1981: *Handicap in a Social World*. Sevenoaks: Hodder and Stoughton in association with the Open University.
Campbell, J. and Oliver, M. 1996: *Disability Politics: Understanding Our Past, Changing Our Future*. London: Routledge.
Coleridge, P. 1993: *Disability, Liberty & Development*. Oxford: Oxfam.
Davis, L. D. 1995: *Enforcing Normalcy: Disability, Deafness and the Body*. London: Verso.
Drake, R. 1999: *Understanding Disability Policy*. London: Macmillan.
Feuer, L. S. (ed.) 1969: *Basic Writings on Politics and Philosophy: Karl Marx and Friedrich Engels*. Glasgow: Collins.
Finkelstein, V. 1980: *Attitudes and Disabled People*. New York: World Rehabilitation Fund.
Finkelstein, V. 1997: Emancipating disability studies. In T. Shakespeare (ed.), *The Disability Studies Reader*, London: Cassell, 28–49.

Foucault, M. 1975: *The Birth of the Clinic: An Archeology of Medical Perception*. New York: Vantage Books.

Foucault, M. 1979: *Discipline and Punish: The Birth of the Prison*, tr. from the French by Alan Sheridan. Harmondsworth: Penguin.

Gleeson, B. 1999: *Geographies of Disability*. London: Routledge.

Goffman, E. 1968: *Stigma: Notes on the Management of a Spoiled Identity*. Englewood Cliffs, NJ: Prentice-Hall.

Gordon, B. O. and Rosenblum, K. E. 2001: Bringing disability into the sociological frame: a comparison of disability with race, sex and sexual orientation statuses. *Disability and Society*, 16(1), 5–19.

Gramsci, A. 1971: *Selections from the Prison Notebooks*. London: New Left Books.

Hasler, F. 1993: Developments in the Disabled People's Movement. In J. Swain, V. Finkelstein, S. French and M. Oliver (eds), *Disabling Barriers – Enabling Environments*. London: Sage in Association with the Open University, 278–84.

Hunt, P. (ed.) 1966: *Stigma: The Experience of Disability*. London: Geoffrey Chapman.

IDF 1998: *World Disabiliy Report*. Geneva: International Disability Forum.

Lenzer G. (ed.) 1975: *August Comte and Positivism: The Essential Writings*. New York: Harper Torchbooks.

Linton, S. 1998: *Claiming Disability*. New York: New York University Press.

Longmore, P. L. and Umansky, L. (eds) 2001: *The New Disability History: American Perspectives*. New York: New York University Press.

Marks, D. 1999: *Disability: Controversial Debates and Psychosocial Perspectives*. London: Routledge.

Meekoshe, H. and Dowse, L. 1997: Enabling citizenship: gender, disability and citizenship in Australia. *Feminist Review*, 57 (Autumn), 45–72.

Mitchell, D. and Snyder, S. 2001: *Narrative Prosthesis: Disability and the Dependencies of Discourse*. Ann Arbor: University of Michigan Press.

Oliver, M. 1983: *Social Work with Disabled People*. London: Macmillan.

Oliver, M. 1990: *The Politics of Disablement*. Basingstoke: Macmillan.

Oliver, M. 1999: Final accounts with the parasite people. In M. Corker and S. French (eds), *Disability Discourse*, Buckingham: Open University Press, 181–93.

Parsons, T. 1951: *The Social System*. New York: Free Press.

Pfeiffer, D. and Yoshida, K. 1995: Teaching disability studies in Canada and the USA. *Disability and Society*, 10(4), 475–500.

Rieser, R. 1990: Internalised oppression: how it seems to me. In R. Rieser and M. Mason (eds), *Disability Equality in the Classroom: A Human Rights Issue*, London: Inner London Education Authority, 29–32.

Rioux, M. H. and Bach, M. 1994: *Disability is not Measles*. Ontario: York University, Roeher Institute.

Rosenhan, D. L. 1975: On being sane in insane places. In S. Dinitz, R. K. Dynes and A. C. Clarke (eds), *Deviance: Studies in Definition, Management and Treatment*, New York: Oxford University Press, 279–81.

Scheff, T. 1966: *Being Mentally Ill: A Sociological Theory.* London: Weidenfeld & Nicolson.

Scott, R. 1969: *The Making of Blind Men.* London: Sage.

Stone, E. (ed.) 1999: *Disability and Development.* Leeds: Disability Press.

Sullivan, M. and Muntford, R. 1998: The articulation and practice: the critique and resistance in Aotearoa. *Disability and Society,* 13 (3), 183–9.

Sutherland, A. T. 1981: *Disabled We Stand.* London: Souvenir Press.

Swain, J., Finkelstein, V., French, S. and Oliver, M. (eds) 1993: *Disabling Barriers – Enabling Environments.* London: Sage in Association with the Open University.

Szasz, T. S. 1961: *The Myth of Mental Illness: Foundations of a Theory of Personal Conduct.* New York: Dell.

Tideman, M. (ed.) 1999: *Handikapp: synsätt principer perspectiv.* Stockholm: Johanson & Skyttmo Förlag.

Townsend, P. 1979: *Poverty in the United Kingdom.* Harmondsworth: Penguin.

UPIAS 1976: *Fundamental Principles of Disability.* London: Union of Physically Impaired Against Segregation.

van Oorschot, V. and Hvinden, B. (eds) 2001: *Disability Policies in European Societies.* The Hague: Kluwer Law International.

Wendell, S. 1996: *The Rejected Body: Feminist and Philosophical Reflections on Disability.* London: Routledge.

WHO 2001: *Rethinking Care from the Perspective of Disabled People: Conference Report and Recommendations.* Geneva: World Health Organizations' Disability and Rehabilitation Team.

Williams, G. 1997: The sociology of disability: towards a materialist phenomenology. In T. Shakespeare (ed.), *The Disability Studies Reader,* London: Cassell, 234–44.

Zola, I. K. 1982: *Missing Pieces: A Chronicle of Living with a Disability.* Philadelphia: Temple University Press.

2

American Pragmatism, Sociology and the Development of Disability Studies

Gary L. Albrecht

Disability is increasingly in the public consciousness for a myriad of reasons. As populations age and world news concerning illness, disease and impairments is broadcast around the globe, disability is becoming recognized as a universal experience (Zola 1989). The visibility of impairments, the personal experience of disability in our lives, the effects of the degraded environment, tobacco, HIV/AIDS, accidents, land mines and civil wars on our well-being and that of others, vulnerability of the food chain to disability-causing agents, neonatal intensive care, and escalating health interventions for the elderly all contribute to our awareness of disability (Albrecht and Verbrugge 2000; Michaud et al. 2001). As these issues are played out in public, disability becomes a case study of the values, worth and position of people in a society. Indeed, a society can be judged on how it treats its children, women, elderly citizens and disabled people.

Disability studies developed as a field in response to the perceived universality of the problem, academic interest in explaining the place and meaning of disability in society, and activist expressions of empowerment, inclusion, normality and the politics of difference. Policy makers and politicians contributed to the growth of the field through their concern with the economic and social costs associated with disability and public discussions of how government support might better be organized to plan for increased numbers of disabled people and the elderly (Chard et al. 1999; Blendon and Benson 2001). Disability studies, then, is an emergent field that spans the boundaries of academia, personal experience, political activism and public policy.

There are six contentious propositions that shape discussion in the field:

1   people interested in disability share a common universe of discourse;
2   leaders and spokespeople in the field represent all disabled people;
3   only disabled people can effectively understand disability or contribute to the field;
4   disability studies is an established field with a home;
5   disability studies share a common history and intellectual tradition across countries and throughout history; and
6   people in the field generally agree on health and welfare policies for disabled people and what constitutes 'reasonable accommodation', 'empowerment' and 'quality of life'.

These propositions provoke heated debates in the disability studies literature and the popular press over the experiences, meanings, context and consequences of disability (Linton 1998; Barnes 1999; Greenhouse 2001). They also represent the fault lines in disability studies, where politically correct values are applied to argue for a position or to silence dissent. For this reason, it is as important to study the values of participants in the disability discourse, the politics and ideologies of the actors, and the attitudes, values, structure and culture of the society in which the discourse takes place, as it is to collect and consider evidence in support of a position. Although there is considerable disagreement among participants in the disability discourse, the passion of their arguments attests to the vitality of the field and importance of the issues (Corker and French 1999; Altman and Barnartt 2000; Albrecht et al. 2001).

While there are universal questions that have been addressed across national boundaries and perspectives, the maturation of a field is dependent on historical context, experience, intellectual tradition, culture and the political economic system. The development of disability studies, then, should be examined and understood in context. I will do this by discussing how pragmatism and American sociology influenced the development of disability studies in the United States, and directly or indirectly addressed the six contentious questions posed above. First, I will consider how pragmatism shaped American thought, social policy and view of the world. Second, I will show how pragmatism combined with the early development of American sociology, including survey research and the social area studies and interactionism of the Chicago school, to provide a framework and method for addressing disability issues. Third, I will

analyse how the disability movement organized, exerted political influence in the American context, and shaped disability studies as a field.
Fourth, I will consider how disability studies in the United States were
influenced by the political economy, embodying the American values of
rugged individualism, capitalism and democracy. Finally, I will reflect on
the future directions of American disability studies.

American pragmatism

Pragmatism is a diverse philosophy that has had a pervasive influence
on American social science and subsequently on disability studies. Pragmatism is a style of philosophy initiated by Charles Sanders Peirce
(1839–1914) and William James (1842–1910) which deeply influenced
the work of Dewey (1968–92), Schiller (1907) and Mead (1964) in the
early twentieth century and the more recent contemporary philosophical
work of Sellars (1973), Quine (1969), Putnam (1978), Rorty (1979,
1991), Haack (1993) and West (1999). Since the tenets of this work
raise many philosophies of science and social policy questions, pragmatism has deeply affected thinking in American social sciences and cultural
studies.

Because of its multiple forms and re-inventions, however, it is difficult
to characterize the work of all pragmatists under one conceptual um-
brella. In searching for a common thread in this work, Susan Haack
(1996: 643) concludes that pragmatism 'is best characterized by the
method expressed in the pragmatic maxim, according to which the
meaning of a concept is determined by the experiential or practical
consequences of its application'.

The early pragmatists worked in the context of the Industrial Revolution and rapid development of knowledge in the physical sciences. They
were attracted by the idea of certainty and the formulation of scientific
laws that had practical applications. Peirce, for example, reacted to the *a
priori* methods traditionally favoured by metaphysicians by arguing for
a scientific method where the inquirer is ready to 'drop the whole
cartload of his beliefs, the moment experience is against them' (Peirce
1931–58: i. 14, 55). According to his perspective, the scientific investi-
gator is a 'contrite fallibilist' in evaluating the beliefs and evidence she
encounters. The purpose was to encourage scholars to pursue truth in a
disinterested way and to produce theories and a body of work that would
withstand multiple, severe tests. This approach to scientific method is
compatible with Popper's principle of falsification, where theories are
proposed and submitted 'to the severest test we can design' (Popper

1972: 16). The attraction of this version of the scientific method is that it emphasized objective knowledge, realism and universality; truth lay in tested theory and in the 'facts'.

William James's emphasis was different from Peirce's. James stressed *praxis*, the practical consequences of believing in a particular concept or social policy. In discussing the complexities of metaphysical and moral questions, he says, for example: 'The pragmatic method in such cases is to try to interpret each notion by tracing its respective practical conse-quences' (James 1907: 28). James also recognized that there might not be scientific evidence to settle every dispute. Therefore, he posited that 'religious beliefs' which in principle cannot be verified or falsified are often used to make decisions because they fit with the believer's life and have practical consequences. He also supported the notion that truth is socially constructed and can change over time. Both his emphasis on 'religious beliefs' and the social construction of truth acknowledge the subjective and relative aspects of knowledge. James's brand of pragma-tism opens the door to later explorations of the subjective meanings of experience.

John Dewey and F. C. S. Schiller moved pragmatism in an increasingly activist direction. Dewey did not engage in the 'quest for certainty' that captured the attention of Peirce. Instead, he recognized that knowing is intimately related to practice (Dewey 1968–92). He was a reformist, in that he advocated that good theories are based on practice, and are modified as experience with a programme demonstrates the success or failure of an idea. Schiller (1864–1937) was more revolutionary than Dewey. He acknowledges the social construction of reality by arguing that truth is relative and means 'valued by us'. A proposition is true if it 'forwards our ends' (Schiller 1907: 8). In terms of social activism, Schiller pointed out how values and subjective experience colour what we think of as being true or right.

A group of neo-pragmatists, including Rorty, Quine, Putnam and Haack, recognize that the 'objective certitude' advocated by early prag-matists is not a feasible goal for science or epistemology. Yet, they are keenly interested in the question of truth, seeking to find a middle ground between dogmatism and scepticism (Haack 1996: 656). This work lays a philosophical foundation for many of the issues debated in contemporary cultural studies, including the following: What constitutes evidence? How is a text to be read? Who can speak about or understand the experience of another? What are human rights? What is just in a given situation?

The confluence of pragmatism,
American sociology and disability studies

Pragmatism was influential in the development of sociology and subsequently of disability studies in the United States, because it provided a conceptual framework for thinking about the critical issues confronting social scientists, and suggested the types of data and analysis that should be used to construct arguments. Social scientists were concerned with developing theories, methods and a body of knowledge addressing social behaviour that would be credible and useful. Over the years, pragmatism shaped the pursuit of these desiderata in the discipline of sociology in three important ways.

First, early pragmatism emphasized that if sociology is to be a science, it should follow the 'scientific method' of the natural sciences by embracing the epistemological principle of falsification. This principle, elaborated and disseminated by Popper (1972), suggests that scientists put forward a theory, initially as an uncorroborated conjecture, and then test its predictions with observations to see if the theory stands up to the test. If carefully designed tests of hypotheses prove negative, the theory is experimentally falsified, and the investigators will modify the theory or build a new one. If, on the other hand, the tests and data support the theory, scientists will continue to use it on the basis of its undefeated hypotheses to further test and extend the theory. According to Peirce, the extension of this approach leads to the development of 'laws', and points to what is true. Thus, pragmatism inculcated an early interest among sociologists in gathering 'objective' data through observations, surveys and censuses that would describe social phenomena, help develop theory, and serve as evidence testing an argument.

Second, the pragmatists, especially William James, encouraged the anchoring of analysis in practical realities and social policies. James stated that a pragmatist 'turns away from abstraction and insufficiency, from verbal solutions, from bad *a priori* reasons, from fixed principles, closed systems, and pretended absolutes and origins. He turns towards concreteness and adequacy, towards facts, towards action, and towards power' (James 1907: 31). Through such arguments, James laid the foundations for grounded theory, the study of social problems, observing behaviour and gathering data in the 'real' world, formulating social policies and testing their effects on behaviour and an examination of the distribution and exercise of power in society. For James, pragmatism involved seeing if theories and policies really made a difference. In this sense, James encouraged social action theory among pragmatists and sociologists alike.

Third, pragmatist thinking moved away from the strict 'objectivism' and application of the scientific method advocated by Peirce towards recognition of the importance of subjective experience, relativistic and culturally different conceptions of behaviour, paradigm shifts in the gathering and interpreting of information, and competing communities of discourse. Rorty (1979, 1991) is an example of these positions. He dismisses claims to objectivity as wishful thinking, arguing that our standards of evidence and our scientific and social policy practices are cultural conventions. Rorty has been a powerful influence on cultural studies, including disability studies, in so far as he stresses the importance of engaging in conversation about issues and analysing texts in an open discourse, taking into account the subjective differences and cultural grounding of the participants. This perspective in social science and the humanities highlights the reading of situations and texts and analysis of both the observer / reader and that which is observed or is the text. Rorty's brand of positivism also emphasizes cultural and historical context. This approach to understanding raises important questions such as: Who has the right to speak and interpret? What constitutes a community of discourse or a community of scholars? What are the criteria of admission to such communities? How is an argument comprised and evidence presented that would convince others of its truth and usefulness? How do cultural context and history affect the definition of a situation and how the 'facts' are interpreted? How are evidence, theory and argument translated into social policies that have the power to change the behaviour of others and rearrange status hierarchies and the structure of institutions? In reviewing this broad range of pragmatic positions and their uses, it is noteworthy that there are not merely different, but radically opposed, forms of pragmatism. However, they do address many of the same fundamental questions of how we acquire and use knowledge, and they share the important principle that knowledge ought to be evaluated in terms of its utility and the consequences of its application to practical problems.

These three themes in pragmatism had a powerful impact on the development of sociology and later of disability studies in the United States. They have conceptual and historical links to five methodological, substantive and theoretical approaches to social research: quantitative, qualitative, historical / contextual, social action / social policy and integrated work. While there is considerable intermingling of these methodological approaches to social research, each has its own constituency undergirded by a particular philosophy of science, intellectual context and projected use of the results.

Quantitative research in the social sciences flowed easily from the desire of sociologists to gain the status of scientists and have their discipline respected for its rigour. According to the dictates of the early pragmatists and the methodologies of the natural scientists, theories should guide research, phenomena under study must be measured accurately, events and units counted, and hypotheses tested in a deductive fashion. The United States Census, which began in 1790, was one of the early sources of such quantitative data. During the last hundred years especially, the United States Public Health Service and medical scientists have been interested in developing epidemiological data to identify population characteristics, define health problems, come up with suitable interventions, and eventually assess the outcomes of those interventions. Quantitative social epidemiology, strongly influenced by the social ecology perspective of the Sociology Department of the University of Chicago in the 1930s, was path breaking in exploring the relationship between social conditions and such social problems as mental disorder (Faris and Dunham 1939). This focus on quantitative research according to the 'scientific method' persists to this day in American sociology. Journals like the *American Sociological Review* and the *Journal of Health and Social Behavior* are replete with articles using quantitative methods to examine the relationship between poverty, race, gender, education, stress, access to resources, and employment and outcome variables such as discrimination, disparity in income, access to opportunities, health, well-being and equal justice for all citizens. Social science publishers like Sage Inc. have instituted series of methodological primers that guide researchers in how better to measure and analyse data, test hypotheses and build ever more sophisticated models of individual, group and organizational behaviour. This vast literature conforms to the spirit of the 'scientific method' proposed by Peirce and legitimized by research in the natural sciences. At the same time, much of this literature is concerned with social problems and issues of justice that carry forth another theme from the pragmatists: the desire to make a difference and to judge the value of research by it practical usefulness.

In the disability arena, these themes were also carried over into rehabilitation and disability research. In the United States, rehabilitation research typically meant *medical* rehabilitation of individuals after trauma or the diagnosis of impairment or *social* rehabilitation through physical and occupational therapy and education that would allow individuals to obtain a job or return to work. Medical rehabilitation research burgeoned after the end of World War II, and particularly from the 1960s to the present. This work was most often directed by physicians and aimed to acquire knowledge that would improve functional status and permit individuals to live independently in the community. Social rehabilitation research was often undertaken by economists and researchers in vocational rehabilitation and special education, sometimes working in conjunction with physicians to develop programmes that would help impaired and disabled people return to work. This has traditionally been the major focus of the Veterans Administration and the branches of the Social Security Administration dedicated to disability. Medical researchers employed the quantitative methods of surveys, targeted sampling strategies, double-blinded clinical trials and evaluation studies to demonstrate patterns and outcomes that would help in implementing programmes to help disabled people be more functionally independent. The social rehabilitation researchers, often including sociologists and economists, also used quantitative methods and statistical models to determine which variables and interventions predicted return to work.

Many disability studies scholars in the United States were trained or heavily influenced by sociologists, so they carried over the social concerns and research paradigms from sociology to disability studies. Quantitative research in disability studies is an illustration of this influence. For example, Fujiura and Rutkowski-Kmitta (2001) point out that counting disability is an important enterprise for disabled people, governments, policy makers and social scientists. Regardless of the heated debates over disability definitions and who and what ought to be measured, if anything, governments need to be able to identify and count disability if they are to provide health insurance and medical and social services and make the environment more accommodating. While there is deep concern over labelling, failing to take disabled peoples' experience into account and paying insufficient attention to the accessibility of the environment, governments could not provide services or even consider altering the environment unless they can identify disabled people and their needs. Fujiura and Rutowski-Kmitta observe that 'Although there are notable exceptions, the organized political state exists to promote the well-being of its people. Data inform this process and help inform the planning and organization of state policy. Thus, the surveillance of health status is both an ancient practice and nearly universal among nation states' (2001: 70). Furthermore, they agree with Obershall's contention (1972) that 'the demand for extensive and detailed information by "social reformers, civic groups and philanthropists" was the foundation of much statistical work in the nineteenth century' (Fujiura and Rutkowski-Kmitta 2001: 70). These goals of disability statistics still pertain today. The difference is that current methodological and statistical techniques allow researchers to address social, cultural and environmental effects in a more precise and integrated fashion (Brown 2001). This exercise has stimulated social scientists and disability scholars to refine the theories and models which they use to understand disability and its effects, health and social interventions, the physical and social environment, and the outcomes of different social policies.

While the purposes of measuring disability and counting disabled people are reasonably clear, these activities are fraught with difficulty and controversy. This is because disability is a 'complicated, multidimensional concept' (Altman 2001: 97), the end purposes of disability measures are multiple, and identification can have negative consequences, such as labelling and discrimination, for disabled people. Debates over these issues can be vividly seen in the ongoing controversies regarding the World Health Organization's development and use of ICIDH codes to classify disability and the Global Burden of Disease Project jointly sponsored by the World Bank and the World Health Organization (Altman 2001; Fujiura and Rutkowski-Kmitta 2001). Regardless of ideological position or predilection for a particular scientific method, this quantitative research on disability reflects the influence of sociology and some key principles of pragmatism on disability studies.

Both the pragmatists and neo-pragmatists exert their influence on contemporary sociology and disability studies. Among qualitative and cultural studies scholars today, there is a strong emphasis on the social construction of reality, the importance of individual experience, culture and context in interpreting behaviour and texts, listening to the 'voices' of the people being studied, and 'discourse' among and between scholars and the people being studied. Harvard University and the University of Chicago were two institutions, among others, where pragmatism and qualitative and socio-historical research provided a foundation for entire areas of sociological work and disability studies. This is not a teleological tale in which there is a direct causal link between individuals, disciplines and departments. Nevertheless, pragmatism and compatible sociological 'schools' have flourished at both Harvard and Chicago for years. William James was at Harvard at the turn of the century, where he had a significant influence on numerous sociologists, including the extraordinary African-American scholar W. E. B. DuBois (1961), who studied with James and called himself a 'realist pragmatist' (Kloppenberg 1998: 539). Today Cornel West and Hilary Putnam are neo-pragmatists at Harvard who have an impact on current sociologists and cultural studies scholars, including William Wilson, a recent past president of the American Sociological Association and Theda Skocpol. Wilson's research on the meaning of work for inner city Blacks, social policies for poor minorities, and social justice is representative of this influence. Skocpol's contributions have been in understanding the welfare state in historical and cultural context. Interestingly, both Wilson and Skocpol came to Harvard from the University of Chicago, another intellectual centre influenced by pragmatism.

Two important early pragmatists, John Dewey and George Herbert Mead, did some of their most important work at the University of Chicago, where there seemed to be a commonality of interests between the pragmatists and groups of sociologists (Bloom 2000). As Abbott (1999) points out, however, there was less a single University of Chicago 'school' than central themes and diverse groups of academics who made significant contributions to sociology in terms of social ecology, social psychology, demography and social organization.

The interactionist perspective in sociology proposed in the work of Weber (1946) and Simmel (1955) emphasizes the importance of understanding the social world from the viewpoint of the individuals who act within it. This approach was influenced by Dewey and elaborated by Mead (1934) and Blumer (1969) at the University of Chicago into what is now known as symbolic interactionism. Blumer later moved to the Department of Sociology at the University of California, Berkeley, where he trained many students in this research tradition. Students of Mead and Blumer at the University of Chicago, like Howard S. Becker (Becker et al. 1961), Erving Goffman (1959, 1961) and Anselm Strauss (Strauss and Glaser 1975; Strauss and Corbin 1990; Strauss 1993), used symbolic interactionism as a framework to produce path-breaking books in medical sociology and in qualitative research methods.

Symbolic interactionism is a form of social psychology that examines the interactions between people in terms of symbols, signs, gestures, shared rules, and written and spoken language. Symbolic interactionism was originally applied to analyses of individuals and groups, but only more recently to organizations and the more encompassing social structure. The essential point of this perspective is that people do not respond to the world directly, but instead place social meanings on it, organize it, and respond to it on the basis of these meanings. Thus, we live in a symbolic as well as a physical world, where social life involves a constant process of assigning meanings to our own acts and those of others and interpreting them within this framework. Other people use similar techniques to understand us and our behaviour. Symbolic interactionism highlights subjective experience and the interpretation of social reality, but also allows individuals to take the place of others symbolically to better understand their behaviour.

This perspective has been used by disability scholars to ask fundamental questions: How does an impairment become a disability? What does disability mean to people with different impairments and in diverse cultures? What is the subjective experience of disability? How do others perceive, define and react to disabled people? Is disability in the individual, in the environment, or in the interaction between the two (Imrie 2000)? How do medical professionals and service providers act towards disabled people, and why? By addressing these questions from a symbolic interactionist perspective, disability scholars have deepened our theoretical and experiential understanding of what it means to be a disabled person.

Social interactionism is well equipped to analyse how social problems, behaviour and institutions are socially constructed. As Robertson (1977: 135) aptly remarks, 'We are not born with any sense of time, of place, or cause and effect, or of the society in which we live. We learn about these things through social interaction, and what we learn depends on the society in which we live and our particular place within it.' According to Berger and Luckmann (1966), reality is socially constructed through three processes: externalization, objectification and internalization. Externalization occurs when people produce cultural products through their social interactions. Examples of this in the disability arena are lip reading and signing among deaf people and group cohesion among spinal cord injured individuals due to the visibility of, and meanings attached to, wheelchair use. Objectification occurs when these externalized products take on a meaning of their own. For example, the wheelchair symbol is used worldwide to denote parking spaces and bathrooms that are intended to be available and accessible to disabled people. Internalization takes place when people learn purported 'objective' facts about reality from others through the socialization process, and make them a part of their own subjective 'internal' consciousness. Thus, individuals socialized in similar cultures share the same perceptions of reality, rarely questioning where these beliefs originated, or why. Stigmatization of, and attitudes towards, persons with mental illness are an example of such an internalization process.

Within this intellectual tradition, Irving Kenneth Zola made a substantial contribution to the development of disability studies as a medical sociologist and a visibly disabled person. He was trained at Harvard in medical sociology, but his work is strongly flavoured with social interactionism and the ethnographic work of Chicago sociologists. Zola's dissertation explored differential perceptions of pain and differences in behaviour when seeking medical help among three diverse cultural groups in Boston: Irish-Americans, Italians and Jews (Zola 1966). His later work highlighted the subjective experience of disability, being an embodied subject, and the universality of disability (Zola 1989, 1991, 1993). He was chair of the Medical Sociology Section of the American Sociological Association, founder of *Disability Studies Quarterly*, which publishes articles, personal statements, book and film reviews, and news of interest to the academic disability community, and a key member of the disability movement responsible for the Americans with Disabilities Act of 1990, accommodations in the environment, and the emergence of disability studies as a field. He was one of the moving forces in establishing the Society for Disability Studies. Here was a scholar in the symbolic interactionist mould who incorporated a critical component of pragmatism into his research by combining academic research and activism. He was, on the one hand, a member of a National Academy of Sciences committee organized to identify the critical research issues in need of funding and, on the other, an activist who could be seen demonstrating on the steps of a court-house about accessibility.

Social movements and politics

As we have seen in the case of Zola, pragmatism and sociology were formative influences on the disability movement. There is a myth that since disabled people have a common experience and a similar view of their social worlds, organizing a disability movement to institute changes in social policy and public attitudes is a natural and easy process. This myth does not reflect the reality. In the United States, disability groups originally formed around types of impairment, age, employment status and military experience. There were, for example, powerful groups that coalesced around visual impairment, deafness, polio, spinal cord injury and mental illness. Some of these groups, like the March of Dimes, concentrated on the young, while others, like the Vocational Rehabilitation Administration focused on returning disabled people with skills and experience to the work-place. Again, the Veterans Administration is an entire government agency devoted to assisting veterans of military service with medical care and rehabilitation. These groups often fought among themselves for the scarce resources available for medical treatment, rehabilitation, social services, independent living and modification of the environment. Behind the scenes, competition rather than co-operation was the rule of the day. That is why the convergence of these groups behind the Americans with Disabilities Act of 1990 (ADA) was such news.

Since Harlan Hahn has a chapter later in this book on disability politics and the disability movement, where he uses a minority group model to understand the evolution of the American disability movement, I will keep my focus on how pragmatism and sociology helped to shape disability studies and crystallize the disability movement. From a social interactionist perspective, the self that people present depends on the role that they are playing. Not all disabled people have disability as their defining role. For example, in an examination of identity, roles and disability culture, Devlieger and Albrecht (2000) discovered that inner city, disabled African-Americans who lived on the near west side of Chicago did not have a strong disability identity or claim a disability culture. Instead, their master status was more likely to be African-American, poor, survivor or gang member. This is one of the reasons why the American disability movement is overwhelmingly composed of white, privileged, educated adults with visible disabilities. When these people speak for all disabled people, many wonder whom they are representing. The disability movement leaders publicly preach unity and inclusion, but where are the poor, the people of colour, the individuals with non-visible disabilities and the intellectually disabled? Power is about representation. If only some are represented in the movement, the others are without voice (Charlton 1998).

The symbolic interactionists have also noted that social life is made predictable through shared expectations and rules. As indicated above, the members of the disability movement, often organized around specific disabilities or issues, were in competition with other disability groups, and excluded those who did not share their disability or viewpoint. As a consequence, their impact was limited, and did not include the majority of disabled people in the nation. Erving Goffman (1959), using a dramaturgical metaphor, studied the aligning actions employed by people to redirect potentially disruptive interactions. He and other symbolic interactionists suggest that finding a common identity and cause, organizing against an outside force, including people with the same interests, developing organizational signs, symbols and culture, presenting a united front, and becoming politically astute are concrete actions that can be taken to unite groups. These are also the strategies most likely to produce social change as expressed in public attitudes, laws, accessible environment and independent living. When the diverse disability groups recognized that they had more to gain by gathering forces co-operatively and organizing behind a common set of strategies, they were able to marshal their energies, conceive a shared plan, take political action, change public opinion and successfully back the Americans with Disabilities Act. Following the dictates of social interactionist theory, leaders in the disability movement employed shared expectations and rules to control internal competition and implement a successful strategy developed around the civil rights model to energize public opinion and pass the ADA. This group cohesion in the disability movement was reinforced by the development of shared signs, symbols and disability culture. People within the movement were able to draw on their subjective experiences and demonstrate that disability is a shared, universal experience, to construct disability as a social problem deserving of attention and resources (Zola 1989). All these strategies combined to produce and reinforce a vigorous disability movement.

American values and the political economy of disability

The preponderance of disability research in the United States has used the individual, families or groups as the unit of analysis. Symbolic interactionism began as a social psychology well suited to these types of analysis. However, there is a need to consider disability from a societal and structural perspective as well. There is analysis at this level using social construction and political economic perspectives to understand societal definitions of disability, the organization of a response to disability and the disability marketplace (Albrecht 1992; Albrecht and Bury 2001).

Gordon and Rosenblum argue that sociologists have failed to cultivate the social constructionist model of disability, and continue 'to frame disability along "traditional" or "individual" lines, that is by focusing on limitations, medicalization, diagnoses, individual adjustment' (2001: 16). They base their observation on a review of 510 articles located in *Sociological Abstracts*, where they found that 'a fairly small proportion' (2001: 15), 17 per cent of the articles surveyed, addressed the social construction of disability. First, this study used only *Sociological Abstracts* as its data source; secondly, 17 per cent of 510 articles (87) is not a trivial number; and third, this review overlooks a number of important books. Gordon's and Rosenblum's sweeping indictment makes a legitimate case, but loses its impact by overstating their argument and overlooking the force of important work in the field. Two key books in the early 1990s, for example, directly address the social construction of disability. Oliver makes the social and cultural production of disability the central argument of *The Politics of Disablement* (1990). Albrecht's book, *The Disability Business: Rehabilitation in America* (1992), is devoted to an analysis of the social construction of disability as a social problem and the development of a rehabilitation industry as an institutional response. While not the dominant themes in disability research, work informed by the social construction of disability, the political economy of disability, and analysis of the disability marketplace contributes significantly to our understanding of disability on the societal and structural levels.

The social construction of disability and political economic forms of institutions are contingent on the values, interests and contexts of the particular society being studied. Therefore, an understanding of disability in the United States requires that American values and ideologies be taken into account, because they influence the ways in which disability is socially constructed and the institutional / political economic response to a defined social problem is organized. In the United States, the key values in the culture – of rugged individualism, capitalism and democracy – have remained remarkably consistent over centuries (DiMaggio et al. 1996). By contrast, European nations, while also espousing democratic values, are generally more benign to those in need, have more comprehensive and complete health and welfare systems, and manifest less extreme differences in income distribution in society and in services available to those in need, such as the unemployed, poor, women, children and disabled people (Ardigó 1995; Evans 1995; Ayanian et al. 2000; Hayward et al. 2000).

In the United States, then, emphasis on rugged individualism, capitalism and the American brand of democracy affect how disability is defined and the shared institutional response. Disability is typically described as an individual problem with which the disabled person must deal. While there are substantial government programmes for disabled people, they emphasize protection for those in politically and economically valuable occupations like the military, transportation workers and government employees, and are often aimed at return to work (Mudrick 1997; Yelin 1997). Whether in the public or the private sector, rehabilitation goods and services are commodities that can be bought and sold. Disability is the focus of a multi-billion dollar business comprised of diverse stakeholders in a capitalistic marketplace, where helping disabled people *and* making money are important goals. The stakeholder groups include health care and medical professionals; hospitals, therapy businesses and home care agencies; assisted care living facilities; the pharmaceutical, medical supply and technology industries and insurance companies; architects, law practices, banks and accounting firms specializing in disability; government and lobby groups; politicians; and last, the consumer (Albrecht and Bury 2001). In this environment, the consumer / disabled person is the stakeholder with the least power.

Such political economic analyses in the United States are important, because the American model of managed care, delivery of technical medicine, definitional processes, and social policies are being exported around the world through multinational companies and government policies. As American capitalism and democracy dictated the definition of, and response to, disability contingent on one's place in, and perceived value to, society in the United States, so these forces will operate in the international arena as health, human services and disability become global businesses. Such analyses are instrumental in helping us understand how values, the political economy and the physical and social environment affect a society's treatment of disabled people and to know best how to intervene.

American exceptionalism and the future of disability studies

As we have seen, American disability studies have been shaped by pragmatism; sociology, including quantitative, symbolic interactionist and political economic analyses; and the particular context in which the discipline has grown in the United States. At the same time, American disability studies have been characterized by a general lack of historical sensibility and a disconcerting insularity. Much-needed contributions on the historical grounding of disability studies are finally appearing (Stiker 1999; Braddock and Parish 2001; Longmore and Umansky 2001; Fleischer and Zames 2001), but there is need for more scholarship like this in the United States and other countries.

Commenting from a British perspective, Colin Barnes (1999) aptly notes disturbing trends in discussing Linton's (1998) recent book, *Claiming Disability*. Barnes argues that disability scholars, exemplified by Linton, are frequently 're-inventing the wheel' because they do not have a deep historical anchoring in their disciplines and do not read the work of others carefully: 'It is clear, however, from the recent body of writing coming out of North America, that some of the emergent crop of "disability scholars" are ignorant of, or choose to overlook, developments on this side of the Atlantic and, indeed, elsewhere' (1999: 577). These remarks are well taken, because it is easy for discipline-based scholars to have myopic vision when they work in a new, interdisciplinary field. The requirement for disability studies to explore the history of disability and to be open to perspectives and research across borders and disciplines is imperative, if it is to acquire maturity as an academic discipline and credibility in the activist world (Barnes et al. 1999; Gleeson 1999; Llewellyn and Hogan 2000; S. J. Williams 2001).

In conclusion, it is an openness to, and respect for, others that will permit a shared universe of discourse, discussions of disability definitions and representations, appreciation of diverse intellectual positions, the experiences of others, the vision of disability studies as a discipline, and how theory and research can bear upon practice (G. H. Williams 2001). Disability studies is a product of the intellectual traditions and the cultural settings where it is evolving. It is most likely to mature as scholars, policy makers and activists listen to each other and engage in respectful discourse about the fault lines, issues, theories and applications of the field to the real world. Let the reciprocal dialogue begin.

REFERENCES

Abbott, Andrew 1999: *Department & Discipline: Chicago Sociology at One Hundred*. Chicago: University of Chicago Press.

Albrecht, Gary L. 1992: *The Disability Business: Rehabilitation in America*. Newbury Park, CA: Sage.

Albrecht, Gary L. and Bury, Michael 2001: The political economy of the disability marketplace. In Gary L. Albrecht, Katherine D. Seelman and Michael Bury (eds), *Handbook of Disability Studies*, Thousand Oaks, CA: Sage, 585–608.

Albrecht, Gary L. and Verbrugge, Lois 2000: The global emergence of disability. In Gary L. Albrecht, Ray Fitzpatrick and Susan C. Scrimshaw (eds), *The Handbook of Social Studies in Health and Medicine*, Thousand Oaks, CA: Sage, 293–307.

Albrecht, Gary L., Seelman, Katherine D. and Bury, Michael 2001: The formation of disability studies. In Gary L. Albrecht, Katherine D. Seelman and Michael Bury (eds), *Handbook of Disability Studies*, Thousand Oaks, CA: Sage, 1–8.

Altman, Barbara M. 2001: Disability definitions, models, classification schemes, and applications. In Gary L. Albrecht, Katherine D. Seelman and Michael Bury (eds), *Handbook of Disability Studies*, Thousand Oaks, CA: Sage, 97–122.

Altman, Barbara M. and Barnartt, Sharon N. (eds) 2000: *Expanding the Scope of Social Science Research in Disability*. Stamford, CT: JAI Press.

Ardigó, A. 1995: Public attitudes and changes in health care systems: a confrontation and a puzzle. In O. Borre and E. Scarbough (eds), *The Scope of Government*, Oxford: Oxford University Press, 388–406.

Ayanian, John Z., Weissman, Joel S., Schneider, Eric C., Ginsburg, Jack A. and Zaslavsky, Alan M. 2000: Unmet health needs of uninsured adults in the United States. *Journal of the American Medical Association*, 284, 2061–2069.

Barnes, Colin 1999: Disability studies: new or not so new directions? *Disability & Society*, 14, 577–80.

Barnes, Colin, Mercer, Geof and Shakespeare, Tom 1999: *Exploring Disability: A Sociological Introduction*. Cambridge: Polity.

Becker, Howard S., Geer, Blanche, Hughes, Everett and Strauss, A. 1961: *Boys in White*. Chicago: University of Chicago Press.

Berger, P. and Luckmann, T. 1966: *The Social Construction of Reality*. Garden City, NY: Doubleday.

Blendon, Robert J. and Benson, John M. 2001: Americans' views on health policy: a fifty-year historical perspective. *Health Affairs*. 20, 33–46.

Bloom, Samuel W. 2000: The institutionalization of medical sociology in the United States, 1920–1980. In C. Bird, P. Conrad and A. M. Fremont (eds), *Handbook of Medical Sociology*, 5th edn, Upper Saddle River, NJ: Prentice-Hall, 11–32.

Blumer, Herbert 1969: *Symbolic Interactionism: Perspective and Method*. Engle-wood Cliffs, NJ: Prentice-Hall.
Braddock, David L. and Parish, Susan L. 2001: An institutional history of disability. In Gary L. Albrecht, Katherine D. Seelman and Michael Bury (eds), *Handbook of Disability Studies*, Thousand Oaks, CA: Sage, 11–68.
Brown, Scott C. 2001: Methodological paradigms that shape disability research. In Gary L. Albrecht, Katherine D. Seelman and Mike Bury (eds), *Handbook of Disability Studies*, Thousand Oaks, CA: Sage Publications, 145–70.
Chard, Jiri, Lilford, Richard and Gardiner, Derek 1999: Looking beyond the next patient: sociology and modern health care. *Lancet*, 353, 486–98.
Charlton, James I. 1998: *Nothing About Us Without Us: Disability, Oppression and Empowerment*. Berkeley: University of California Press.
Corker, Mairian and French, Sally (eds) 1999: *Disability Discourse*. Buckingham: Open University Press.
Devlieger, Patrick J. and Albrecht, Gary L. 2000: Your experience is not my experience: the concept and experience of disability on Chicago's near west side. *Journal of Disability Policy Studies*, 11, 51–60.
Dewey, John 1968–92: *The Collected Works of John Dewey, 37 vols*. Carbondale: Southern Illinois University Press.
DiMaggio, P., Evans, J. and Bryson, B. 1996: Have Americans' social attitudes become more polarized? *American Sociological Review*, 102, 690–755.
DuBois, W. E. B. 1961: *The Souls of Black Folk*. Greenwich, CT: Fawcett.
Evans, G. 1995: Why is America different? Explaining cross-national variation in support for welfare distribution. *Working Paper Series, Centre for Research into Elections and Social Trends*, Oxford: Nuffield College, 36, 1–28.
Faris, Robert E. L. and Dunham, H. Warren 1939: *Mental Disorders in Urban Areas*. Chicago: University of Chicago Press.
Fleischer, Doris Z. and Zames, Freida 2001: *The Disability Rights Movement: From Charity to Confrontation*. Philadelphia: Temple University Press.
Fujiura, Glenn T. and Rutkowski-Kmitta, Violet 2001: Counting disability. In Gary L. Albrecht, Katherine D. Seelman and Michael Bury (eds), *Handbook of Disability Studies*, Thousand Oaks, CA: Sage, 69–96.
Gleeson, Brendon 1999: *Geographies of Disability*. London: Routledge.
Goffman, Erving 1959: *The Presentation of the Self in Everyday Life*. New York: Doubleday.
Goffman, Erving 1961: *Asylums: Essays on the Social Situation of Mental Patients and Other Inmates*. Chicago: Aldine.
Gordon, Beth O. and Rosenblum, Karen E. 2001: Bringing disability into the sociological frame: a comparison of disability with race, sex, and sexual orientation statuses. *Disability and Society*, 16, 5–19.
Greenhouse, Linda 2001: Justices accept two cases to clarify protection for disabled. *New York Times*, 17 April, p. A13.
Haack, Susan 1993. *Evidence and Inquiry: Towards Reconstruction in Epistemology*. Oxford: Blackwell.

Haack, Susan 1996. Pragmatism. In N. Bunnin and E. P. Tsui-James (eds), *The Blackwell Companion to Philosophy*, Oxford: Blackwell, 643–61.

Hayward, Mark D., Crimmins, Eileen M., Miles, Toni P. and Yang, Yu 2000: The significance of socioeconomic status in explaining the racial gap in chronic health conditions. *American Sociological Review*, 65, 910–30.

James, William 1907: *Pragmatism*. Cambridge, MA: Harvard University Press.

Imrie, Rob 2000: Disabling environments and the geography of access: policies and practices. *Disability and Society*, 15, 5–24.

Kloppenberg, James A. 1998: Pragmatism. In R. W. Fox and J.T. Kloppenberg (eds), *A Companion to American Thought*, Oxford: Blackwell, 537–40.

Linton, Simi 1998: *Claiming Disability: Knowledge and Identity*. New York: New York University Press.

Llewellyn, A. and Hogan, K. 2000: The use and abuse of models of disability. *Disability and Society*, 15, 157–65.

Longmore, Paul K. and Umansky, Lauri (eds) 2001: *The New Disability History: American Perspectives*. New York: New York University Press.

Mead, George Herbert 1964 (1934): *Selected Writings: George Herbert Mead*, ed. A. J. Reck, New York: Bobbs-Merrill.

Michaud, Catherine M., Murray, Christopher J. L. and Bloom, Barry R. 2001: Burden of disease-implications for future research. *Journal of the American Medical Association*, 285, 535–9.

Mudrick, Nancy R. 1997: Employment discrimination laws for disability: utilization and outcomes. *Annals of the American Academy of Political and Social Science*, 549, 53–70.

Obershall, A. 1972: The sociological study of the history of social research. In A. Obershall (ed.), *The Establishment of Empirical Sociology: Studies in Continuity, Discontinuity, and Institutionalization*, New York: Harper & Row, 2–14.

Oliver, Michael 1990: *The Politics of Disablement*. New York: St Martin's Press.

Peirce, C. S. 1931–58 *Collected Papers*, ed. C. Hartshorne, P. Weiss and A. Burks. Cambridge, MA: Harvard University Press.

Popper, Karl R. 1972: *Objective Knowledge: An Evolutionary Approach*. Oxford: Clarendon Press.

Putnam, Hilary 1978: *Meaning and the Moral Sciences*. London: Routledge and Kegan Paul.

Quine, W. V. O. 1969: *Ontological Relativity and Other Essays*. New York: Columbia University Press.

Robertson, Ian 1977: *Sociology*. New York: Worth Publishers Inc.

Rorty, R. 1979: *Philosophy and the Mirror of Nature*. Princeton, NJ: Princeton University Press.

Rorty, R. 1991: *Objectivity, Relativism and Truth*. Cambridge: Cambridge University Press.

Schiller, F. C. S. 1907: *Studies in Humanism*. London and New York: Macmillan.

Sellars, W. 1973: Givenness and explanatory coherence. *Journal of Philosophy*, 61, 123–39.

Simmel, Georg 1955: *Conflict and the Web of Group Affiliations*. New York: Free Press.
Stiker, Henri-Jacques 1999: *A History of Disability*. Ann Arbor, MI: University of Michigan Press.
Strauss, A. 1993: *Continual Permutations of Action*. New York: Aldine De Gruyter.
Strauss, A. and Corbin, J. 1990: *Basics of Qualitative Method*. Newbury Park, CA: Sage.
Strauss, A. and Glaser, B. 1975: *Chronic Illness and the Quality of Life*. St Louis, MO: Mosby.
Weber, Max 1946: *From Max Weber: Essays in Sociology*, tr. and ed. H. H. Gerth and C. Wright Mills. New York: Oxford University Press.
West, Cornel 1999: *The Cornel West Reader*. New York: Basic Civitas Books.
Williams, Gareth H. 2001: Theorizing disability. In G. L. Albrecht, K. D. Seelman and M. Bury (eds), *The Handbook of Disability Studies*, Thousand Oaks, CA: Sage, 123–44.
Williams, Simon J. 2001: Sociological imperialism and the profession of medicine revisited: where are we now? *Sociology of Health & Illness*, 23,135–58.
Yelin, Edward H. 1997: The employment of people with and without disabilities in an age of insecurity. *Annals of the American Academy of Political and Social Science*, 549, 117–28.
Zola, Irving K. 1966: Culture and symptoms: an analysis of patients presenting complaints. *American Sociological Review*, 31, 615–30.
Zola, Irving K. 1989: Toward the necessary universalizing of disability policy. *Milbank Memorial Fund Quarterly*, 67 (suppl. 2), 401–28.
Zola, Irving K. 1991: Bringing our bodies and ourselves back in: reflections on the past, present and future of medical sociology. *Journal of Health and Social Behavior*, 32, 1–16.
Zola, Irving K. 1993: Disability statistics: what we count and what it tells us. *Journal of Disability Policy Studies*, 4, 9–39.

3

Disability Theory: Key Ideas, Issues and Thinkers

Carol Thomas

Introduction

'Disability' is a commonplace term. Its meaning, at one level, is beguilingly obvious – not being able to do something. In lay terms, referring to people with impairments as disabled signals that they belong to that group of people who cannot engage in 'normal' activities because of their 'abnormal' bodily or intellectual 'deficit' or 'incapacity'. Disability studies (DS) activists and writers in Britain have overturned this everyday meaning of disability, together with derivatives of it adopted in many academic disciplines. In contrast, DS proponents assert that the inability of people with impairments to undertake social activities is a consequence of the erection of barriers by the non-disabled majority. These social barriers – both physical and attitudinal – limit activity and constrain the lives of people with impairment. In short, these barriers socially exclude and work to oppress those with a socially ascribed impairment. The term 'disability' now refers to a type of social oppression, and disablism enters the vocabulary alongside sexism, racism and other discriminatory practices.

This simple exposition of the revolutionizing of the meaning of disability gives no hint of the political and conceptual struggles involved in its achievement, or of those yet to come in the advancement of the social status of disabled people and the related theorizing of their social position. In reality, the key ideas, issues and thinkers informing this new understanding of disability did not, and will not, belong exclusively to the academy. This chapter on key ideas, issues and thinkers – past and present – recognizes that the gaining of new knowledge about disability involves a dynamic interplay of, as well as conflict between, forces at a number of levels: the individual and the collective, the broader political, and the more narrowly academic and disciplinary.

The first part of the chapter outlines the social model of disability – its distinguishing ideas and political roots. This is followed by a review of more traditional ideas about disability that have been challenged by the disabled people's movement and DS – perspectives found in biomedicine, the rehabilitative sciences and services, and in medical sociology. This includes a discussion of the influential *International Classification of Impairments, Disabilities and Handicaps (ICIDH)* and its new incarnation as *ICIDH-2*. The next section of the chapter reviews ideas about disability within DS, outlining, in turn, materialist perspectives on the economic roots of disability, and feminist, postmodernist and poststructuralist views on the cultural generation of disability and the significance of impairment. The conclusion summarizes the chapter themes and considers the issues that lie ahead for disability studies thinkers.

The social model of disability

In Britain, the reformulating of disability as a form of social oppression as opposed to a purely medical or welfare concern began in the 1970s. Disabled individuals and groups began to self-organize to resist, among other things, their relegation to residential institutions, their exclusion from the labour market and the opportunity to earn a living wage, and their enforced poverty. The history of these early activities and pre-occupations of the disabled people's movement in Britain is now well documented (Oliver 1996c; Campbell and Oliver 1996; Barton and Oliver 1997) and archived (http://www.leeds.ac.uk/disability-studies/archiveuk/index.html). These political struggles in turn gave birth to radical new ideas about disability. One of the founding organizations in this movement, the Union of the Physically Impaired Against Segregation (UPIAS) bequeathed an important statement that played a key role in shifting the concept of disability into the realm of the social:

> [Disability is] the disadvantage or restriction of activity caused by a contemporary social organisation which takes no or little account of people who have [...] impairments and thus excludes them from the mainstream of social activities. (UPIAS 1976, cited in Oliver 1996c: 22)

This socio-political recasting of disability led the activist and scholar Mike Oliver to talk of 'the social model of disability'. The possibility was opened up that the restrictions of activity and myriad disadvantages experienced by people with impairments could be placed at the door of society, seen as a consequence of the social relationships between the impaired and the non-impaired, rather than as caused by impairment *per se*. Ideas about disability in lay, medical, welfarist and other cultural discourses – that restrictions of activity and social disdavantage are the inevitable and tragic consequence of being impaired – could be challenged and refuted. In fact, these traditional ideas could be understood to be a key part of the oppressive apparatus determining the lives of people with impairment (Finkelstein 1980; Oliver 1990; Barnes 1991; Morris 1991; Barton 1996; Barton and Oliver 1997).

The social modellist idea that disability is the outcome of social arrangements that work to restrict the activities of people with impairments through the erection of social barriers has become the leitmotif of disability studies in Britain. The social model of disability is the rallying call for disability organizations identifying with the disabled people's movement. When disabled individuals encounter the social model, the effect is often revelatory and liberatory, enabling them, perhaps for the first time, to recognize most of their difficulty as socially caused. Disabling barriers in all areas of social life come into view – in housing, education, employment, transport, cultural and leisure activities, health and welfare services, civil and political rights, and elsewhere.

What are the key antagonistic ideas that social modellists have been attempting to combat in the academy and among those in the medical and rehabilitative professions who have seen disability as their territory of expertise?

Ideas about disability to be challenged

Biomedicine and rehabilitation

Biomedicine has as its focus individual deviations of body and mind from socially recognized norms. Impairment *per se* is of central concern – its detection, avoidance, elimination, treatment and classification – though chronic and degenerative diseases remain hard nuts to crack. Much biomedical hope and expectation are currently invested in a fast-moving genetic science which appears to its practitioners to offer a brave new world of disease eradication and radical new treatments for the restoration of normal functioning. In this 'medical model' perspective, disability continues to be equated with the impairment itself – 'the disability' is the impairment. The emergence of the social model of disability has had little or no impact on constructions of disability in the heartlands of Western scientific medicine.

In the domain of rehabilitative science and services, the biomedical perspective on disability continues to have a weighty presence in training and practice, although the focus is on a different set of issues: the adjustment and adaptation of disabled individuals to a life 'as near normal' as possible. The same is true of social care or welfare services, although new entrants to professions such as social work in Britain are likely to have been introduced to social modellist thought in their training (Oliver and Sapey 1999). The social disadvantages associated with impairment are certainly recognized, and some therapists may attribute many of these to discrimination and inequality structured into the wider social environment. Nevertheless, at the core of this rehabilitative world-view is a strong adherence to the idea that impairment inevitably leads to social difficulties and exclusions, and that most of the latter can be causally attributed to impairment. This combination of ideas – that impairment causes limitations in activity, but so too do restrictions built into the wider social environment – has drawn many in the rehabilitative services towards the *International Classification of Impairments, Disabilities and Handicaps* (*ICIDH*). The influential and authoritative ideas embodied in the *ICIDH* require some attention.

The ICIDH

The *ICIDH* was developed for the World Health Organization by Philip Wood, Elizabeth Bradley and Mike Bury in the 1970s. Published in 1980 (Wood 1980), the *ICIDH* represented an important attempt to move away from a biomedical view of disability. Bury has expressed this as follows:

> These were very exciting days for the three of us. As we saw it, the [WHO] was moving away from a narrow medical model of health and disease – one primarily concerned with body systems and aetiologies – to one which recognised the consequences of health-related phenomena. We were particularly concerned to argue for a clearer recognition of social disadvantage – the focus of handicap codes in the classification. Our aim was to bring such disadvantages to the fore. (Bury 2000: 1073)

Handicap was defined in the *ICIDH* schema as 'a disadvantage for a given individual, resulting from an impairment or a disability, that limits or prevents the fulfillment of a role that is normal (depending on the age, sex, social and cultural factors) for that individual' (cited in Oliver

1996a: 40–1). The schema's definition of disability reflected the term's literal and lay meaning of 'lack of ability': 'a disability is any restriction or lack (resulting from impairment) of ability to perform an activity in the manner or within the range considered normal for a human being' (ibid.).

Thus disability (restricted activity) was not equated with impairment, but was seen as caused by it in large measure. Bury argues that the schema allowed the social disadvantages (handicaps) experienced by disabled people to come into view; there was room for the possibility that some restrictions of activity could be seen to be caused, or influenced, by social factors (Bury 1997, 2000). These ideas were used in a significant seam of social policy and sociological research on disability in the 1980s and 1990s (reviewed in Bury 1997, 2000). However, despite this move in the direction of social consequences and determination, most social modellists have opposed the *ICIDH* on the grounds that it retains a medical model causal link between impairment and disability such that the former determines the latter (Oliver 1996c), and because the term 'handicap' (as well as being offensive because of its 'begging' associations: cap-in-hand) just does not do the job of re-centring the problems of disability in social arrangements and practices.

The WHO's *ICIDH* schema has recently been revised in the form of *ICIDH-2* (Pfeiffer 1998, 2000; Bickenbach et al. 1999; Bury 2000). The term 'disability' has been replaced with 'disablement', with a focus on limits to activities, and 'handicap' is superseded by considerations of 'participation'; impairment remains as before – loss or abnormality of psychological, physiological or anatomical structure or function. Do these changes in terminology represent a shift in thinking in the direction of social modellist ideas? The authors of *ICIDH-2* have certainly acknowledged the voices of disabled people's organizations in Britain and internationally, and have wanted to give an upbeat spin to 'disablement'. However, the many voices of those with a professional interest in the schema have also been attended to. The end result is a schema that differs from the original *ICIDH* in its use of language and in details, but not in its three-tier 'impairment–disability–handicap' structure, although the old causal links from level one to level three are not so clearly in evidence:

> The *ICIDH-2* embodies what is now termed the 'biopsychosocial' model, a synthesis of the medical and social approaches to disablement. Each dimension of disablement is conceptualized as an interaction between intrinsic features of the individual and that person's social and physical environment. (Bickenbach et al. 1999: 1183)

Within DS, opinions differ on whether *ICIDH-2* has anything to offer disabled people (Pfeiffer 2000; Hurst 2000). The outcome of the present period of field-testing *ICIDH-2* will be of interest to all.

Medical sociology

The *ICIDH* was the definitional approach to disability favoured by medical sociologists in Britain. As an architect of the *ICIDH* schema, the medical sociologist Mike Bury has defended its use in the field known as 'the sociology of chronic illness and disability' (Bury 1997). Bury has been one of the few sociologists to publicly engage with social modellist ideas, although he finds little of value in them (see also the debate in Barnes and Mercer 1996). In his view (Bury 2000: 1074), the key problem with the social model of disability is its 'oversocialised' character as witnessed in Oliver's (1996a, 1996c) denial of any causal link between impairment and restricted activity (disability). For Bury, chronic illnesses such as stroke, arthritis and multiple sclerosis undeniably cause restricted activity. Advocates of the social model have created

> what has frequently seemed to me to be a confusing and confused 'radical' alternative to disablement: by turns Marxist, constructionist and deeply individualistic. I do not believe that the 'social model' has really engaged with the real issues facing the vast majority of disabled people, and, despite its rhetoric and undoubted attractions for some, it has not produced a cogent approach which can serve the real practical needs of disabled people, or indeed the research community. (Bury 2000: 1075)

I have discussed the difference in positions adopted by Bury and Oliver at length elsewhere (Thomas 1999). Writing from a social modellist stance, I can see the logic in Bury's argument about oversocialization in cases where the social model is presented in a rather crude form. My own argument can be briefly summarized as follows. *If* the social model position were that *all* restrictions of activity experienced by people with impairment are caused by social barriers (and this is how it sometimes appears), then this would indeed be an oversocialized stance. But this is not the claim made in the UPIAS reformulation of disability cited above. The UPIAS statement asserts that disability comes into being when aspects of contemporary social structure and practice operate to disadvantage and exclude people with impairments through a restriction of their activity. Disability is not equated with restricted activity *per se*, as it is in the *ICIDH* schema. The potential for impairment to limit activities is not denied, but such restrictions do not constitute *disability*; I have used the term 'impairment effects' to distinguish these kinds of limits on activity (Thomas 1999). The important point here is that medical sociologists, social policy writers and other social scientists have grossly underestimated, and frequently ignored, socially engendered restrictions, disadvantages and exclusions – that is, disability. Impairment effects are focused upon at the expense of what really troubles most people who live with impairment – disability. Restrictions of activity are frequently attributed solely to impairment effects when they are actually the result of disablism (or a combination of the two). To put it in a way that makes use of the *ICIDH*'s own terminology, a sociology of *handicap* is woefully underdeveloped. A large body of sociological research on 'handicap' simply has not come into being (see Blaxter 1976 for an early example of what could have been built on).

There is a weighty literature in the sociology of chronic illness and disability regarding the phenomenology of the experience of living with chronic illnesses and other impairments (Anderson and Bury 1988; Conrad 1990; Bury 1991, 1997; Radley 1993, 1994; Kelly and Field 1996). In the interpretivist tradition, attention has been focused on how 'sufferers' give meaning to, and cope with, their changed identity and sense of purpose in the wake of a chronic illness diagnosis or major injury. Key concepts in this field are biographical disruption, illness narrative, coping, illness management and negotiated orders. While having the merit of highlighting some of the important existential and ontological dimensions of experiences that had previously been viewed solely through biomedical lenses, this research has thrown little light on the material and wider social dimensions of being or becoming impaired. Gareth Williams (1996: 209–10), who has written in both the medical sociology and DS camps, puts it well:

> the work of many sociologists starts off by viewing the experience of chronic illness and disablement in its context of social and economic circumstances, but gets side-tracked into increasingly solipsistic explorations of identity and self.

In my view (a view not shared by many in DS) this literature in medical sociology is of interest and value, but it is *not* a sociology of disability. It does not begin to address the issues of pressing concern to many disabled people: independent living, poverty, employment, education, communication, transportation, accessing built environments and civil rights. By dismissing the social model of disability as oversocialized, Bury and others actually side-step the necessity to engage with the idea that disability is a form of social oppression, something that they are happy to contemplate in other sets of social relationships associated with gender, 'race', sexuality and class.

Another significant literature in sociology that appears to have something important to say about disability is 'the sociology of the body', a growing preoccupation in the 1980s and beyond, signalling the considerable impact of postmodernist and poststructuralist ideas on a wide range of disciplines in the academy. As we shall see in the next section, some writers *within* disability studies have also drawn upon these theoretical perspectives, but as far as the wider literature on the sociology of the body is concerned, very little has been said about impairment or disability.

The sociology of the body

The 'missing' impaired and disabled body in the sociology of the body is, in part, a reflection of the fact that 'real' bodies – material and organic – of any type are absent. The social constructionist character of much of the theorizing ensures that it is the cultural representations and discursive positionings of bodies (that is, of 'normal' bodies) that is the focus of interest. The 'fixed', material, body has been viewed as a complex of ideas manufactured by essentialist, though powerful, cultural discourses including the biological sciences and medicine (Turner 1992). However, this constructionist sociology of the body has recently become the subject of critique, and there are some calls for the real material body to be brought back in. Of particular note is the work of Simon Williams and Gillian Bendelow in their book *The Lived Body* (1998). These authors reject the 'shifting sands' social constructionist project of reducing the body to a series of representations, while at the same time retaining what they see as some of the valuable insights that a constructionist perspective offers. They argue that sociologists, as embodied subjects themselves, need to move from the theorization 'of' the body (in which the body is objectified) to an embodied sociology:

> theorising not so much *about* bodies (in a largely disembodied male way) but *from* bodies as *lived* entities, including those of its practitioners as well as its subjects. Social institutions and discursive practices cannot be understood apart from the real lived experiences and actions of embodied human beings across time and space. Social theory must therefore be rooted in the problems of human embodiment. (Williams and Bendelow 1998: 209)

Whether such a move would bring the sociology of the body into a serious engagement with impairment and disability is uncertain, and perhaps unlikely. It is significant that in their extended argument about the need to return to 'real', 'lived', bodies, Williams and Bendelow (1998) barely mention disability, either in the traditional medical sociological sense of restricted activity or in the social modellist sense of social oppression. Thus it appears that ideas in the field of the sociology of the body have yet to offer anything of significance on the subject of disability.

Debates within disability studies

In asserting that disability is socially caused and a form of social oppression, the social model of disability unleashes a series of new sociological questions, not least: How can this social phenomenon be theorized? What is its social history? In the newly emerging British disability studies of the 1980s, some of the leading thinkers sought answers to these questions in Marxist or materialist paradigms (Finkelstein 1980; Oliver 1990; Barnes 1991). With the gathering of interest in DS, these influential ideas have been challenged by a growing number of disability studies writers employing other theoretical systems, particularly feminism(s), postmodernism and poststructuralism (Priestley 1998; Thomas 1999). There is now lively debate about the nature of both disability and impairment in DS, and some of the key issues shall be explored.

Materialist perspectives on disability

Building on the early insights of Vic Finkelstein (1980), Mike Oliver (1990) examined the relationship between disability and capitalist relations of production. The issue is as follows: if disability is the restriction of activity imposed on people with impairment by contemporary social structures and practices, how did this come into being? In Oliver's view the answer lies in the emergence of industrial capitalism. In brief, when the wage–labour relation became increasingly bound up with large-scale industry from the late eighteenth century in Britain, people with impairment began to be systematically excluded from direct involvement in economic activity. Long hours of labour in factory environments required a standardized dexterity, speed and intensity of work. Many people with impairments were unable to sell their labour power under such conditions; they were increasingly socially positioned as dependants, excluded in the economy of generalized commodity production. During the nineteenth century, large-scale industry increasingly usurped small-scale manufacture and petty commodity production, the dependency of impaired people was consolidated, and the policy solution to the 'social problem' they posed was found in institutionalization and medicalization (for a more detailed account of the argument, see Oliver 1990; Thomas 1999). The exclusions and dependency that disabled people experienced in the twentieth century – barriers in employment, education, welfare services, housing, transport, cultural and leisure domains, whether in institutional or community settings – could be traced back to this earlier economic relegation of the impaired to the category of the 'non-productive' and the dependant. Oliver summarizes his position as follows:

> Hence the economy, through both the operation of the labour market and the social organisation of work, plays a key role in producing the category disability and in determining societal responses to disabled people. Further, the oppression that disabled people face is rooted in the economic and social structures of capitalism which themselves produce racism, sexism, homophobia, ageism and disablism. (Oliver 1996b: 33)

The Australian-based scholar Brendan Gleeson (1997, 1999) has considerably developed this materialist perspective on the historical emergence of disability, marshalling evidence for the argument that disability has its origins in the transition from feudal to capitalist social relations of production. These kinds of analyses make the decisive point that disability is not a transhistorical, ubiquitous, social phenomenon, but is bound up with social relationships at specific historical junctures. This enables us to move beyond simplistic ideas about disability being a type of always occurring 'restricted activity'; disability is located spatially, temporally and economically.

In my view, this materialist perspective on the economic roots of disability, where disability is viewed in a social-relational sense (a phenomenon of social relationships between groups of people in socio-structural circumstances), is of great interest and value. However, materialist writers in disability studies need to be able to update their analyses to take theoretical account of contemporary developments in capitalist economic systems. The challenge is to examine whether economic arrangements characteristic of a global capitalism, or hypercapitalism (Scholte 2000) – with its multi- and trans-national corporations, supra-territorial money and finance systems, and burgeoning information and communications industries – is changing, perhaps transforming, the social position of people with impairments, for better or worse. Do people with impairments now occupy an entirely different relationship to the wage–labour economy because 'new technologies' no longer automatically exclude their participation? Perhaps it depends on the type of impairment. What new divisions, exclusions and dependencies are opened up? The analysis of such questions has begun in DS (Roulstone 1998; Sapey 2000; Beresford and Holden 2000), but a great deal remains to be examined.

How has this materialist, or Marxian, rendering of the basic social modellist proposition that disability is the socially produced restrictions on activity experienced by people with impairments been challenged within British DS?

The foregrounding of 'difference' and culture

Disability studies in Britain has been enriched by the growing presence of perspectives and issues that have challenged the materialist prioritization of the economic roots of disability and the contemporary operation of structural barriers in the wider social environment. Questions have been posed about the adequacy of this agenda in dealing with matters of difference among disabled people, especially those associated with gender, 'race', sexuality or type of impairment (e.g., Corbett 1994; Warmsley 1997; Morris 1996; Crow 1996; Appleby 1994; Vernon 1996; Corker 1998). Taking deafness as an example, perhaps people with particular forms of impairment experience forms of disablism that are as much about language, communication and cultural systems as they are about the disabling barriers traditionally identified in social modellist thought (Corker 1998)? Or perhaps disabled women occupy different kinds of social locations to disabled men, because more than one system of oppression is in operation, so that they have priorities not addressed in conventional social modellist thinking (Morris 1991, 1993, 1996). The writing that has emerged through an engagement with such questions has drawn upon feminist, postmodernist, poststructuralist and other social constructionist theoretical ideas. The work of feminists in disability studies is of particular note, but this should not be mistaken for a single set of ideas. Wider feminist thinking has fragmented into several feminisms, each linked to other theoretical traditions, some materialist and some social constructionist (Thomas 1999, 2001, 2002).

The social model of disability itself has come into the firing line: is it too limited, exclusive, inadequate, in need of adaptation, transformation or replacement? Vigorous debate is ongoing. Here, two issues of significance in the exchange of ideas will be discussed: culture and disability, and the need to theorize impairment.

Culture and disability

Writers such as Tom Shakespeare (1997) and Mairian Corker (1998, Corker and French 1999) have argued that much social modellist thinking seriously downplays the importance of cultural processes and discourses in the generation of disability and disablism:

> A determinist view, [materialism] does not give much explanatory space or autonomy to the realm of culture and meaning. (Shakespeare 1997: 224)

> Because human agency is lost in the materialism of the social model and because discourse is seen to be a side-effect of social structure, neither can be the focus for social change. (Corker 1998: 39)

In the minds of these writers, materialism mistakenly sees culture as either of little significance or as secondary to, and determined by, the economic – as part of an ideological superstructure. In contrast, considerable emphasis is placed on the disability-engendering role played by cultural ideas, always negative, about people with impairment: these ideas position those with culturally ascribed bodily and behavioural differences, 'abominations', in locations of powerlessness and dependency, profoundly undermining their sense of self-worth and identity. Foucauldian notions of the self-disciplining of the body in the shadow of powerful medical and welfarist discourses on impairment are seen to offer ways of understanding the subordination experienced by disabled people (Price and Shildrick 1998).

Postmodernist and poststructuralist perspectives on the cultural construction of our social worlds involve the rejection of what are seen to be rationalist, modernist ideas. The materialist view of the roots of disability being located in capitalist social relations of production is dismissed as mistakenly modernist. Emphasis is placed on the need to transcend the dualistic thinking attributed to modernism, wherein the body is separated from the mind, the biological from the social, and the cultural from the economic. Rather, all social phenomena, including disability and impairment, should be understood to be woven through, and out of, cultural ideas and discursive practices: there is no 'reality' independent of ideas concerning it.

Materialistically oriented writers have, in turn, critiqued the position of those who attach such overriding significance to the cultural, although it is acknowledged that more attention to cultural and ideological forces in the shaping of disablism is required (Barnes 1996; Oliver 1996c). Barnes, for example, objects to what he suggests is a reduction of explanations for social phenomena to 'thought processes' (Barnes 1996: 49). Some in disability studies see the possibility of drawing on the strengths of both the materialist and the social constructionist arguments: '[This form of oppression] needs to be considered as a product of both cultural values and material relations of power (such as political economy, patriarchy and imperialism)' (Priestley 1998: 87). We await with interest the further elaboration of arguments on these issues.

Impairment

One issue over which materialist, social constructionist and feminist perspectives within DS have clashed is the relevance and nature of impairment (Thomas 1999, 2001, 2002). Social modellists like Oliver (1996c) and Barnes (1998) have argued that the personal experience of living with impairment is not the concern of disability studies, and that intellectual and political energies should be concentrated on understanding and tackling the wider social causes *of disability*. They see a focus on impairment as posing a danger to the gains made by the social model's conceptual severing of impairment from disability – it gives succour to the 'impairment causes disability' positions in the medical model of disability, medical sociology and other disciplines.

The argument for the necessity of paying attention to impairment has been made on a number of grounds. First, feminist writers like Jenny Morris (1996) and Liz Crow (1996) have argued that the social modellist relegation of impairment to the domain of 'the private and personal' is a reflection in DS of a patriarchal separation of 'the personal' from 'the public', the private from the social (Thomas 2001). Jenny Morris sees this as problematic:

> there was a concern amongst some disabled women that the way our experience was being politicised didn't leave much room for acknowledging our experience of our bodies; that too often there wasn't room for talking about the experience of impairment, that a lot of us feel pressurised into just focusing on social barriers. (Morris 1996: 13)

A plea was being made for impairment experiences to be acknowledged, discussed and shared in disability politics and DS; bringing to life the 'personal is political' feminist slogan. It was seen as anti-holistic and unacceptable to construct impairment in terms of the 'private'. Further, it was suggested that impairment *did* restrict activities in important ways (Morris 1996; Crow 1996; French 1993; Wendell 1996), a position seen as particularly problematic by those social modellists who equate disability with 'restricted activity' (see the discussion in Thomas 1999). Clearly, on this point, there is some overlap with the medical sociological arguments of Mike Bury discussed earlier, about a causal link between illness and disability.

A second variant in this line of argument is the contention of social constructionist feminists that the distinction between disability (as social) and impairment (as biological, of the body) is a product of modernist, 'essentialist', dualistic thinking (Shildrick and Price 1996; Price and Shildrick 1998; Corker 1998; Corker and French 1999). In this view, *both* impairment and disability are discursively constructed social categories, the former having no relationship to a supposedly underlying biological reality, itself another construct. The postmodernist feminist writers Janet Price and Margrit Shildrick express this as follows:

> The postmodernist claim that there is no essential biologically given corpus upon which meaning is inscribed, and no unmediated access to a body prior to discourse, remains contentious. It is not that the materiality of the body is in doubt, but that materiality is a process negotiated through the discursive exercise of what Foucault (1980) calls power/knowledge. To both the biomedical profession with its fantasy of descriptive objectivity, and to the [disabled people's movement] with its investment in the notion that impairment can be separated off from disability, the claim is anathema. While both may subscribe to the view that health care practices are both normative and normalising, there is little recognition that those practices are also constitutive of the body. As Judith Butler puts it... 'there is no reference to a pure body which is not at the same time a further formation of that body' (1993:10). What that means is that the physical impairments of the body, and the socially constructed disability are equally constructs held in place by regulatory practices that produce and govern all bodies. (Price and Shildrick 1998: 234)

So, for Price and Shildrick, powerful discourses in medicine and other regulatory domains work to represent, construct and position some people as 'impaired' or 'disabled' and others as 'normal'. In this view, there is nothing inherent, or 'pre-social', in individuals' bodily states that can sustain the idea of 'real' bodily differences – 'impaired' and 'disabled' people are entirely discursively constructed.

A third argument in a similar vein is found in the work of DS writers Bill Hughes and Kevin Paterson (1997; Hughes 2000):

> there is a powerful convergence between biomedicine and the social model of disability with respect to the body. Both treat it as a pre-social, inert, physical object, as discrete, palpable and separate from the self. The definitional

separation of impairment and disability which is now a semantic convention for the social model follows the traditional, Cartesian, western meta-narrative of human constitution. (Hughes and Paterson 1997: 329)

The apparent social modellist relegation of impairment to the realm of the biological is thus seen as an example of untenable dualistic thinking; impairment is naturalized when it should be thought of as *social*. However, unlike postmodernist thinkers, Hughes and Paterson do not want to deny the 'reality' of impairment and the materiality of bodies. Their solution lies with a future sociology of impairment, one that draws on phenomenological perspectives in particular, emphasizing the importance of the lived experience of impairment.

In response to the earlier feminist calls for impairment to be taken seriously, and for it to become a concern within DS, Mike Oliver (1996c) has acknowledged that a sociology of impairment may well constitute a field of study, but has also stuck to his guns, that impairment is not the business of DS. Not all materialistically oriented DS writers have agreed with this stance. Paul Abberley (1987, 1996), for example, has long argued against the social modellist naturalization of impairment through its relegation to the realm of the biological (leaving it, unchallenged, in the hands of the biomedics). However, unlike social constructionist thinkers, Abberley has drawn attention to the 'real' social production of impairment – the material creation of impairment in capitalist and other societies. Impairment is produced through a myriad of social production and other processes: accidents and injury in work-places; accidents in transportation; medical mistakes, drug therapies and surgical advances (extending the life expectancy of many people with impairment); wars, street and domestic violence, and so forth. Thus impairment is as much social as it is biological. This is an important argument, suggesting that DS should encompass the study of both disability and impairment.

The arguments about the nature and relevance of impairment are ongoing. One thing is certain: impairment will not go away in DS debates; it is an issue that requires further theoretical and political attention. This is a particularly pressing matter given the rising star of the genetic sciences and associated technologies, whose advances have profound implications for disabled people.

Conclusion

This chapter has reviewed a range of competing ideas about disability. 'Traditional' ways of thinking about disability – in biomedicine, rehabilitative science and services, and in medical sociology – have been outlined, as has the challenge to these ideas forged through the political struggle of disabled people against their day-to-day subordination and oppression.

The emergence of DS as an academic discipline in Britain saw the conceptual elaboration of the social model of disability. In the early stages, the flesh that was added to the bones of this model had a materialist cast: the roots of the socially engendered restriction of activity experienced by people with impairment were sought in the social relations of the capitalist system of commodity production. Contemporary exclusions were located in the operation of socio-structural 'social barriers'. More recently, and as DS has gathered strength, other theoretical perspectives, much influenced by social constructionist thought, have also made their presence felt in DS. The social model itself has, in turn, been criticized and vigorously defended. Ensuing debates about disability have demanded an engagement with the significance of culture in the creation of disability, and with the matter of impairment itself. The intersection of disability with other forms of oppression – gender, 'race', sexual orientation (and, to a lesser extent, class and age) – has been placed on the theoretical agenda by feminists and others. The need to recognize and deal conceptually with 'difference' among disabled people has also been a growing theme in DS. This has demanded both that the difference in the lived experiences of categories of disabled people (men, women, straight, gay, with learning difficulty and/or physical impairment and/or mental 'illness', and so on) are better understood *and*, in a postmodernist sense, that these categories are themselves deconstructed because they are essentialist and discursively generated.

Debates within DS, and between DS writers and those in other traditions – especially medical sociologists – are engines for the formulation of an ever more sophisticated sociology of disability. In my view, the deepening of a materialist theorization of disability, but one that encompasses questions of culture, difference and impairment, is required (Thomas 1999, 2001, 2002). I have also argued for the recognition and theorization of what I have called the psycho-emotional dimensions of disability – those disablist practices that undermine the psychological and emotional well-being of people with impairment – something largely unacknowledged as a form of disablism in social modellist thought (Thomas 1999). Other writers will set different priorities for DS, but whatever our agendas, a considerable amount of research and theorizing lies ahead. Thought needs to be further applied to many disability issues, not least the impact of globalization, disability in developing societies, information technology: communication systems, genetic science and medical practices, independent living, welfare system change, the achievement of full civil rights, media representations – the list goes on.

Disability studies is a young discipline, with an encouraging rate of expansion. However, it should not be forgotten that its radical edge and its relevance to disabled people in our communities hinges on its ability to maintain its close alliance and involvement with the ongoing political struggles of disabled people.

REFERENCES

Abberley, P. 1987: The concept of oppression and the development of a social theory of disability. *Disability, Handicap and Society*, 2, 5–20.
Abberley, P. 1996: Work, utopia and impairment. In L. Barton (ed.), *Disability and Society: Emerging Issues and Insights*. London: Longman, 61–79.
Anderson, R. and Bury, M. (eds) 1988: *Living with Chronic Illness: The Experience of Patients and their Families*. London: Unwin Hyman.
Appleby, Y. 1994: Out in the margins. *Disability and Society*, 9 (1), 19–32.
Barnes, C. 1991: *Disabled People in Britain and Discrimination*. London: Hurst & Co.
Barnes, C. 1996: Theories of disability and the origins of the oppression of disabled people in western society. In L. Barton (ed.), *Disability and Society: Emerging Issues and Insights*. London: Longman, 43–61.
Barnes, C. 1998: Review of *The Rejected Body* by Susan Wendell. *Disability and Society*, 13 (1): 145–6.
Barnes, C. and Mercer, G. (eds) 1996: *Exploring the Divide: Illness and Disability*. Leeds: Disability Press.
Barton, L. (ed.) 1996: *Disability and Society: Emerging Issues and Insights*. London: Longman.
Barton, L. and Oliver, M. (eds) 1997: *Disability Studies: Past, Present and Future*. Leeds: Disability Press.
Beresford, P. and Holden, C. 2000: We have choices: globalisation and welfare user movements. *Disability and Society*, 15 (7), 973–89.
Bickenbach, J. E., Chatterji, S., Badley, E. M. and Ustun, T. B. 1999: Models of disablement, universalism and the international classification of impairments, disabilities and handicaps. *Social Science and Medicine*, 48, 1173–87.
Blaxter, M. 1976: *The Meaning of Disability*. London: Heinemann.
Bury, M. 1991: The sociology of chronic illness: a review of research and prospects. *Sociology of Health and Illness*, 13 (4), 167–82.
Bury, M. 1997: *Health and Illness in a Changing Society*. London: Routledge.
Bury, M. 2000: A comment on the *ICIDH2*. *Disability and Society*, 15 (7), 1073–7.
Butler, J. 1993: *Bodies that Matter: On the Discursive Limits of 'Sex'*. London: Routledge.

Campbell, J. and Oliver, M. 1996: *Disability Politics: Understanding our Past, Changing our Future*. London: Routledge.

Conrad, P. 1990: Qualitative research on chronic illness: a commentary on method and conceptual development. *Social Science and Medicine*, 30 (11), 1257–63.

Corbett, J. 1994: A proud label: exploring the relationship between disability politics and gay pride. *Disability and Society*, 9 (3), 343–57.

Corker, M. 1998: *Deaf and Disabled, or Deafness Disabled?* Buckingham: Open University Press.

Corker, M. and French, S. (eds) 1999: *Disability Discourse*. Buckingham: Open University Press.

Crow, L. 1996: Including all of our lives: renewing the social model of disability. In C. Barnes and G. Mercer (eds), *Exploring the Divide: Illness and Disability*, Leeds: Disability Press, 55–73.

Finkelstein, V. 1980: *Attitudes and Disabled People: Issues for Discussion*. New York: World Rehabilitation Fund.

French, S. 1993: Disability, impairment or something in between? In J. Swain, V. Finkelstein, S. French, and M. Oliver (eds), *Disabling Barriers – Enabling Environments*, London: Sage, 17–24.

Gleeson, B. J. 1997: Disability studies: a historical materialist view. *Disability and Society*, 12 (2), 179–202.

Gleeson, B. J. 1999: *Geographies of Disability*. London: Routledge.

Hughes, B. 2000: Medicine and the aesthetic invalidation of disabled people. *Disability and Society*, 15 (4), 555–68.

Hughes, B. and Paterson, K. 1997: The social model of disability and the disappearing body: towards a sociology of impairment. *Disability and Society*, 12 (3), 325–40.

Hurst, R. 2000: To revise or not to revise? *Disability and Society*, 15 (7), 1083–7.

Kelly, M. and Field, D. 1996: Medical sociology, chronic illness and the body. *Sociology of Health and Illness*, 18 (2), 241–57.

Morris, J. 1991: *Pride Against Prejudice: Transforming Attitudes to Disability*. London: Women's Press.

Morris, J. 1993: Gender and disability. In J. Swain, V. Finkelstein, S. French, and M. Oliver (eds), *Disabling Barriers – Enabling Environments*, London: Sage, 85–92.

Morris, J. (ed.) 1996: *Encounters with Strangers: Feminism and Disability*. London: Women's Press.

Oliver, M. 1990: *The Politics of Disablement*. London: Macmillan.

Oliver, M. 1996a: Defining impairment and disability: issues at stake. In C. Barnes and G. Mercer (eds), *Exploring the Divide: Illness and Disability*, Leeds: Disability Press, 139–54.

Oliver, M. 1996b: A sociology of disability or a disablist sociology? In L. Barton (ed.), *Disability and Society: Emerging Issues and Insights*, London: Longman, 18–42.

Oliver, M. 1996c: *Understanding Disability*. London: Macmillan.

Oliver, M. and Sapey, B. 1999: *Social Work With Disabled People*. 2nd edn. Basingstoke: Macmillan.

Pfeiffer, D. 1998: The *ICIDH* and the need for its revision. *Disability and Society*, 13 (4), 503–23.

Pfeiffer, D. 2000: The devils are in the details: the *ICIDH2* and the disability movement. *Disability and Society*, 15 (7), 1079–82.

Price, J. and Shildrick, M. 1998: Uncertain thoughts on the dis / abled body. In M. Shildrick and J. Price (eds), *Vital Signs: Feminist Reconfigurations of the Biological Body*, Edinburgh: Edinburgh University Press, 224 – 49.

Priestley, M. 1998: Constructions and creations: idealism, materialism and disability theory. *Disability and Society*, 13 (1), 75–95.

Radley, A. (ed.) 1993: *Worlds of Illness: Biographical and Cultural Perspectives on Health and Disease*. London: Routledge.

Radley, A. (ed.) 1994: *Making Sense of Illness*. London: Sage.

Roulstone, A. 1998: *Enabling Technology: Disabled People, Work and New Technology*. Buckingham: Open University Press.

Sapey, B. 2000: Disablement in the informational age. *Disability and Society*, 15 (4), 619–36.

Scholte, J. A. 2000: *Globalization: A Critical Introduction*. Basingstoke: Palgrave.

Shakespeare, T. 1996: Disability, identity, difference. In C. Barnes and G. Mercer (eds), *Exploring the Divide: Illness and Disability*, Leeds: Disability Press, 94–113.

Shakespeare, T. 1997: Cultural representation of disabled people: dustbins of disavowal? In L. Barton and M. Oliver (eds), *Disability Studies: Past, Present and Future*, Leeds: Disability Press, 217–36.

Shildrick, M. and Price, J. 1996: Breaking the boundaries of the broken body. *Body and Society*, 2 (4), 93–113.

Thomas, C. 1999: *Female Forms: Experiencing and Understanding Disability*. Buckingham: Open University Press.

Thomas, C. 2001: Feminism and disability: the theoretical and political significance of the personal and the experiential. In L. Barton (ed.), *Disability, Politics and the Struggle for Change*. London: David Fulton Publications, 45–58.

Thomas, C. 2002: The 'Disabled' Body. In M. Evans and E. Lee (eds), *Real Bodies*, Basingstoke: Macmillan (forthcoming)

Turner, B. S. 1992: *Regulating Bodies: Essays in Medical Sociology*. London: Routledge.

Vernon, A. 1996: A stranger in many camps: the experience of disabled black and ethnic minority women. In J. Morris (ed.), *Encounters with Strangers: Feminism and Disability*, London: Women's Press, 48–68.

Warmsley, J. 1997: Including people with learning difficulties: theory and practice. In L. Barton and M. Oliver (eds), *Disability Studies: Past, Present and Future*, Leeds: Disability Press, 62–77.

Wendell, S. 1996: *The Rejected Body: Feminist Philosophical Reflections on Disability.* London: Routledge.

Williams, G. 1996: Representing disability: some questions of phenomenology and politics. In C. Barnes and G. Mercer (eds), *Exploring the Divide: Illness and Disability,* Leeds: Disability Press, 194–212.

Williams, S. and Bendelow, G. 1998: *The Lived Body: Sociological Themes, Embodied Issues.* London: Routledge.

Wood, P. 1980: *International Classifications of Impairments, Disabilities and Handicaps.* Geneva: World Health Organization.

4

Disability and the Body

Bill Hughes

Introduction

The relationship between disability and the body – once settled and non-controversial – has become, since the 1960s, a highly contested domain. The long historical partnership between modernity and medicalization produced a hegemonic conception of disability as an outcome of bio-physical or mental impairment. Disabled people were people with broken bodies or faulty minds. It is the fate of breakage – as matter out of place – to be swept up and disposed of. To the modern mind, in particular, to appear to be 'broken' or 'faulty' was to offend against the sense of order, to represent a hint of chaos in a context dominated by clarity and perspective. As Alain Touraine (1995: 201) put it, 'The triumph of rationalist modernity rejected or forgot anything that seemed to resist the triumph of reason, or else confined it in repressive institutions.' If the history of modernity is, as Touraine suggests, one of forgetfulness, exclusion and confinement, then surely the most exemplary particular instance of this history is the modern experience of disabled people.

The definition of disability as a corporeal problem has meant that, for the most part, throughout modernity, disabled people have come under the jurisdiction, control and surveillance of (bio)medicine. This process of locating disability within the disciplinary scope of medicine has influenced profoundly the state of knowledge about it. Disability has been understood as a sickness, and disabled people have been understood as invalids. The medicalization or corporealization of disability suggests, therefore, that the life of a disabled person must be understood in terms of incapacity and confinement. Social policy has followed through with this discourse such that, in modernity, disabled people have been confined, indeed incarcerated, socially excluded, stripped of their social responsibilities and constituted as the epitome of dependency. The application of the label 'invalid' to disabled people has contributed to their 'invalidation'– that is, to their constitution as strangers (Hughes 1999; 2000). This argument suggests that the production of medical knowledge about disabled people has itself been disabling.

However, a materialist critique of the medical model of disability has developed apace since the 1960s. The 'social model of disability' (Oliver 1990; Finkelstein 1980) developed as the intellectual expression of the movement of disabled people. It embodies the argument that disability should be understood not as a corporeal deficit but in terms of the ways in which social structure excludes and oppresses disabled people. By separating physical or mental impairment from social processes of discrimination, exclusion and oppression, the social model of disability was able to make the case that disability was a public issue rather than a personal trouble (Barnes et al. 1999). In so doing, however, the social model instituted an analytical distinction between impairment and disability. Ironically, just as sociology – through (the new) sociology of the body – was trying to deconstruct the duality of body and society (Williams and Bendelow 1998), disability studies – by consigning impairment to a pre-social domain – was constructing a new dualism. In the early 1990s the sociology of the body and disability studies seemed to be ships passing in the night. The problem for the sociology of the body was that the accusations of disablism that were made against it were warranted (Hughes and Paterson 1997). The problem for disability studies was that it had cut itself off from the possibility of developing a sociology of impairment (Hughes and Paterson 1997). I think that it is probably fair to say that disability studies has made more progress with its problem than the sociology of the body has made with its.

This chapter is divided into three sections, entitled 'Thesis', 'Antithesis' and 'Synthesis'. This is not an attempt to claim a particular philosophical heritage for what follows. It is simply a heuristic device that I have used to try to map out the relationship, in modernity, between the body and disability. Mapping sociology into the relationship between the body and disability has been a relatively simple task, because I have accepted the 'orthodox' sociology of the body account which argues that the body in sociology has been – until recently – an 'absent presence' (Shilling 1993, Williams and Bendelow 1998). Medicine has dominated the interpretation of disability for most of modernity. Consequently,

disability has been construed in corporeal terms as an outcome of physical or mental impairment, and sociology has been – with respect to the
interpretation of disability – an 'absent presence' in which the 'presence'
– as the first section will demonstrate – is often difficult to detect. In the
post-World War II period, medical sociology began to offer explanations
of disability. Yet, despite the partial advances offered by labelling theory
and Goffman's (1968) account of stigma, as a body of knowledge,
medical sociology tended to confirm the physicians' view that disability
was a sickness (Barnes and Mercer 1996). It was the antithesis of the
conception of disability as a corporeal essence, provided by disability
studies, as it emerged from the 'social model of disability', that made
sociology a truly valuable frame of reference for reflections on disability.
However, the social model pushed the study of impairment to the fringes
of disability studies, and it is only recently that it and the sociology of the
body have combined to try to map out the case for a 'sociology of
impairment' (Hughes and Paterson 1997).

Thesis

*The ontological essence of disability is a physical or mental impairment
or a biological 'deficit' or 'flaw' that limits what disabled people can do.*

The dominant framework for understanding disability in the modern
period has been the medical model (Oliver 1990). From the early nineteenth century onwards, biomedicine legitimated the view that biophys-
ical 'abnormality' or 'maladaptation' leads to, or is the cause of, social
'abnormality' or 'maladaptation'. In other words, to be defined as a
'flawed' body is simultaneously to be defined as incapable of adequate
social participation. The corporealization of disability meant, in practical
terms, the segregation of those so labelled. The logic of the medical
model runs from diagnosis to social response. In causal terms, there
seem to be three linked elements in the chain: impairment leads to
disability, which in turn leads to confinement or 'institutionalization'.
The social response to the 'flawed' body – particularly in the nineteenth
century – was anthropoemic. This concept refers to the expulsion or exile
of alien persons. The Victorian penchant for excluding people from social
participation on the ground of what today might be called 'difference'
was summed up by Foucault's (1969) notion of the 'great confinement'.
The segregation associated with confinement was not only equivalent to
a custodial sentence – often for life – but was also a sentence of 'social
death', which was – in itself a sort of tacit legitimation for the denial of

human rights and the application of oppressive practices of care (Barnes 1990). These institutional spaces of exclusion, into which disabled people were cast, were, after all, 'civilized' by medical jurisdiction. The very authority that had objectified disabled people by reducing them to their impairments now had the opportunity to define disabled people's needs and, in many cases, act *in loco parentis*.

However, the transformation of impairment into a social problem is not simply a story of medical intervention. Political economy was a major protagonist (Finkelstein 1980: Oliver 1990). The capitalist system that emerged in full-blooded form out of the rapid economic changes of the early to mid nineteenth century made wage slavery – for the vast majority of people – the sole option for survival. Disabled people did not have this option. They were excluded from industrial production on the grounds that their labour power was impaired. The labour market, which prized above all the skill of corporeal repetition that was matched to a pace set by machinery and later the production line, was closed to 'cripples'. 'Mechanised production required a uniform work-force, who could perform similar tasks and work was not organised to cater for the range of intellectual and bodily differences between people' (Marks 1999: 80). Further, the pool of disabled people was refreshed continuously as other people became – to use a contemporary military euphemism – 'collateral damage' of the capitalist mode of production. Not regarded as 'fit' to join the reserve army of labour, in a society where labour power determined one's place, disabled people became materially constituted as a waste product. At best, they were defined as a class of unfortunates who had better be thankful that the goodness of the community or the largesse of the infant 'therapeutic state' (O'Neil 1986) was on hand to save them from destitution and starvation.

The medical model of disability is, and has been, strongly associated with the potentially reactionary theme that 'biology is destiny', and is embedded in popular culture by the 'naturalization' of the view that natural aptitudes determine life chances. Nurture is causally impotent. In the social world, it is natural endowment that is the most efficacious variable. At its worst, in the nineteenth century, the medicalization of disability dovetailed with what Foucault called 'the racisms of the state' (1979: 54), with the Darwinist and eugenicist perspectives which promised to cleanse the social body of impurity, imperfection, degeneracy and defectiveness. Even in the twentieth century, not only in Fascist Germany, but also in post-World War II Social Democratic Sweden, the view that disability represents a contaminant within and a threat to the physical and moral integrity of the population was manifest in state-sponsored programmes of sterilization (Muller-Hill 1994). In the United States,

Margaret Sanger, a major proponent of birth control, declared in 1919: 'More children from the fit, less from the unfit – that is the chief issue of birth control' (quoted in Lupton 1994: 139). The concept of 'fitness' was used, in such contexts, as a criterion for making 'humanity' – defined in terms of aesthetic ideals of embodiment – into a relative term. Modernity is riddled with such eugenic conceptions of 'social hygiene'. They are based on the view that disabled people are either 'unfit' to be in society or to reproduce. The eugenic gaze proposes collective solutions to the contaminant that disabled bodies represent, but does not propose collectivist explanations. It is imprisoned in the repertoire of socio-biology and social Darwinism, and treats disability as an error of nature that should be righted. When wedded to a rigid concept of heredity, biological reductionism may – at its worst – translate into a politics of genocide.

At the level of culture, impairment, or bodily 'abnormality', is interpreted and represented, ubiquitously, as a personal tragedy (Oliver 1990). Consequently, the non-disabled gaze is structured by pity and fear, and such negative emotional responses tend to have an 'elective affinity' with social responses that are characterized by a policy mix of alms and segregation or, to put it another way, charitable paternalism and exclusion. The dominance of such ablist practices inform institutional, social, cultural and even emotional responses to disabled people. At work in this process is a crude visual materialism in which the truth of a disabled person is read off from physical appearance. Such judgements are self-fulfilling prophecies because they take place in a cultural context in which values regarding physical appearance are not only inseparable from moral order, but also inform a system of aesthetic stratification (Synnott 1993), the foot of which is over-represented by the most battered and bruised proletarians. The impact of early capitalism on labouring bodies is a matter of record: 'Women made unfit for childbearing, children deformed, men enfeebled, limbs crushed, whole generations wrecked, afflicted with disease and infirmity, purely to fill the purses of the bourgeoisie' (Engels 1987: 184). And, the author might have added, it was these very 'unfortunates' who provided the bourgeoisie with the opportunity to do charitable works, which might include the funding of places of asylum for mendicants or people damaged in the process of production. Impaired bodies might have been surplus to economic value, but they had emotional value for the dominant class and can be credited, therefore, with at least one useful function.

In the twentieth century, the medical model of disability developed beyond the strategy of confinement. Rehabilitation became the watchword and objective of a practical, 'normalizing' strategy in which biomedical authorities took the view that the impaired body could benefit from rationalization and reform (Seymour 1998). The goal of rehabilitation was to fix or improve the 'performance' of broken bodies and thus make them 'fit', once again, to carry out their social roles and responsibilities:

> The rehabilitation role obligates its occupants to resume as many of their previous roles as possible, or develop new capabilities. It is also expected that the person with the impairment will take their cue from rehabilitation professionals and fully co-operate in attempts to develop ways to retrieve some element of normality. (Barnes, et al. 1999: 41–2)

It was in the guise of post-Parsonian functionalism that sociology first entered – with any serious intent – the debate about disability. Sociology accommodated itself to the medical agenda. Nomenclature was testimony; the study of disability was located within medical sociology. Disability was a sickness, a particular form of social deviance based on individual physical or mental 'incapacity'. In adopting an uncritical approach to the medical distinction between 'the normal and the pathological' (Canguilhem 1991), medical sociology simply reiterated the thesis that impairment was invalidity, and thereby reinforced the modernist agenda by which the medicalization of disability had ensured the social and cultural invalidation of disabled people.

Antithesis

Disability is not a medical or personal problem but a set of physical and social barriers that constrain, regulate and discriminate against people with impairments.

For disabled people the legacy of modernity was one of invalidation. This originated in the processes that excluded 'impaired labour power' from the work-force and in medical systems of classification in which disability came to mean a 'faulty' or abnormal body. A disabled person was a victim of the cruel whim of nature or circumstance and became the kind of person that her body allowed her to be. The barriers to citizenship, to living a full and active life, were – tragically and unfortunately – physical and internal. The ontological essence of disability was impairment. For example, with respect to people with mobility impairments, the medical model suggests that 'their immobility is their own fault or the consequence of a deviant corporeality which requires medical care, or, failing that, the application of charitable works' (Imrie 2000: 1652).

The antithesis of this perspective began to evolve in the 'counter-culture' of the late 1960s. In this historical moment of convention-breaking reflexivity, a great many taken-for-granted ideas were put to the test. Sexual mores, gender relations, civil rights for people of colour, the scope and operation of state power, relations between the generations were just some of the issues that were transformed, rapidly, from matters of consensus to sources of conflict and division. This was the breeding ground for new social movements and struggles for citizenship and emancipation fought out in the name of a variety of excluded groups. It was the cradle of identity politics (Nicholson and Seidman 1995), the inspiration for radical and liberal sociology's championing of the underdog which claimed that disabled people were stigmatized, and that their 'deviance' was amplified by negative social reactions and pejorative labels (see, e.g., Goffman 1968 and Lemert 1972). It was also the historical locus for the rise of the Independent Living Movement (ILM) (Barnes et al. 1999).

These developments were linked, and provided a dynamic in which the discourses of dependency, charity and medicalization that had defined disability from the Industrial Revolution onwards came under challenge. However, what gave this challenge its cutting edge was not so much the general climate of emancipatory discourse, which, in fact, was largely absorbed into consumer culture by the late 1970s, but rather the fact that the challenge came, primarily, from disabled people themselves. In the 1970s, the Union of the Physically Impaired Against Segregation (UPIAS) advocated organized struggle against disability discrimination on the grounds that disability was a social problem rather than the outcome of a 'natural' (f)law. In what might be described as its 'manifesto', entitled *The Fundamental Principles of Disability*, UPIAS redefined disability as 'the disadvantage or restriction of activity caused by a contemporary social organisation which takes little or no account of people who have physical impairments and thus excludes them from participation in the mainstream of social activities' (1976: 14).

This was a radical departure from the tradition that put natural 'abnormalities' and the science of pathology at the aetiological core of disability. Impairment was cut loose from disability. The biological and the social were separated into distinct domains, and disability became a concept that was allocated to the latter. The ontological essence of disability was transformed from a physical or mental deficit into a matter of exclusion and discrimination. To be a disabled person was to be oppressed. 'Disability' was transformed in its implications – in the USA – into a claim for civil rights (Driedger 1989), and described, in Great Britain, as a form of collective political agency that had all the hallmarks of a 'new social movement' (Oliver 1996b). The distinction between disability and impairment was the theoretical move that grounded the 'social model of disability' (Oliver 1990). It split disability discourse into a professional, non-disabled frame of reference that was biological and an activist praxis that was political and social. The study of disability had undergone a transformation that might be described as a 'paradigm shift' (Kuhn 1970). The 'social model of disability' transformed disability from an objective medical fact derived from the universal body of knowledge known as clinical pathology into an outcome of relations of power. How these relations of power are expressed in social patterns which exclude disabled people was the question posed by the social model.

With the body removed from the definition of disability, it became possible to rewrite disability as a socio-political discourse and thus to outline the range, form and types of discrimination that made the world a hostile place for disabled people (Barnes 1991). It also became possible to express the experience of disabled people, in contemporary Western society, in terms of the 'barriers' that block the paths to social, cultural and political participation (Swain et al. 1993). These accounts of disability lead to its characterization as a form of (social) oppression (Oliver 1990; Barnes 1996):

> The defining feature of disability theory has been its focus on the social exclusion and oppression of disabled people. The barriers are embedded in policies and practices based on the individualistic, medicalized approach to disability. Consequently the removal of such obstacles involves far more than gaining control over material resources and the range and quality of services. It requires a fundamental reappraisal of the meaning and hence medicalization of disability and recognition that the multiple deprivations experienced by people with accredited impairments are the outcome of hostile physical and social environments: in other words, the way society is organised. (Barnes et al. 1999: 168)

The social model of disability, the disability movement and disability studies are all manifestations of the fact that, in the last twenty years disability has been transformed, and that the dominance of the biomedical conception of disability has been contested by a political discourse. Decarcerated disabled people have refused to accept the view that they are victims of defective bodies or that they need care, cure or charity. Passivity and disability are no longer synonymous. Disability politics is no stranger to direct action, and slogans such as 'Rights not charity' represent criticisms of traditional views of disabled people. They also express demand for cultural and political change, as opposed to the usual diet of 'improvements' in medical services (Paterson and Hughes 2000).

Synthesis

Impairment is social and disability embodied.

The claim that to complement the 'social model of disability' a 'sociology of impairment' might be necessary has to be understood in the context of the emergence of what Turner (1996: 1) has called the 'somatic society'. This is a society 'within which major political and personal problems are both problematised within the body and expressed through it'. This term suggests that, in the contemporary world, the body has come to be recognized as the key domain in which struggles over power and control are contested. 'Bio-politics' has come to dominate contemporary politics to the extent that we have witnessed a 'somatic turn'.

> Once social scientists became uncomfortable with the distinction between nature and culture, the idea of the body as a pre-social object became very difficult to sustain. The impact of post-Cartesian philosophy – particularly in its phenomenological and poststructuralist guises – was such that sociologists felt compelled to interrogate the place of embodiment in social life and a world disgruntled by rationality went in search of sensuality, pleasure and desire. Meanwhile the body was making itself ever-present in social and political life, be it in the shape of a battered woman, a terminated foetus, a victim of torture or televised war, a proud celebration of womanhood, disability, colour or homosexuality, an organ in transit for transplantation, a human-machine stepping on the moon, a sample of DNA under the microscope, a man who was a woman or vice versa, a body transformed by diet, exercise or the surgeon's knife, a homeless person camped on the streets of the world's richest nation, a mass grave, another world record smashed. (Hancock et al. 2000: 17)

Yet, as sociology rushed headlong to embrace all things somatic, disability studies had banished the body from its debates. Whilst sociology was responding to the 'deafening chorus to "bring the body back in"' (Williams and Bendelow 1998: 9), disability studies was consigning impairment to the margins of its agenda (Hughes and Paterson 1997). The dualism that consigned impairment to biological explanation and disability to sociological explanation had been a better servant of disability politics than of disability theory. The sociology of the body was, in itself, a recognition of the coming of age of a post-Cartesian agenda (Burkitt 1999), which – following in the wake of feminist debates about the relationship between sex and gender – was reconfiguring sociological debates about time (Adam 1995), nature and the environment (Spaargaren et al. 2000) and the emotions (Williams 2000). These aspiring sociological agendas delved into the largely unexplored spaces in which nature and culture collided.

These agendas were motivated philosophically by feminist, poststructuralist and phenomenological ideas (Turner 1996; Williams and Bendelow 1998). Disability studies, on the other hand, had its roots in historical materialism, rather than a critique of the Cartesian subject, and was therefore, understandably, much more concerned with advancing the cause of disabled people than with the cognitive contortions associated with bringing mind, body and society into an intellectually satisfying symbiosis. In addition, attention to corporeality and reactionary politics had been, for many disabled people throughout modernity, two sides of the same coin. Furthermore, as Shakespeare (1992: 40) argued, 'the achievement of the disability movement has been to break the link between our bodies and our social situation and to focus on the real cause of disability, i.e. discrimination and prejudice'. However, the advantages of forgetting the body with all its negative associations needed to be balanced against Deborah Marks's (1999: 115) claim that 'To leave out impairment means that it becomes difficult to distinguish disability from other forms of oppression'.

This important practical difficulty could be traced to a theoretical problem at the core of the social model. The social model – in the dualistic tradition – defined impairment solely in biological terms and thus denied its social nature (Hughes and Paterson 1997). If impairment was the opposite of disability, and disability was socially constituted, then impairment must be biologically constituted. Impairment must, therefore, be taken to refer to that palpable and pathological fleshy object that constitutes the subject matter of medical science. If follows that impairment must be devoid of social meaning and separate from the self. As such, impairment could make claim to epistemological validity only as a form of biological dysfunction, and could be identified solely by the authority of the medical gaze. In other words, the Cartesian approach to impairment and disability sponsored by the social model compelled it to adopt a concept of the body that was indistinguishable from the one promoted by biomedicine. This was a curious, even ironic, affinity. The political radicalism of disability studies was underpinned by a theoretical conservatism that conceded impairment to medical hegemony. Thus the social model, conceived as the intractable opponent of all things associated with the medical model of disability, came to share with it a common conception of the body as a domain of corporeality untouched by culture. This body, devoid of history, affect, meaning and agency was 'typically assumed to be a fixed, material entity subject to the empirical rules of biological science, existing prior to the mutability and flux of cultural change and diversity and characterised by unchangeable inner necessities' (Csordas 1994: 6).

The more telling contradiction is that within disability studies, despite the theorization of impairment in purely objectivist and politically neutral terms, there is a tradition in which disabled people have discussed their impairments as integral to their experience of discrimination (Oliver et al. 1988; Morris 1989). It was feminists who, as proponents of the social model (Morris 1989, 1991; Crow 1996), developed 'insider critiques' which suggested that, if the personal was political and the experience of impairment was personal, then it must be political. This argument exposed the dualistic approach to impairment and disability as theoretically problematic. Yet the norm of conflating impairment with (personal) experience persisted, partly because, at this stage in the development of the politics of disablement, there was understandable reluctance to accept the argument that disability might be personal and that such a claim might also be political. If one claims that oppression is embodied (Paterson and Hughes 1999) – that is, lived and felt by disabled people in the course of their daily lives – then one has to collapse the distinction between private troubles and public issues. One has to take the view that the analytical utility of this dualistic axiom which has been accepted by both sociology and disability studies has had its day. Once the legacy of post-Cartesian ideas began to bite at the theoretical core of a discipline/movement (think of the experience of women's studies/feminism), either as deconstructionism or as the phenomenological politicization of the experience of everyday life, then its modernist dualistic inheritance rapidly became indigestible.

One can see how this process worked with respect to disability studies. Recognition of the impaired body as a social issue began to be registered itself in a number of ways. Mike Oliver (1996a) gave, albeit reluctant and limited, legitimacy to the deconstruction of the impairment–disability duality when he accepted the possibility of a 'social model of impairment'. Almost a decade before this, an influential figure in disability studies, Paul Abberley (1987: 14) had argued that for disabled people 'the body is the site of oppression, both in form and what is done with it'. Colin Barnes (1996: 57) has recently developed a materialist account of cultural responses to impairment. He argues that the 'interaction between the material and cultural forces' that sustain the 'myth of the body perfect' should provide a starting point for 'future sociological accounts of disability and, indeed, other forms of societal oppression'. In other words, even within the materialist tradition that was the original inspiration for both disability studies and the social model of disability, there is a growing interest in developing some kind of sociological agenda for impairment. Carol Thomas (1999: 143), for example, has developed a feminist materialist 'non-reductionist ontology of the body' which highlights what she calls 'impairment effects'.

The cultural, somatic and linguistic 'turns' that have produced post-structuralism and re-animated phenomenological approaches have also been influential in making links between impairment and oppression (see, e.g., Corker 1999, Corker and French 1999; Hughes and Paterson 1997; Hughes 1999, 2000; Paterson and Hughes 1999; Shakespeare 1994; Shildrick 1997). An important testimony to both the growth of theoretical eclecticism in disability studies and the development of an agenda around the social aspects of impairment is the breadth of the theoretical and 'somatic' content of a recent and important 'disability' Reader that appeared in the USA in 1997 (Davis 1997).

The body disappeared from disability discourse because, as Tom Shakespeare (1992: 40) put it, 'to mention biology, to admit pain, to confront our impairments has been to risk the oppressors seizing on evidence that disability is really about physical limitation after all'. It appears that disabled people, through the mouthpiece of disability studies, are prepared to take that risk. Such confidence is the outcome of struggle, of a developing praxis in which impairment is transformed by the agency of disabled people themselves into a matter of pride. As disabled people have begun to rescue their bodies from the aesthetic priorities and discriminatory perceptions of the non-disabled gaze (Hughes 1999), they have recognized that interpretation of impairment cannot be left exclusively to the normalizing sciences of biomedicine.

Indeed, the sociology of impairment makes the case that 'the impaired body has a history and is as much a cultural phenomenon as it is a biological entity' (Paterson and Hughes 1999: 600). From a Foucauldian position, the impaired body is inseparable from the power that is visited upon it. As a discursive construction, impairment is culturally complex. It is a product of the intense disciplinary practices that produce it. In her poststructuralist critique of the Disability Living Allowance (DLA), Margrit Shildrick (1997: 53) argues that the questionnaire used to determine eligibility for the allowance is comprehensive, a monument to the intensity and voyeurism of state surveillance in respect of disabled people's physical and social lives. 'No area of bodily functioning escapes the requirement of total visibility, and further the ever more detailed subdivision of bodily behaviour into a set of discontinuous functions speaks to a fetishistic fragmentation of the embodied person'.

The governance of impairment, as Shildrick's argument indicates, is administratively dense, but it is also mediated by complex processes of cultural constitution in which, increasingly, judgements of authenticity and moral worth are based on aesthetic criteria. Worth is reduced to appearance, performance (Russell 2000; Featherstone 1992) and superficial concepts of competence. With the collapse of aesthetics into ethics, the ideal of physical beauty and perfection has become the not-so-new tyranny for a new millennium (Glassner 1992). There is a struggle in contemporary culture between an agenda that celebrates physical difference and one that valorizes impossibly rigid regimes of bodily maintenance and consumer asceticism. The narrowing of norms about the ideal body creates an environment in which physical capital becomes a much more important indicator of cultural capital. Impairment has been politicized by aesthetic discrimination:

> Beautyism, and its attendant fascism, the prejudice and discrimination in favour of the beautiful and attractive (however defined) and against the ugly and less attractive are virtually institutionalised in our society and are the last major bastion of inequality.... The pursuit of beauty.... is widely regarded as an excellent investment with substantial psychic, social and economic returns and for these reasons it is increasing in salience in Europe, North America and around the world. (Synnott 1993: 100)

Disabled people are right to be wary of the potential ossification of aesthetic discrimination. Contemporary ideas which suggest that the body is very amenable to reconstruction and re-formation by way of regimes of maintenance and enhancement imply that the 'body we have is the body we deserve'. What might be called 'body fascism' arises from the confusion of the ethical subject with the aesthetic ideal of embodiment, and when this confusion meets the ideology of the flexible body, then disabled people should expect and be ready to fight prejudice and discrimination.

However, discrimination and impairment meet in other less obvious ways: for example, through the ways in which non-impaired carnality constitutes itself as the corporeal blueprint for 'being in the world'. The social world and the built environment are carnally constituted or, to put it another way, deeply informed by carnal norms (Paterson and Hughes 1999). The spaces and places that people carve out for themselves are not only products of bodies (what existentialists call 'projects', combinations of schemes of the imagination and the physical and mental labour that make them possible). They are also designed with particular kinds of bodies in mind. For example, the world made by and for *Homo erectus* is alien to the wheelchair user, and the visual culture of postmodernity excludes visually impaired people. The contemporary carnal order is not only profoundly disablist, but also a stubborn material factor in the constitution of disability as a specific form of oppression. Disabled people do not recognize themselves in the way in which space and time are organized, precisely because they have played little or no part in the constitution of the carnal order of modernity. This is hardly surprising, since disabled people's experience of modernity has been largely one of incarceration and segregation. Decarceration made disability access a political problem because impaired bodies encountered the barriers erected by a world which was a reflection of, and dominated, by the temporal, spatial and mobility needs of non-impaired people (Paterson and Hughes 1999; Imrie 2000). A phenomenological sociology of impairment seeks to demonstrate that the carnal presuppositions that inform and structure the world of institutional as well as inter-subjective relations, including embodied norms of communication, are experienced by disabled people as places of exclusion.

Discrimination is built into the everyday world in such a way that impaired bodies '*dys*-appear'. This describes the process whereby the impaired body-as-subject – in the process of everyday social encounters – is objectified, and thus experiences itself as an awkward presence (Paterson and Hughes 1999). In other words, the body, 'normally' taken for granted by most people in most situations, becomes a palpable factor in social encounters only when attention is drawn to it. Invariably, people with visible impairments, in the context of everyday social encounters, experience their bodies as an influential presence largely because their bodies are treated as such by non-disabled social actors. The encounter is thereby transformed from an encounter between two persons to one between a person and an object. Dys-appearance therefore refers to the dehumanization of disabled people, as well as the immanent experience of alienation that is associated with it.

Furthermore, the disability movement has been able to demonstrate clearly that forms of exclusion from physical and social space are ubiquitous (Imrie and Kumar 1998), and that the movement and mobility of people with impairments is constrained. This is because the physical and social worlds are made, by and large, in the image and likeness of non-disabled bodies (Imrie 2000). Even where buildings and public spaces are designed to meet the access needs of disabled people, they are usually profoundly inappropriate with respect to 'concerns about aesthetics, privacy, sociability and comfort' (Marks 2000: 52). The carnal hegemony of non-disabled bodies is designed into the fabric of everyday living and the amenities that help to make of it a pleasurable experience. As some doors open to people with impairments, it is becoming apparent that there are multiple barriers on the other side. It is a bit like being invited to a party and then discovering, on arrival, that one is not welcome. The more that disabled people enter the spaces of modernity from which they have been excluded hitherto, the more they are likely to recognize the ways in which disability discrimination is embodied in the carnal norms that constitute the 'objective' status of the taken-for-granted world. The greatest figure in modern architecture, Le Corbusier, argued 'that all men have the same organism and the same functions. ... The same needs' (quoted in Imrie 1996: 81). Such a universal claim – typical of liberal modernity – cuts across bodily difference and suggests a homogeneous aesthetic of the built environment which will, by definition, exclude disabled people. Architectural practice is informed by 'normalising discourses which serve to alienate impaired bodies and to prioritise what one might term the "mobile body"' (Imrie 2000: 1641).

Conclusions

It seems clear that the contemporary neo-liberal state has set its sights on an individualistic response to disability. However, the discourse of rights that grounds this response is not wholly indebted to the medical model and the 'flawed' body school of disability. The neo-liberal perspective recognizes the validity of anti-discrimination legislation, and therefore shifts the debate about disability from corporeal and cognitive impairment to opportunities. Disability activists have every right not to be too impressed by this development, given that the gap between opportunities and reality is massive. Furthermore, although 'trendy' doctrines of social inclusion have acquired some of the rhetoric of the social model of disability, there is no real evidence that the exclusion experienced by disabled people has been mitigated in any fundamental way. As the sociology of impairment develops, one thing is becoming evident. As limited opportunities open up for disabled people, they reveal the extent to which non-impaired carnality is the 'constitutional' force behind norms about space, movement, mobility and temporality. What is interesting about all these domains is that, like the body, they occupy an ambivalent territory that straddles the traditional distinction between nature and culture, and reveal new ways in which disability discrimination is embodied in contemporary social relations. However, if modernity 'begins' with a biologically reductionist view of disability and 'ends' with one in which the meaning of disability is contested at the level of politics, one is tempted by tempered optimism and even encouraged to invoke that rather tattered value called progress.

However, where there are opportunities, there are threats. The very cautious optimism expressed in the last paragraph glosses the fact that abroad in the contemporary world is a reactionary, disablist discourse which threatens to upset disabled people's bumpy ride towards inclusion and emancipation. One might call this the discourse of bodily perfection. Whilst it has a long history in Western culture (Stone 1995; Synnott 1993) and can claim the eugenic movement as one of its most infamous 'triumphs', it has been reinvigorated of late by two important developments. The first derives from contemporary scientific work, in particular the exponential growth of the 'new genetics' and the 'geneticization' of explanations of human behaviour (Shakespeare 1995; Steinberg 1997; Spallone 1998). The second arises from popular culture: in particular, the processes that constitute the aesthetic invalidation of disabled people (Hughes 1999; 2000). Both are connected to the aestheticization of everyday life (Welsch 1996), and how this produces new forms of discrimination that are focused on embodiment and appearance. One of the potential dangers of the 'somatic society' (Turner 1996) is that 'cultural capital' (Bourdieu 1984) may come to be defined, increasingly, in terms of physical attributes. This might mean that distinction, hierarchy and the emotive judgements that might accompany an aestheticized system of power relations could deepen the prejudice, exclusion and oppression that disabled people have experienced throughout modernity. Disability studies and the disability movement, it could be argued, could use the sociology of impairment as a tool to measure and counter the nature and extent of these contemporary, cultural threats.

In this chapter, I have argued that there are three key 'moments' in the development of the relationship between disability and the body. The first corresponds to the medicalization of disability, and emerged from the historical collision of modernity, medicine and impairment. From this confluence of forces, disability emerged as a social identity that was predicated on the presence of physical or mental impairment – that is, on an 'objective fact' of embodiment. Disability became a pathology that could be detected in an individual's corporeal and / or mental disposition. The second 'moment' constituted the antithesis of the first. The political movement of disabled people recast the concept of disability in terms that drew upon the dialectic of emancipation. The 'problem' of disability was reformulated as a problem of social organization rather than corporeal status, a problem of politics rather than nature. The third 'moment' arises out of the erosion of the legitimacy of a world conceived in dualistic terms. The post-Cartesian age is one of 'body politics', in which society is 'somatic' (Turner 1996), disability embodied, and impairment social.

References

Abberley, P. 1987: The concept of oppression and the development of a social theory of disability. *Disability, Handicap and Society*, 2, 5–19.

Adam, B. 1995: *Timewatch: The Social Analysis of Time*. Cambridge: Polity.

Barnes, C. 1990: *Cabbage Syndrome: The Social Construction of Dependency*. London: Palmer Press.

Barnes, C. 1991: *Disabled People in Britain and Discrimination*. London: Hurst and Co.

Barnes, C. 1996: Theories of disability and the origins of the oppression of disabled people in western society. In L. Barton (ed.), *Disability and Society: Emerging Issues and Insights*, London: Longman, 43–60.

Barnes, C. and Mercer, C. 1996: *Exploring the Divide: Illness and Disability*. Leeds: Disability Press.

Barnes, C., Mercer, J. and Shakespeare, T. 1999: *Exploring Disability: A Sociological Introduction*. Cambridge: Polity.

Bourdieu, P. 1984: *Distinction*. London: Routledge & Kegan Paul.

Burkitt, I. 1999: *Bodies of Thought: Embodiment, Identity and Modernity*. London: Sage.

Canguilhem, G. 1991: *The Normal and the Pathological*. New York: Zone Books.

Corker, M. 1999: Differences, conflations and foundations: the limits to accurate theoretical representation of disabled peoples experiences? *Disability & Society*, 14 (5), 627–42.

Corker, M. and French, S. (eds) 1999: *Disability Discourse*. Buckingham: Open University Press.

Crow, L. 1996: Including all our lives: renewing the social model of disability. In J. Morris (ed.), *Encounters with Strangers: Feminism and Disability*, London: Women's Press, 36–51.

Csordas, T. 1994: *Embodiment and Experience: The Existential Ground of Culture and Self*. Cambridge: Cambridge University Press.

Davis, L. (ed.) 1997: *The Disability Studies Reader*. New York and London: Routledge.

Driedger, D. 1989: *The Last Civil Rights Movement: Disabled Peoples International*. London: Hurst and Co.

Engels, F. 1987 [1845]: *The Conditions of the Working Class in England in 1844*. Harmondsworth: Penguin.

Featherstone, M. 1992: Postmodernism and the aestheticization of everyday life. In S. Lash and J. Friedman (eds), *Modernity and Identity*, Oxford: Blackwell, 104–12.

Finkelstein, V. 1980: *Attitudes and Disabled People: Issues for Discussion*. New York: World Rehabilitation Fund.

Foucault, M. 1969: *Madness and Civilisation*. London: Tavistock.

Foucault, M. 1979: *Discipline and Punish*. Harmondsworth: Penguin.

Glassner, B. 1992: *Bodies: The Tyranny of Perfection*. Los Angeles: Lowell House.

Goffman, I. 1968: *Stigma: Notes on the Management of Spoiled Identity*. Harmondsworth: Penguin.

Hancock, P., Hughes, B., Jagger, L., Paterson, K., Russell, R., Tulle-Winton, E. and Tyler, M. 2000: *The Body, Culture and Society: An Introduction*. Buckingham: Open University Press.

Hughes, B. 1999: The constitution of impairment: modernity and the aesthetic of oppression. *Disability and Society*, 14 (2), 155–72.

Hughes, B. 2000: Medicine and the aesthetic invalidation of disabled people. *Disability & Society*, 15 (4), 555–68.

Hughes, B. and Paterson, K. 1997: The social model of disability and the disappearing body. *Disability and Society*, 12 (3), 325–40.

Imrie, R. 1996: *Disability and the City: International Perspectives*. London: Paul Chapman Publishing.

Imrie, R. 2000: Disability and discourses of mobility and movement. *Environment and Planning*, 32, 1641–56.

Imrie, R. and Kumar, M. 1998: Focusing on disability and access in the built environment. *Disability and Society*, 13 (3), 357–74.

Kuhn, T.S. 1970: *The Structure of Scientific Revolutions*. Chicago: University of Chicago Press.

Lemert, E. 1972: *Human Deviance, Social Problems and Social Control*. Englewood Cliffs, NJ: Prentice-Hall.

Lupton, D. 1994: *Medicine as Culture: Illness, Disease and the Body in Western Societies*. London: Sage.

Marks, D. 1999: *Disability: Controversial Debates and Psycho-social Perspectives*. London: Routledge.

Marks, D. 2000: Secure base? disabling design. In L. McKie and N. Watson (eds), *Organizing Bodies: Policy, Institutions and Work*, Basingstoke: Macmillan, 42–53.

Morris, J. 1989: *Able Lives: Women's Experience of Paralysis*. London: Women's Press.

Morris, J. 1991: *Pride Against Prejudice: Transforming Attitudes to Disability*. London: Women's Press.

Muller-Hill, B. 1994: Lessons from the dark and distant past. In A. Clarke (ed.), *Genetic Counselling: Principles and Practices*, London: Routledge, 131–41.

Nicholson, L. and Seidman, S. 1995: *Social Postmodernism: Beyond Identity Politics*. Cambridge: Cambridge University Press.

Oliver, M. 1990: *The Politics of Disablement*. Basingstoke: Macmillan.

Oliver, M. 1996a: Defining impairment and disability: issues at stake. In C. Barnes and G. Mercer (eds), *Exploring the Divide: Illness and Disability*, Leeds: Disability Press, 39–54.

Oliver, M. 1996b: *Understanding Disability: From Theory to Practice*. London: Macmillan.

Oliver, M., Zarb, G., Silver, J., Moore, M. and Salisbury, V. 1988: *Walking into Darkness: The Experience of Spinal Injury*. London: Macmillan.

O'Neil, J. 1986: The disciplinary society. *British Journal of Sociology*, 37 (1), 42–62.

Paterson, K. and Hughes, B. 1999: Disability studies and phenomenology: the carnal politics of everyday life. *Disability & Society*, 14 (5), 597–610.

Paterson, K. and Hughes, B. 2000: Disabled bodies. In P. Hancock, B. Hughes, E. Jagger, K. Paterson, R. Russell, E. Tulle-Winton and M. Tyler (eds), *The Body, Culture and Society: An Introduction*, Buckingham: Open University Press, 29–44.

Russell, R. 2000: Ethical bodies. In P. Hancock, B. Hughes, E. Jagger, K. Paterson, R. Russell, E. Tulle-Winton, and M. Tyler (eds), *The Body, Culture and Society: An Introduction*, Buckingham: Open University Press, 101–16.

Seymour, W. 1998: *Remaking the Body: Rehabilitation and Change*. London: Routledge.

Shakespeare, T. 1992: A response to Liz Crow. *Coalition*, September, 40–2.

Shakespeare, T. 1994: Cultural representations of disabled people: dustbins for disavowal. *Disability and Society*, 9 (3), 283–301.

Shakespeare, T. 1995: Back to the future? New genetics and disabled people. *Critical Social Policy*, 44/5, 22–35.

Shildrick, M. 1997: *Leaky Bodies and Boundaries: Feminism, Postmodernism and (Bio)Ethics*. London: Routledge.

Shilling, C. 1993: *The Body and Social Theory*. London: Sage.

Spaargaren, G., Mol, A. and Buttel, F. 2000: *Environment and Global Modernity*. London: Sage.

Spallone, P. 1998: The new biology of violence: new geneticisms for old. *Body and Society*, 4 (4), 47–65.

Steinberg, D. L. 1997: *Bodies in Glass: Genetics, Eugenics and Embryo Ethics*. Manchester: Manchester University Press.

Stone, S. D. 1995: The myth of bodily perfection. *Disability and Society*, 10 (4), 413–24.

Swain, J., Finkelstein, V., French, S. and Oliver, M. 1993: *Disabling Barriers – Enabling Environments*. London: Sage.

Synnott, A. 1993: *The Body Social: Symbolism, Self and Society*. London: Routledge.

Thomas, C. 1999: *Female Forms: Experiencing and Understanding Disability*. Milton Keynes: Open University Press.

Touraine, A. 1995: *Critique of Modernity*. Oxford: Blackwell.

Turner, B.S. 1996: *The Body and Society*, 2nd edn. London: Sage.

UPIAS 1976: *Fundamental Principles of Disability*. London: Union of the Physically Impaired Against Segregation.

Welsch, W. 1996: Aestheticization processes: phenomena, distinctions and prospects. *Theory, Culture and Society*, 13 (1), 1–24.

Williams, S. J. 2000: *Emotion and Social Theory*. London: Sage.

Williams, S. J. and Bendelow, G. 1998: *The Lived Body: Sociological Themes, Embodied Issues*. London: Routledge.

5

Theorizing Divisions and Hierarchies: Towards a Commonality or Diversity?

Ayesha Vernon and John Swain

Introduction

Payne claims that the idea of ' "social divisions" is one of the most useful and powerful tools available' (2000a: 1) in understanding ourselves, society and why society operates as it does. Certainly the notion of social division has a long history in social theory, particularly in association with understandings of inequality and hierarchies in power relations. Membership of a category in a social division can confer unequal opportunities of access to desirable resources of all kinds, including wealth, privilege and the production and consumption of resources. Social theory has associated social divisions of class, race and gender, and more recently sexuality and disability, with inequalities which are woven into the very structure and fabric of British society and organizations. The development of the social model of disability has, in a general sense, brought disability into this arena of sociology, to be considered and analysed alongside other social divisions in general texts such as Alcock (1996) and Payne (2000b). It is a way of understanding that applies to, and connects, the experiences of disabled people with those of Black and ethnic minority groups, gays and lesbians, old people and women. The commonalities in issues of racism, sexism, homophobia and disablism can be explored through themes such as prejudicial attitudes and discriminatory language (Thompson 1997). Alcock (1996), for instance, explicitly compares the 'discrimination and disadvantage' experienced by disabled people with that experienced by people within other social divisions.

Nevertheless, this is also an arena of considerable complexity and debate, as is evident in a comparison between the following two quotations. Rachel Hurst of Disabled People's International states:

> When you come together with other disabled people, you have the time and opportunity to discuss what the situation really is – what oppression is – who is oppressing you; where oppression comes from, what discrimination is and where it comes from. (Coleridge 1993: 54)

On the other hand, Abu-Habib, talking about the work of OXFAM with disabled women, particularly in the Middle East, states:

> We soon saw that we needed to consciously reject simplistic analyses which focus on disability in isolation from other important issues and social relations. Most importantly, we recognised that disabled people are not sexless: they are men and women with different interests, different characteristics including age, economic status, aspirations and different life experiences. (1997: 11)

Whilst the orientation of the first quotation is toward commonality or universality, the second speaks to diversity and difference. In various guises, this interplay between commonality and diversity is central to reflections on developing disability theory from the vantage point of 'divisions and hierarchies'.

From this viewpoint we reflect first on the forms of discrimination faced by different groups, particularly groups whose day-to-day experience involves multiple discrimination. Though our remit is broad, our main focus is the experiences of disabled women from Black and ethnic minority communities. We reflect on how such experiences have been analysed by the people themselves, and on the argument that the interaction of social divisions creates simultaneous oppression. We then turn to questions of identity as a key concept in the politics of social divisions. In particular, we explore evolving positive identities in relation to new social movements, in contrast to the possibilities for fragmented identities in the interaction among social divisions. On this basis we explore the implications for disability theory *per se*, contrasting the sociological position of historical materialism with that of the growing influence of postmodernity. Finally, we look towards future possibilities for building disability theory founded in commonality but speaking to diversity. This chapter draws upon research conducted by Vernon (1998b), which examined the underlying complexity that makes up the experience of multiple oppression, given the multi-faceted nature of each of the component identities that shape, in particular, Black and ethnic minority disabled women's daily existence.

Reflecting on experience: simultaneous oppression?

Social divisions overlap, of course. A person's employment position, for instance, may be associated with class, gender, age, ethnicity or disability, or indeed any combination of contributing factors. In particular, we are going to explore how social divisions, particularly of gender, race and disability, conjoin and interact with one another in Black and ethnic minority disabled women's lived experiences. From this viewpoint, gender, class, race, sexuality, age and disability combine in important and varying ways to exacerbate or modify the experience of disablism, sexism and/or racism.

The simultaneous discrimination faced by disabled people from Black and ethnic minority communities manifests itself in many ways in day-to-day living. The evidence relating to this particular group is sparse, but points to major barriers at all levels of institutional discrimination. Two studies of the families of Asian people with learning difficulties (ADAPT 1993; Azmi et al. 1996), for instance, provided evidence of high levels of poverty, with 69 per cent of families having no full-time wage earner, and half of the families being on income support. In terms of attitudes, 'there is a lack of understanding among the majority population concerning the life-style, social customs and religious practices of people from ethnic minority groups' (French and Vernon 1997: 62)

Discrimination within the provision of services has received particular attention. One consistent finding suggests that discrimination has been denied and rationalized by service providers through myths that, for instance, Black families prefer 'to look after their own' (Baxter 1995). The documented views of Black disabled people consistently speak to experiences of segregation and marginalization within services. For instance, in their research into the views and experiences of young Black disabled people, Bignall and Butt (2000) found feelings of segregation due to racism in settings segregated due to disablism, as evident in the following quotations from two participants:

> I felt – well, it was alright after a while, but I think some of the teachers were a bit racist against me because I was the only brown one there. I felt a bit out of place, but it was all right after a while. (Pinky)

You feel like, oh why wasn't there, you know, someone your age as well and who's Asian, you know. You always see the white people but I used to get on with them as well... but you do think but why, where are the Asian people you know, sometimes. (Tubassam)

Summarizing the evidence from several studies, Butt and Mirza state:

The fact that major surveys of the experience of disability persist in hardly mentioning the experience of black disabled people should not deter us from appreciating the messages that emerge from existing work. Racism, sexism and disablism intermingle to amplify the need for supportive social care. However these same factors sometimes mean that black disabled people and their carers get a less than adequate service. (Butt and Mirza 1996: 94)

In their study of young Black disabled people's experiences and views, Bignall and Butt conclude:

Our interviews revealed that most of these young people did not have the relevant information to help them achieve independence. Hardly any knew of new provisions, such as Direct Payments, which would help with independent living. Most people did not know where to get help or information they wanted, for example, to move into their own place or go to university. (Bignall and Butt 2000: 49)

Language is often seen as the main barrier to effective service provision. It is therefore assumed that an adequate supply of leaflets and interpreters in appropriate languages would solve the problem. However, communication consists of more than language skills and literacy. The research suggests that even among British-born English-speaking Asians, there is considerable lack of knowledge of what services are on offer. Research by Banton and Hirsch bears out the findings of previous research. They state:

Communication problems are identified in all work in this area. Such problems are partly to do with language differences, but also arise from the separate lives led by different ethnic groups in our society and the consequent unlikely coincidence of communications about services arising through informal contacts. (Banton and Hirsch 2000: 32)

Perhaps the most consistent recommendation from research has been the necessity for the direct involvement of disabled clients, including Black disabled clients, in the planning of services (Butt and Box 1997). Again, this needs to be understood within the context of multiple discrimination. Concluding their study with Asian deaf young people and their families, Jones, Atkin and Ahmad state:

identities are not closely tied to single issues and young people and their families simultaneously held on to different identity claims. To this extent, it is not a question of forsaking one claim for another and choosing, for instance, 'deafness' over 'ethnicity', but to negotiate the space to be deaf and other things as well. It is only through addressing these tensions that services will adequately respond to the needs of Asian deaf people and their families. (Jones et al. 2001: 68)

In her analysis of experiences of multiple oppression, Vernon (1998b) suggests that, to some extent, it is of no relevance whether it was sexism, racism or disablism that contributed to a particular experience. Laila, one of the participants in her research, echoed feelings shared by many in the study: 'I feel oppression is the denial of opportunity. There are lots of things you have to battle against and if they don't get you on one, they will get you on another.' Black and ethnic minority disabled women's awareness of particular issues changes according to the circumstances and situations they are confronted with. For example, if they cannot use women's health centres because of steps at the entrance, then disablism at that point may be the most significant aspect of their oppression. If, on the other hand, a male doctor accuses them of being hysterical, then sexism will be their greatest concern at that moment in time. In the latter situation it would be difficult to determine how much of the doctor's response is related to his attitude to women and how much to his perception that disabled people are asexual. As Begum states:

> The very nature of simultaneous oppression means that as Black Disabled men and women, and Black Disabled lesbians and gay men, we cannot identify a single source of oppression to reflect the reality of our lives. No meaningful analysis of multiple oppression can take place without an acknowledgement that Black Disabled people are subject to simultaneous oppression and as a consequence of this we cannot simply prioritise one aspect of our oppression to the exclusion of others. (Begum 1994: 35)

Thus, as argued by Stuart, Black disabled people are subjected to a unique form of institutional discrimination which is different from the sum of racism experienced as a Black person and disablism experienced as a disabled person. Their experiences 'isolate Black disabled people and place them at the margins of the ethnic minority and disabled populations' (1993: 95). Hill drew attention to the extremes of oppression faced by Black disabled people. She stated that the cumulative effect of discrimination is such that Black disabled people are 'the most socially, economically and educationally deprived and oppressed members of society' (1991: 6).

Comparable analyses of the experiences of the interaction of other social divisions – for example, disabled and old, disabled and female, disabled and gay or lesbian, and disabled and working class, indicate that there are parallels. For instance, in the most extensive research into the views and experiences of disabled lesbians and bisexual women, there was evidence that they felt marginalized by the lesbian and gay groups: 'many disabled lesbian and bisexual women have experienced alienation rather than nurturing and support from the lesbian and gay community' (Gillespie-Sells et al. 1998: 57).

The association between social divisions and experiences of discrimination is complex, particularly in the interplay of factors. Bhavnani has pointed out that

> Black women's experience cannot always be assumed to be different from white women, Black men or white men in all contexts. The interplay of factors such as 'race', gender, class, age and disability create a multiplicity of discrimination. These may, in some contexts, suggest similarities with, as well as differences between, white women and Black and white men. (Bhavnani 1994: p. viii)

The experience of racism may certainly be modified or exacerbated by an individual's class position. On the axes of privilege / penalty (Hill-Collins 1990), social class is an important determinant of many critical factors. As class privilege increases, the effects of other penalties is likely to decrease. Equally, the effect of other penalties may be exacerbated by lower social class positioning. Moreover, disablism and racism significantly lessen the chances of disabled people and Black and ethnic minority people progressing higher up the social class ladder, a fact evident in their high unemployment rates as well as their concentration in low-paid and low-skilled jobs (Brown 1984; Oliver 1991).

The importance of the socio-economic context for disabled people's lives is aptly illustrated by Morris (1991) when she contrasts the situation of two people who are both extensively paralysed, yet whose options and life-styles are very different: a lawyer, who owns several homes and bought 'all the technology he needs to create independence for himself' (p. 141), and a young woman with no material resources who was consigned to a long-stay hospital. Clearly, then, class privilege can be a powerful diluter of discrimination, both economically and socially. Thus, although the potential for discrimination is greatly increased for those who possess multiple identities, because the ideologies of oppression do not operate independently of one another (Hill-Collins 1990; Miles 1989), their effects cannot be assumed to be invariably experienced simultaneously. For some, their privileged class position may modify the intersection of gender, race and / or disability. For others, their working-class background and / or sexuality may heighten the experience of gender, race and / or disability. Hence, the experience of disablism, racism or sexism may be modified or exacerbated by the presence of privileges or other penalties respectively.

Furthermore, multiple penalties may increase the experience of one penalty. For example, disabled women's experience of sexism is often exacerbated by the intersection of gender and disability (Lloyd 1992; Lonsdale 1990). Gender, class, race, sexuality, age and disability are not, however, invariably experienced at the same time. Although Black and ethnic minority disabled women are simultaneously subject to institutional manifestations of gender, race and disability, on an individual level the experience varies considerably from day to day, depending on the context. Sometimes, the oppression relates to disability in an obvious manner, so, for example, when two participants in Vernon's (1998b) research, Nelam and Laila, were refused interviews after, but not before, their potential employers had knowledge of their having an impairment. At other times, it may be any combination of disability, race and gender exacerbating their experience. For example, Emma (also from Vernon's research) was denied a mainstream management post on the assumption that because of her visual impairment she would 'not cope'. The assumption and pronouncement that she would not 'cope' are disabling in themselves. However, Emma felt that the underlying reason was racism, because they did not want a Black person as a manager in the council. Thus, disability seems to have been used to mask racism, although it is possible that both disability and race played a part in the denial of promotion for Emma. In her research with physiotherapists French (2001) also found that it can be difficult to know whether it was age, gender, disability or something else about the participants that prevented promotion.

To summarize, it would seem that factors of gender, race, class and disability interact and impinge differently in different situations, sometimes in combination and sometimes individually, either exacerbating or modifying the experience of discrimination, depending on the context.

Reflecting on identity

The concept of identity has increasingly come to prominence in areas of inquiry across the social sciences (Jenkins 1996). In relation to social divisions, questions of identity take analysis explicitly into the political arena. Hetherington suggests that identity has become significant through resistance to dominance in unequal power relations:

> One of the main issues behind this interest in identity and in identity politics more generally has been the relationship between marginalisation and a politics of resistance, and affirmative, empowering choices of identity and a politics of difference. (Hetherington 1998: 21)

In relation to disability, Vernon (1998b) found a complex relationship between experiences of multiple oppression and identity. In the case of the following participant, for instance, race and cultural ethnic identity seemed to predominate over disability identity. Shazia felt that because her impairments are hidden, racism is more predominant in her experience when she is away from her family, as the visibility of her skin colour is there for all to see and to mark her out as being different:

> For thirty years I have experienced racial discrimination on a daily basis and it's something that defines me. That's why I say Black and Asian before disabled for me. It's absolutely fundamental to my life. It doesn't matter where I have been, at home, on the street, in education I have faced it and I am still facing it. My impairments I live with. Being a woman I am proud of. I don't see them as negatively as I do being Black. It's not being Black that's negative, but it's the experience of it which is such that you think, unless you are Black you are not going to understand this, the fear on a daily level, the fear of being attacked because of your skin colour.

Although the threat of racism is far more predominant in Shazia's life, if her impairments had been more visible, it may be that her sense of vulnerability would have been greater rather than less.

It is apparent, then, that the more overt the discrimination, the more heightened one's awareness and sense of vulnerability around that particular identity. There is a clear interrelationship between disability identity and disability politics. As Monks states:

> People who are socially excluded and oppressed, and who are often also defined as lacking qualities of a normative social being, may find solidarity in the shared experience of exclusion itself....The 'communities' which emerge may become politically active...Experience of the interdependence, mutuality and solidarity which arise from shared activities and communication is an important part of membership, even of direct political action. (Monks 1999: 71)

The growth of the disabled people's movement and the emergence of the social model of disability were the fertile grounds for the positive affirmative of disabled identity. Barnes, Mercer and Shakespeare (1999: 178) suggest that involvement in social protest has been the 'catalyst to a more positive disabled identity'. Oliver and Barnes state that 'The re-evaluation of a disabled identity within a political context involves processes which challenge traditional views of disabled people as incapable, powerless and passive' (1998: 71). Richard Wood summarizes these developments as follows:

> Discovering our identity as disabled people is very, very important. It's still important today, otherwise people won't value themselves. I think that is probably the biggest success that the movement has been able to point to. It is our movement, nobody else owns it. We know who we are. I think we're fairly clear about where we're going and why we're going there. (Campbell and Oliver 1996: 124)

Furthermore, the roots of disability arts lie in the politicizing of disability issues. As Shakespeare et al. state: 'Drama, cabaret, writing and visual arts have been harnessed to challenge negative images, and build a sense of unity' (1996: 186). Finkelstein, who was one of the founders of the London Disability Arts Forum (LDAF) in 1987, stated that it is 'essential for us to create our own public image, based upon free acceptance of our distinctive group identity' (Campbell and Oliver 1996). This development of identity has indeed been central to disability arts, challenging the values that underlie institutional discrimination. Through song lyrics, poetry, writing, drama and so on, disabled people have celebrated difference and rejected the ideology of normality wherein disabled people are devalued as 'abnormal'. They are creating images of strength and pride, the antithesis of dependency and helplessness (Swain and French 2000).

Whilst new social movements have produced new foci for the politics of collective identities, for many social scientists the broad picture is one of fractured, fluid, multiple and contested identities. According to Bradley (1996: 23), for instance, identity is no longer predominantly class-based, and people can now draw their sense of identity from a much broader range of sources, including gender, age, marital status, sexual preference, consumption patterns and, we would add, disability. Furthermore, identity is a matter of 'becoming' rather than simply 'being':

> Far from being eternally fixed in some essentialized past, they are subject to the continuous 'play' of history, culture and power...identities are the names we give to the different ways we are positioned by, and position ourselves within, the narratives of the past. (Hall 1990: 225)

In a context of diversity and fluidity, identity is contested within conflicts of interest and power inequalities. Marsh provides the following example:

> [A] Catholic male homosexual from a working-class background in Ireland who is the head of a suburban girls' comprehensive school in Yorkshire will have to juggle with a range of separate and competing claims on his self image which raise questions of gender, sexuality, religion, nationality, class and ethnicity. (Marsh 2000: 31)

New social movements are expressions of collective identity, but they are also sites of contested identities. Williams shows how the commonality between women stressed by the feminism of the 1970s has been challenged:

> Feminism based on Black, lesbian and disabled politics has pointed to the need to deconstruct the category of 'woman' in order to understand the complex and inter-connected range of identities and subject positions through which women's experiences are constituted, as well as the ways these also change over time and place. (Williams 1996: 69)

Modood (1997) has traced the complex changes in patterns of ethnic identity for second- and third-generation members of minority ethnic groups in Britain. He suggests that identities are more consciously chosen, publicly celebrated, debated and contested.

Numerous commentators have identified parallel patterns of fragmentation in disabled identities. A number of related arguments can be identified. Perhaps first is the possibility of fragmentation within the movement. Monks, for instance, claims that:

> By the early 1990s there was undeniable differentiation of the movement motivated by claims of *particular* experience of disablement. A current major dilemma for the movement, then, lies in the membership's recognition of peculiarities of experience being coupled with a commitment to collective political action. (Monks 1999: 75)

Morris writes:

> Black disabled people and disabled gay men and lesbians express their particular concerns in particular contexts...such groups should not be treated as an 'added on' optional extra to a more general analysis of disability. (Morris 1991: 12)

Such criticisms are repeatedly endorsed from different viewpoints by Campbell and Oliver (1996). For instance, Hill states:

I got fed up to the back teeth of being told by white disabled people that as black disabled people we shouldn't be concerned with issues of race and disability; that we should be concerned only with issues of disability because that was the fight; that was the most important element in our character. I am of the belief that black disabled people share a lot in common with white disabled people. We have lots of issues in common but we cannot ignore the fact that to a very large extent there still is that added element of racism that we have to encounter as black people. I didn't think that the white disability movement was taking that on board. (Campbell and Oliver 1996: 132)

This fragmentation is potentially limitless with the interaction of different social divisions. For example, REGARD is a campaigning organization of disabled lesbians and gay men established to address the heterosexism that exists within the disabled people's movement and communities. However, the research by Gillespie-Sells, Hill and Robbins suggests that this group is not representative of all disabled lesbians and gay men:

Discussion with REGARD revealed a reluctance on behalf of Black disabled lesbians to 'come out' and be identified. The reason put forward was homophobia in the disability community.... There were also problems of anti-lesbianism within families and minority ethnic communities; in addition there was a lack of support to tackle the hostility that asserting their sexuality aroused. (Gillespie-Sells et al. 1998: 62)

Disabled refugees and asylum seekers are another more recent addition to the list of groups whose interests are not fully taken into account by single issue movements. They 'constitute one of the most disadvantaged groups within our society' (Roberts 2000: 945). Disabled refugees and asylum seekers are 'lost in the system' because both 'the disability movement and the refugee community focus their attention...on issues affecting the majority of their populations and fail to engage adequately with issues which affect a small minority'.

This is a feature of most social movements. It is ironical that the very thing they are united on is also the very thing that leads to division between them – that is, 'identity and difference'. Thus, as a Black feminist writer, Audrey Lorde, has stated:

Somewhere on the edge of consciousness, there is what I call a *mythical norm*...this norm is usually defined as white, thin, male, young, heterosexual, Christian and financially secure. It is with this mythical norm that the trappings of power reside within this society. Those of us who stand outside that power often identify one way in which we are different, and we assume that to be the primary cause of all oppression, forgetting other distortions around difference, some of which we ourselves may be practising. (1984: 37)

The experience of Black disabled people within the disabled people's movement demonstrates this, as Hill stated:

> As was the case within society generally, so it was within the disabled communities – two societies were developing, one black, one white – separate and unequal. . . . as far as the disability movement was concerned, disablism always took precedence, not only over racism but also over other human rights. (Hill 1994: 75)

This attitude is also prevalent in the Black community, as McDonald's experience of his family's reaction demonstrates: 'to fight for the rights of black people is one thing; to fight for the rights of disabled people is something else, there is not enough time and energy to fight two different wars' (1991: 3).

Social movements organized around single issue politics force individuals with multiple negative identities – such as disabled Black people – to prioritize one or the other struggle. The interplay between identity, difference, politics and power is far more complex. As Anita explained in Vernon's (1998b) research:

> Lot of the time you can't separate it. I think that your gender, race and disability combine at times to create a discriminatory experience. For example, in education it was disability, in work it was race and disability and at home it is being a woman that predominates one's experience. By separating it, you lose the totality of the person's experience.

Jackie, who is a woman, a Black person and a person with learning difficulties, expressed a similar view: 'My view is that I can't separate them. This is me. I relate to them all in different ways' (Walmsley and Downer 1997: 45). It can be argued that the oppression that different groups experience is unique, and thus underpins different identities: 'it may be necessary to move away from the unitary, essentialist disability identity and think of a variety of disability identities' (Shakespeare 1996: 110).

To summarize, identity – or rather, identities – can be viewed as multifaceted and fluid. Indeed, it is questionable whether Black and ethnic minority disabled people, for instance, can or should be considered as a heterogeneous group, or 'Black and disabled' as a stable identity. Williams states, 'At one or many moments, in one or many places issues of disability may be highlighted; at another moment the inequalities of class may predominate for the same person or group' (1992: 215). From this viewpoint, in a social context of rapid change, there is an ever expanding range of identity choices and explanations of the social world in terms of 'large-scale and relatively stable social categories which do violence to the complexity of the everyday experiences of individuals' (Mason 2000: 111).

Reflecting on disability theory

Turning to disability theory *per se*, notions of social divisions and hierarchy are central. The foundations of the social model, and hence disability theory, lie in historical materialism, with the most often cited texts being Finkelstein (1980) and Oliver (1990). In a more recent statement Oliver explains: 'the economy, through both the operation of the labour market and the social organisation of work, plays a key role in producing the category disability and in determining societal responses to disabled people' (1996: 33). In this account, disability, in present-day Western society, is a production of the economic and social power relations of capitalism, and disability theory is rooted in materialist theory of the production of social division. The foundation of disability theory, it can be argued, associates disability with social class as the form of social inequality that has received the most attention in sociology (Bradley 1996). In Marxist theory, inequalities of wealth and power are a direct product of the developing capitalist system, widening the gap between those who own the means of production, the bourgeoisie, and the working class, or proletariat:

> The epoch of the bourgeoisie possesses...this distinctive feature: it has simplified the class antagonisms. Society as a whole is more and more splitting into two great hostile camps, into two great classes directly facing each other – bourgeoisie and proletariat. (Marx and Engels 1934: 10)

The same theoretical basis offers a framework that incorporates the analysis of disabling power relations alongside other social divisions: 'The oppression that disabled people face is rooted in the economic and social structures of capitalism which themselves produce racism, sexism, homophobia, ageism and disablism' (Oliver 1996: 33). A materialist account of the creation of disability places ideology at the centre of the analysis of social division. Thompson (1997) suggests that a dominant ideology operates in a number of ways, by:

1   legitimizing social inequalities, power relations and structures;
2   establishing 'what is 'normal' and therefore, by extension, what is 'abnormal'' (Thompson 1997: 25);
3   defining cultural values and desirable goals;
4   being 'naturalised, taken for granted and almost all-embracing' (Barnes 1996b: 48).

As we have mapped earlier, however, recognition of diversity of experience and identity in terms of multiple social divisions challenges the development of a comprehensive theoretical account. Perhaps the most straightforward references to other social divisions and movements is through comparison to inform and understand developments within the disabled people's movement and disability theory. Priestley, for instance, suggests that:

> For an emergent movement, the recognition of difference may give rise to fears of fragmentation. As the experience of the women's movement or the Black civil rights movement shows, such fears are easily manifested in a reluctance to acknowledge separatism or specific interest groups. Consequently, there may be much for the Disabled People's Movement to learn from issues of difference within other social movements. (Priestley 1999: 66)

Such insights are not as recent as Priestley might seem to imply – at least not for Finkelstein, who was imprisoned and then deported having actively fought against apartheid in South Africa: 'So some of the arguments I was raising about oppression of disabled people originated from oppression of Black people' (quoted in Campbell and Oliver 1996: 120).

Two related bodies of critique have emanated from feminist academics and activists and from writers in postmodernist schools of thought. It needs to be emphasized that both are broad sources rather than single coherence perspectives. Two recent contributions to the feminist(s) analysis of disability issues, for instance, are grounded in radically different stances, Thomas (1999) being a materialist feminist and Fawcett (2000) a postmodernist feminist. It is difficult to capture these substantial and complex analyses within succinct summaries, though the conflicting foundations are clear. Thomas in her book is

> starting out with a social-relational conception of disability, and seeking to explain disablism in terms of its roots in the level of development of the productive forces, the social relations of production and reproduction, and the cultural formations and ideologies in society. (Thomas 1999: 143)

Postmodernists eschew grand narratives, overarching frameworks and all-encompassing theoretical perspectives. Postmodernists critique any emphasis on commonalities and coherence and celebrate fragmentation. Fawcett writes of critiques of materialist accounts from a postmodernist orientation:

> Such critiques include universalist conceptions of basic human need . . . and notions of inalienable human rights based on fundamental citizenship entitlements. Postmodern orientations can therefore be seen to remove the very foundation of disability rights movements based on the social model of disability and to severely challenge modernist feminist movements. (Fawcett 2000: 125)

The fragmentation of experience and identity finds its theoretical expression in strong postmodernist orientations. Williams (1996) traces parallel developments in feminism, and in doing so refers to disability politics, which is ironic, given the general neglect of disability issues by feminist analysis and activism (Morris 1996):

> Feminism based on Black, lesbian and disabled politics has pointed to the need to deconstruct the category 'woman' in order to understand the complex and inter-connected range of identities and subject positions through which women's experiences are constituted, as well as the way these also change over time and place. (Williams 1996: 69)

The same line of reasoning points to the need to deconstruct the category of 'disabled people'.

Whilst postmodernist thought has proved very influential in the social sciences, including disability studies, there has been a backlash and a reassertion of modernity, though 'one less sure of itself, more uncertain, detraditionalised, provisional and risk ridden – in general, more a reflective modernity' (Hetherington 1998: 7). In terms of disability theory, Barton (1996: 9) warns against the 'regressive relativism of particular forms of postmodernism'. Linking theoretical development with developments within the movement, Finkelstein states:

> Emancipatory movements are usually started by people on the political left but as the new-born movement manages to fumble its way through the first muddy barriers, not without casualties, individuals to the centre and right of the political spectrum all too often 'discover' the movement's message and claim it for their own. (Finkelstein 2001: 13)

Perhaps the most serious criticism of postmodernity (or forms of postmodernity), and one which takes us into our concluding section, is that posited by Crook: 'An inability to specify possible mechanisms of change, and an inability to state why change is better than no change' (1990: 59).

To summarize, the concepts of division and hierarchy have a substantial and contested role to play within social theory generally, and disability theory in particular. Essentially, the debate addresses the politics of disability in terms of theorizing day-to-day experience, personal identity, collective identity and social change.

Conclusion

As many disabled commentators recognize, disabled people will not judge disability theory by its contribution to academic or research discourses, but ultimately by its role in social change, in the emancipation of disabled people. It is in these terms that the consideration of social divisions needs to inform the development of disability theory. Again, debates in feminism are pertinent. Ramazanoglu (1989) put forward the view, endorsed by others, that feminists should work positively with the contradiction that women are simultaneously united through the imbalance of power relations between women and men in the economic and social structures of society, but divided through multiple social divisions. Langan states:

> This involves challenging the nature of power, whoever holds it, including being sensitive to the power some women have over other women, and the need, for example, for white feminists to confront their own racism. This approach places a greater emphasis on the active, resisting role of women. (Langan 1992: 5)

As we have illustrated in this chapter, similar contradictions of oppression are apparent for disabled people. Jackie Downer, who has been a central figure in the Black People First movement, states:

> Black People First? If you see one you can tell me – no such thing. It was gonna exist but it doesn't. People need space and choice – Black, gay men and women, children. I set up a Black friendly group and it was stressful. People were saying 'Why can't we have mixed groups, what's wrong with us?' You can segregate yourself, people need to unite and segregating doesn't help the movement. (Quoted in Goodley 2000: 83)

Indeed, it can be argued that fragmentation has played a major role historically in the social oppression of disabled people. Segregated schooling, for instance, not only separated disabled people from non-disabled people in schools and in their local communities; it separated disabled people from other disabled people, as categorized by impairments, and continues to do so. Disabled people were, and still are, separated by charity organizations, in day centres, residential homes and so on. In some 'homes', such as the large-scale hospitals for people labelled 'mentally handicapped', women with learning difficulties have been separated from men with learning difficulties, as an expression of policy and service provision of eugenics.

The challenges of addressing the contradictions of commonality and diversity are critical to disability theory evolving from the social model of disability and promoting emancipation from social oppression. They involve theorizing the relationship between disability, ethnicity, sexuality, age and gender, to promote the realization of inclusive disability theory and an inclusive disabled people's movement. Barnes states:

> The politics of disablement is about far more than disabled people; it is about challenging oppression in all its forms.... Like racism, sexism, heterosexism and all other forms of social oppression, [disability] is a human creation. It is impossible, therefore, to confront one type of oppression without confronting them all and, of course, the cultural values that created and sustain them. (1996a: p. xii)

Vernon endorses this view, arguing that:

> The experience of disabled Black people, women, gay men and lesbians, older people and those from the working class is fully integrated to take account of the fact that the experience is often exacerbated by the interaction of other forms of oppressions. The politics of eradicating disability, therefore, must take into account the whole oppressive structure of our society and be careful to challenge all forms of oppression wherever it is found. (1998a: 209)

It is the nature of oppression in the capitalist system, at least in present-day Western societies, that oppression fragments social divisions and casts one group against another – including poor white people against poor Black people, disabled people against poor people, disabled people against women, and Black disabled women against white disabled men. Thus, 'disabled people have no choice but to attempt to build a better world because it is impossible to have a vision of inclusionary capitalism: we all need a world where impairment is valued and celebrated and all disabling barriers are eradicated. Such a world would be inclusionary for all' (Oliver and Barnes 1998: 62). Disabled people, too, have no choice but to struggle towards this vision collectively, to unity that gives full recognition to diversity.

How might we summarize the implications for future theoretical developments? To paraphrase Hetherington (1998), we do so only with uncertainty and provisionally. Yet there are signposts. First, theorizing disability should retain and strengthen analyses of the material forces that create poverty, unequal structures and power relations, and institutionalized discrimination. The second imperative for developing theory is that it 'put disabled people in a leading role for constructive social change – a complete reversal of expectations about disabled people' (Finkelstein 2001: 11). Finally, theoretical development should recognize that emancipation of disabled people can never be realized in a society that sustains racism, sexism, homophobia and ageism. Theorizing disability from the viewpoint of social divisions and hierarchies is generated by the recognition of both commonalities and diversity.

REFERENCES

Abu-Habib, L. 1997: *Gender and Disability: Women's Experiences in the Middle East.* Oxford: OXFAM.
ADAPT 1993: *Asian and Disabled: A Study into the Needs of Asian People with Disabilities in the Bradford Area.* West Yorkshire: Asian Disability Advisory Project Team, The Spastics Society and Barnardos.
Alcock, P. 1996: *Social Policy in Britain: Themes and Issues.* Houndmills: Macmillan.
Azmi, S., Emerson, E., Caine, A. and Hatton, C. 1996: *Improving Services for Asian People with Learning Difficulties and their Families.* Manchester: Hester Adrian Research Centre / The Mental Health Foundation.
Banton, M. and Hirsch, M. M. 2000: *Double Invisibility: Report on Research into the Needs of Black Disabled People in Coventry.* Coventry: Warwickshire County Council.
Barnes, C. 1996a: Foreword to J. Campbell and M. Oliver, *Disability Politics: Understanding our Past, Changing our Future*, London: Routledge, pp. ix–xiii.
Barnes, C. 1996b: Theories of disability and the origins of the oppression of disabled people in western society. In L. Barton (ed.), *Disability and Society: Emerging Issues and Insights*, London: Longman, 43–61.
Barnes, C., Mercer, G. and Shakespeare, T. 1999: *Exploring Disability: A Sociological Introduction.* Cambridge: Polity.
Barton, L. (ed). 1996: *Disability and Society: Emerging Issues and Insights.* London: Longman.
Baxter, C. 1995: Confronting colour blindness: developing better services for people with learning difficulties from Black and ethnic minority communities. In T. Philpot and L. Ward (eds), *Values and Visions: Changing Ideas in Services for People with Learning Difficulties*, Oxford: Butterworth-Heinemann.

Begum, N. 1994: Mirror, mirror on the wall. In N. Begum, M. Hill and A. Stevens (eds), *Reflections: Views of Black Disabled People on their Lives and Community Care*, London: Central Council for Education and Training in Social Work, 17–32.

Bhavnani, R. 1994: *Black Women in the Labour Market: A Research Review* Manchester: Equal Opportunities Commission.

Bignall, T. and Butt, J. 2000: *Between Ambition and Achievement: Young Black Disabled People's Views and Experiences of Independence and Independent Living*. Bristol: Policy Press.

Bradley, H. 1996: *Fractured Identities: Changing Patterns of Inequality*. Cambridge: Polity.

Brown, C. 1984: *Black and White in Britain: The Third PSI Survey*. Oxford: Heinemann.

Butt, J. and Box, L. 1997: *Supportive Services, Effective Strategies: The Views of Black-Led Organisations and Social Care Agencies on the Future of Social Care for Black Communities*. London: Race Equality Unit.

Butt, J. and Mirza, K. 1996: *Social Care and Black Communities*. London: Race Equality Unit.

Campbell, J. and Oliver, M. 1996: *Disability Politics: Understanding our Past, Changing our Future*. London: Routledge.

Coleridge, P. 1993 *Disability, Liberation and Development*. Oxford: OXFAM.

Crook, S. 1990: The end of radical social theory? Radicalism, modernism and postmodernism. In R. Boyne and A. Rattansi (eds), *Postmodernism and Society*, London: Macmillan, 46–76.

Fawcett, B. 2000: *Feminist Perspectives on Disability*. Harlow: Prentice-Hall.

Finkelstein, V. 1980: *Attitudes and Disabled People: Issues for Discussion*. Monograph 5. New York: World Rehabilitation Fund.

Finkelstein, V. 2001: A personal journey into disability politics. www.leeds.a-c.uk / disability-studies / links.htm.

French, S. 2001: *Disabled People and Employment: A Study of the Working Lives of Visually Impaired Physiotherapists*. Aldershot: Ashgate.

French, S. and Vernon, A. 1997: Health care for people from ethnic minority groups. In S. French (ed.), *Physiotherapy: A Psychosocial Approach*, 2nd edn., Oxford: Butterworth–Heinemann, 59–73.

Gillespie-Sells, K., Hill, M. and Robbins, B. 1998: *She Dances to Different Drums: Research into Disabled Women's Sexuality*. London: King's Fund.

Goodley, D. 2000: *Self-Advocacy in the Lives of People with Learning Difficulties*. Buckingham: Open University Press.

Hall, S. 1990: Cultural identity and diaspora. In J. Rutherford (ed.) *Identity: Community, Culture and Difference*, London: Lawrence and Wishart.

Hetherington, K. 1998: *Expressions of Identity: Space, Performance, Politics*. London: Sage.

Hill, M. 1991: Race and disability: In The Open University (ed.), *Disability – Identity, Sexuality and Relationships: Readings*, K665Y course. Milton Keynes: The Open University.

Hill, M. 1994: They are not our brothers: the disability movement and the black disability movement. In N. Begum, M. Hill and A. Stevens (eds), *Reflections: Views of Black Disabled People of their Lives and Community Care*, Paper 32.3. London: Central Council for Education and Training in Social Work.

Hill-Collins, P. 1990: *Black Feminist Thought: Knowledge, Consciousness and the Politics of Empowerment*. Oxford: Unwin–Heinemann.

Jenkins, R. 1996. *Social Identity.* London: Routledge.

Jones, L., Atkin, K. and Ahmad, W. I. U. 2001: Supporting Asian deaf young people and their families: the role of professionals and services. *Disability and Society*, 16(1), 51–70.

Langan, M. 1992: Introduction: women and social work in the 1990s. In M. Langan and L. Day (eds), *Women, Oppression and Social Work: Issues in Anti-discriminatory Practice*, London: Routledge, 1–12.

Lloyd, M. 1992: 'Does she boil eggs?' Towards a feminist model of disability. *Disability, Handicap and Society*, 7(3), 207–21.

Lonsdale, S. 1990: *Women and Disability: The Experience of Women with Disability*. London: Macmillan.

Lorde, A. 1984: *Sister Outsider*. California: Crossing Press Feminist Series.

Marsh, I. 2000: *Sociology: Making Sense of Society*, 2nd edn., Harlow: Prentice-Hall.

Marx, K. and Engels, F. 1934: *Manifesto of the Communist Party*. London: Lawrence and Wishart.

Mason, D. 2000: Ethnicity. In G. Payne (ed.), *Social Divisions*, Houndmills: Macmillan, 91–119.

McDonald, P. 1991: Double discrimination must be faced now. *Disability Now*, March 8.

Miles, R. 1989: *Racism*. London: Routledge.

Modood, T. 1997: Culture and identity. In T. Modood, R. Berthoud, J. Lakey, J. Nazroo, P. Smith, S. Virdee and P. Beishon (eds) *Ethnic Minorities in Britain*, London: Policy Studies Institute, 290–339.

Monks, J. 1999: 'It works both ways': belonging and social participation among women with disabilities. In N. Yuval-Davis and P. Werbner (eds), *Women, Citizenship and Difference*, London: Zed Books.

Morris, J. 1991: *Pride Against Prejudice: Transforming Attitudes to Disability*. London: Women's Press.

Morris, J. 1996: Introduction to J. Morris (ed.), *Encounters with Strangers: Feminism and Disability*, London: Women's Press.

Oliver, M. 1990: *The Politics of Disablement*. Basingstoke: Macmillan.

Oliver, M. 1991: Disability and participation in the labour market. In P. Brown and R. Scase (eds), *Poor Work: Disadvantage and the Division of Labour*, Buckingham: Open University Press, 132–47.

Oliver, M. 1996: A sociology of disability or a disablist sociology? In L. Barton (ed.), *Disability and Society: Emerging Issues and Insights*, London: Longman, 18–43.

Oliver, M. and Barnes, C. 1998: *Disabled People and Social Policy: From Exclusion to Inclusion.* London: Longman.

Payne, G. 2000a: An introduction to social division. In G. Payne (ed.), *Social Divisions,* Houndmills: Macmillan, 1–20.

Payne, G. (ed.) 2000b: *Social Divisions.* Houndmills: Macmillan.

Priestley, M. 1999: *Disability Politics and Community Care.* London: Jessica Kingsley.

Ramazanoglu, C. 1989: *Feminism and the Contradictions of Oppression.* London: Routledge.

Roberts, K. 2000: Lost in the system: disabled refugees and asylum seekers in Britain. *Disability and Society,* 15(6), 943–8.

Shakespeare, T. 1996: Disability, identity, difference. In C. Barnes and G. Mercer (eds), *Exploring the Divide: Illness and Disability,* Leeds: Disability Press, 94–114.

Shakespeare, T., Gillespie-Sells, K. and Davies, D. 1996: *The Sexual Politics of Disability.* London: Cassell.

Stuart, O. 1993: Double oppression: an appropriate starting-point? In J. Swain, V. Finkelstein, S. French and M. Oliver (eds), *Disabling Barriers – Enabling Environments,* London: Sage, 93–100.

Swain, J. and French, S. 2000: Towards an affirmative model of disability. *Disability and Society,* 15(4), 569–82.

Thomas, C. 1999: *Female Forms: Experiencing and Understanding Disability.* Buckingham: Open University Press.

Thompson, N. 1997: *Anti-Discriminatory Practice,* 2nd edn, Houndmills: Macmillan.

Vernon, A. 1998a: Multiple oppression and the disabled people's movement. In T. Shakespeare (ed.), *The Disability Reader: Social Science Perspectives,* London: Cassell, 201–11.

Vernon, A. 1998b: Understanding 'simultaneous oppression': the experience of disabled Black women in education and employment (unpublished Ph.D., University of Leeds).

Walmsley, J. and Downer, J. 1997: Shouting the loudest: self-advocacy, power and diversity. In P. Ramcharan, G. Roberts, G. Grant and J. Borland (eds), *Empowerment in Everyday Life: Learning Disability,* London: Jessica Kingsley, 35–48.

Williams, F. 1992: Somewhere over the rainbow: universality and diversity in social policy. In N. Manning and N. Page (eds), *Social Policy Review,* London: Social Policy Association, 200–19.

Williams, F. 1996: Postmodernism, feminism and the question of difference. In N. Parton (ed.), *Social Theory, Social Change and Social Work,* London: Routledge.

6

History, Power and Identity

Anne Borsay

Introduction

History is a missing piece of the jigsaw in disability studies. Whereas the field has expanded from its origins in social theory and social policy to include politics, culture, leisure and the media, historical perspectives across the entire range of disabled people's experiences are virtually non-existent. The purpose of this chapter is to show why it is important to study the past and how it is done. An evaluation of the historical models developed by social scientists is used to launch a social history of disability in which materialism and culturalism are complementary rather than mutually exclusive. A comprehensive historical survey is not attempted. Rather, attention focuses on the interface between physical impairment, charity and medicine in the late nineteenth and early twentieth centuries. Surveillance procedures, and resistance to them, will be examined with the help of a case study of the Nottingham and District Cripples' Guild, thus demonstrating the use of a historical source. And the chapter will conclude by exploring the place of the past in shaping the present identities of disabled people. But it is appropriate to begin by looking at the relationship between sociology and history.

Sociology and history

The neglect of history is largely due to the formative influence of sociology in disability studies. Both history and sociology emerged from the same intellectual stable, sharing in later nineteenth-century Britain a positivist commitment to the objective understanding of the human condition (Bentley 1999; Warren 1998). At this early stage in the growth of modern academic disciplines, the boundaries between the humanities and the social sciences were more permeable than they are today. Therefore, the founding fathers of sociology were not averse to addressing the historical processes of social change. Herbert Spencer (1820–1903), for example, anticipated Darwin in arguing that societies evolved like biological organisms through peaceful adaptation and ferocious combat (Burrow 1966). Similarly, Marx (1818–83) posited a transition from ancient to feudal, capitalist and socialist modes of production, driven by class conflict which arose when economic forces and social relations clashed (Marx 1961). Yet, in tracking how societies evolved, these first sociologists were already employing a methodology which differed from that of their contemporary historians.

The divide opening up was between the 'nomothetic' and the 'idiographic' approaches. Sociologists adopted a nomothetic methodology, which sought 'universals rather than particulars', amalgamated individual events into abstractions, privileged 'structure over human agency', and took 'pride in conceptual rigour'. Contrariwise, historians followed an idiographic methodology, which addressed the particular rather than the universal, eschewed the abstract for the concrete, gave priority to agency rather than structure, and engaged in the meticulous scrutiny of empirical evidence (Wilson 1993: 36). The recent postmodernist assault on rationality has challenged the desire of both disciplines for objective knowledge (Jenkins 1991; Lyon 1994). According to Anthony Giddens, however, the nomothetic / idiographic dichotomy is untenable. Giddens insists that:

> Structure, or structural properties, . . . exist only in so far as there is continuity in social reproduction across time and space. And such continuity in turn exists only in and through the reflexively monitored activities of situated actors, having a range of intended and unintended consequences.

Therefore, 'every research investigation in the social sciences or history is involved in relating action to structure', and '[n]o amount of juggling with abstract concepts could substitute for the direct study of such problems in the actual contexts of interaction' (Giddens 1984: 212, 219, 358, 362).

But however plausible in theory, this fusion has not materialized in practice. Historians, whilst making considerable use of sociological ideas, have resisted the 'mechanical' application of models or polar types; and any theoretical enterprises have been pragmatic, flexible and 'grounded' in 'the materials themselves' without 'adherence to a pre-existing theory' (Jordanova 2000: 68–70). It follows that most historians do not deal readily with the conceptual strategies which are the stuff of sociology. No less an impediment to collaboration are differing stances towards empirical evidence. Though the quantitative and qualitative social survey personifies sociology's distinguished empirical tradition, data are collected to test for the general validity of theoretical concepts. History, conversely, starts from the empirical detail. Initially preoccupied with the written documentary record (e.g., diaries, Parliamentary Papers, minute-books, and the press), it has now come to recognize the importance of oral testimonies, literary texts and visual representations (e.g., art, architecture, film and photography). But all these sources are subjected to a forensic examination, which scrutinizes their provenance and content. Are they authentic? Who was the author? Why were they produced? And what do they disclose about the historical problem under review (Marwick 1970)? From the answers to these questions, historians are more likely to construct narratives of individual agency than analyses of social structure. And, as a result, their work may be inaccessible to social scientists trained to think in conceptual ways.

Compounding the problem of methodology is the orientation of historical subject matter. When the discipline began to professionalize in Britain, from the 1860s, it converged on the state and became preoccupied with constitutional, administrative, legal, ecclesiastical, imperial and diplomatic history. This bias persists, but from the outset social history snapped at the heels of its stronger sibling. In his famous *English Social History*, published during World War II, G. M. Trevelyan defined the subject 'negatively as the history of a people with the politics left out' (1973: p. vii). Trevelyan was continuing a literary genre which pre-dated the 1860s and targeted the 'popular' market. Since the late nineteenth century, however, 'professional' social histories had appeared for an academic readership. As in sociology, evolutionary writers produced accounts based on the Darwinian 'survival of the fittest' (Traill and Mann 1895), and Marxist writers produced accounts based on the evils of the economic system (Hammond and Hammond 1934). Marxism was the more influential, ultimately inspiring a generation of historians after 1945. However, it was not until the 1960s that social history in Britain became a mature sub-discipline with the proficiency to locate social issues such as disability within their historical contexts (Bentley 1999; Wilson 1993).

Though regarded by some as economically determinist, the best Marxist historiography fashioned sophisticated arguments that were anchored to a close analysis of historical records (Warren 1998). In *The Making of the English Working Class* (1963), for instance, Edward Thompson complemented economic conditioning with individual agency, acquired from a growing awareness of change and from socio-political experiments directed at inequalities. Equally important was the way in which such initiatives encouraged reflection about the nature of history. First, there was greater receptiveness to ideas from other disciplines. Contributing to the *Times Literary Supplement* in 1966, Keith Thomas thus maintained that the social sciences would augment the historian's 'social vocabulary', that statistical methods would permit the more accurate measurement of historical trends, and that social anthropology and social psychology would bring exciting insights. Equipped with these new tools, the social historian would be able to explain 'the workings of human society and the fluctuations in human affairs' which had long defeated the mainstream discipline. Second, there was a commitment 'to rescue the poor ... from the enormous condescension of posterity' (Thompson, 1963: 13). The result was a more catholic agenda, in which the ordinary lives of everyday people joined the dominant narrative of political élites. But though we now have vibrant social histories of class, gender and race, the marginality of disabled people has prevented them from penetrating territory won by other disadvantaged groups. Social exclusion has been matched by intellectual exclusion.

Histories of disability

So far we have attributed the shortage of disability histories to three factors: the alien nature of historical methodology to social scientists, the late arrival of social history as a specialism within historical scholarship, and the translation of disabled people's social discrimination to academic discourse. As a consequence, the histories of disability which have been constructed are largely framed within the nomothetic mode of the social sciences. Indebted to Marxism and underpinned by the materialism of the social model, these studies have favoured a developmental approach, homing in on the transition from feudalism to modern industrial capitalism. Vic Finkelstein began the debate in 1980 with his provocative but imprecise identification of three 'phases'. In phase 1, impaired people were congregated at the bottom of the economic pile in the company of poorly paid workers, the unemployed and the mentally ill. Phase 2 saw the emergence of segregated disability institutions in response to 'a new productive technology'. '[L]arge scale industry with production-lines geared to able-bodied norms' excluded impaired people who had previously been integrated, socially active members of their class and community. Furthermore, the growth of hospital-based medicine encouraged the expansion of professionals whose expert knowledge was disabling. But, paradoxically, public services also helped disabled people to acquire social independence and tackle the professional control of their lives. It was this critique which gave birth to the social model and the onset of phase 3 (Finkelstein 1980: 8–11).

Finkelstein's schema was valuable for the way in which industrialization was highlighted. On his own admission, however, it sought 'to say something about the context in which attitudes are formed', and was not 'a historical analysis of disability' (Finkelstein 1980: 8). Therefore, the dynamics of the industrial process and its social and political outcomes were not made plain. Michael Oliver has tackled these deficiencies. First, he complicated the influence of the 'economic base' by arguing that whereas fully-fledged capitalism was exclusive, 'agriculture or small-scale industry ... did not preclude the great majority of disabled people from participating in the production process'. Next, the 'mode of thought' and the problem of order were added to the impact of the economy. Essentially, Oliver argued that the evolution of intellectual concepts, 'from a religious interpretation of reality' to a metaphysical and then a scientific one, interacted with the disruption thrown up by the rise of capitalism to alter 'historical perceptions of disability' and to propagate new medical and institutional methods for subduing deviancy. This tripartite model of economy, ideology and politics advanced a far more subtle understanding of economic development than Finkelstein's, and the dissection of social policies was situated within a political matrix which included beliefs and values and the policing of disorder (Oliver 1990: 27–30). Nevertheless, Oliver endorsed the supposition that impairment in pre-industrial Britain was for the most part unproblematic: a trap into which Brendan Gleeson has also fallen.

Gleeson's distinctive contribution was his geographical insight: the argument that 'the historical production of space' was 'a contested process where the exercise of power largely determines who benefits and who loses from the creation of new places and landscapes'. What he advocated was an 'embodied materialism', in which disability was 'seen as part of a broader process of social embodiment – the ascription of roles and representations to body types that varies in time and space'. This theoretical standpoint was executed in a comparison of feudal England and the industrial city. Gleeson maintained that physical impairment was so commonplace among the medieval peasantry that it was 'probably a general feature of peasant social space'; bodily impairment may have 'marked itself out', but only when it had 'spiritual significance' or threatened leprosy. With the gradual shift to industrial capitalism and urban living, this inclusion was sacrificed.

> One disabling feature of the ...city was the new separation of home and work, a socio-spatial phenomenon which was all but absent in the feudal era.... In addition, industrial workplaces were structured and used in ways that disabled 'uncompetitive' workers .... The rise of mechanised forms of production introduced productivity standards that assumed a 'normal' (that is to say, usually male and non-impaired) worker's body and disabled all others.

The upshot of this 'labour market exclusion' was 'socio-spatial marginalisation', whether through incarceration, home working, or street trading. Therefore, even those disabled people who were visible on the thoroughfares of the Victorian city were not engaged in the customary pedestrian activities of shopping, socializing or circulating. Rather, the street was 'a place of subsistence' which also served as a stage that 'constantly retold the story of their social difference' (Gleeson 1999: 33, 34, 93–6, 106–10).

Towards a cultural perspective

Running throughout these histories of disability, which span twenty years, is a common emphasis on the material implications of the economy for social and political life. Prior to the Industrial Revolution of the late eighteenth century, disabled people were part of an undifferentiated mass poor, and hence clustered at the lower reaches of society but not excluded from it. After industrialization, new technologies debarred them from the work-force and set in train segregatory state policies implemented by professional experts. Colin Barnes has shown that discrimination long pre-dated this era, finding examples in 'Greek culture, Judaeo-Christian religions and European drama and art since well before the renaissance' (1996: 51–2). However, the economic and political, as well as the cultural, chronology of materialist histories is faulty.

First, the doctrine of economic rationality was widely upheld before the late eighteenth century. 'Regularly labouring people are the Kingdom's greatest treasure and strength,' insisted the Quaker cloth merchant and social thinker John Bellers in 1714; 'for... if the poor labourers did not raise much more food and manufacture than what did subsist themselves, every gentleman must be a labourer and every idle man must starve' (1987: 204; see also Borsay 1998). Given such espousal of the work ethic, the pre-industrial labour market may not have been very hospitable to impaired participants. Second, the impact of economic change was variable, and the onset of factory employment was far from rapid; in 1841, for instance, only 6 per cent of the total labour force worked in textile plants, the one sector where mechanization was significant (Evans 1983). Finally, the evolution of the state was complex. Though the nineteenth century did witness an expansion of collectivist legislation, the non-statutory services kept a vital role that was particularly extended in the area of disability. Yes, there were workhouses for the destitute, built under the Poor Law Amendment Act of 1834 (Crowther 1981). Yes, the state had required the erection of lunatic asylums since 1845 (Scull 1993) and mental deficiency institutions since 1913 (Thomson 1998). But much of the segregated provision for physically impaired adults and children was provided by charitable bodies which were increasingly drawn into partnerships with government (Parker 1965; Topliss 1975). Therefore, it is difficult to see the incarceration of disabled people as simply the outcome of an oppressive state.

The assumption that industrialization ushered in a concentration of economic power in big, mechanized factories and a concentration of political power in a centralized, professionalized state is not only historically flawed. There is also a conceptual problem: the omission of a cultural dimension. The social model from which histories of disability have been derived already stands accused of an 'arid materialism' (Paterson and Hughes 1999: 599), which rides roughshod over the multiplicity of disabled peoples' experiences (Barnes et al. 1999). The architects of the model have pitted themselves against any concessions, warning that they reduce 'explanations for cultural phenomena...to the level of thought processes, thus detracting attention away from economic and social considerations' (Barnes 1996: 49). In some respects, however, the polarity is exaggerated, because phenomenology has 'long emphasized the "social construction of reality"', whilst cultural Marxists 'have stressed the importance of thought and imagination in the production of..."society"' (Burke 1992: 120). What historical study requires is a conceptual framework which holds materialism and culturalism – or structure and agency – in tension. As Peter Burke has amplified:

> The current emphasis on cultural creativity and on culture as an active force in history needs to be accompanied by some sense of the constraints within which that creativity operates. Rather than simply replacing the social history of culture by the cultural history of society we need to work with the two ideas together and simultaneously, however difficult this may

be. In other words, it is most useful to see the relation between culture and society in dialectical terms, with both partners at once active and passive, determining and determined. (Burke 1992: 123)

In the remainder of this chapter, I attempt the endeavour that Burke outlines, applying a cultural concept of power to the surveillance procedures that charity and medicine deployed to police disabled people between the late Victorian period and the outbreak of World War II.

Moral surveillance

Whereas materialism envisages the state as a unitary structure, culturalism fragments it into 'one segment of a much broader play of power relations'. Not only are professionals and bureaucracies, leisure pursuits and cultural representations encompassed (Barns et al. 1999: 8), but so is a mixed economy of welfare with inputs from the voluntary, commercial and informal sectors (Kidd 1999). On this scenario, social policy ceases to be a statutory 'tool to regulate a population from the top down' and becomes 'more diffuse' (Shore and Wright 1997: 5). Foucault's concept of disciplinary power captures this dismemberment. For him, discipline could not be tied to an institution or an apparatus, but comprised 'a whole set of instruments, techniques, procedures, levels of application, targets' (Foucault 1991: 215). Therefore, power penetrated the social body, tailoring the 'docile' subject to modern economic and political demands by means of 'continuous surveillance and monitoring, [and] the application of endless rules of conduct, manner, attitude and appearance' (O'Brien and Penna 1998: 116). It follows that the community is no less a site for the transaction of power than the institution, and that charities are no less conduits than the state.

Charitable activity in Britain accelerated rapidly from the late eighteenth century. The new philanthropic organizations were frequently patronized by the middle classes, imbued with the fervour of evangelical religion and increasingly affluent due to commercial and industrial growth. Their aim was to ensure that, in the aftermath of the French Revolution and political radicalism at home, the poor behaved as orderly and economically productive citizens (Borsay 1999; Prochaska 1988). In the case of impairment, the effects were differential. Blind and deaf people, denied access to the word of God, appealed to Christian sympathies, particularly since new methods of teaching them to communicate offered a justification for schools. Employment facilities often followed, as ex-pupils struggled to find work in the open labour market

(Topliss 1975). Provision for physical, as opposed to sensory, impairments, on the other hand, was slower to materialize. Some projects did date from the early nineteenth century. In 1817, for example, a small General Institution for the Relief of Persons labouring under Bodily Deformity was established in Birmingham (White 1997). Similar institutions followed elsewhere (Cholmeley 1985). But despite the toll of factory accidents, and their exploitation in the campaign for legislative reform (Gray 1996), foundations for physically impaired people burgeoned only in the late Victorian period.

The thrust behind this philanthropic impulse was 'the "social" discovery of the "crippled child"', itself part of a broader reconfiguration of childhood in which the 'wage-earning "non-child" of the labouring poor was transformed into the economically worthless "child-scholar"'. Therefore, between 1870 and 1914 – during which time state schools joined charitable and commercial schools to provide elementary education that was free and compulsory – more than forty voluntary agencies for 'crippled' children appeared. At first, their ethos was sentimental, as the names bring out only too clearly: the Crutch and Kindness League, the League of Hearts and Hands, the Guild of the Brave Poor Things. In 1893, however, the Charity Organization Society (COS) published an influential report on *The Epileptic and Crippled Child and Adult*. Renowned for a rabid belief in personal responsibility since set up in 1867, the COS promoted a scientific brand of philanthropy in which, through collaboration with statutory and voluntary bodies, it sought to direct charitable assistance only towards the deserving poor who were predisposed towards self-help. Therefore, 'crippled' children were schooled in the virtues of independence, their alleged triumph over disaster potently endorsing the flagging ideology of individualism (Cooter 1993: 53–9).

The self-help mentality was not the monopoly of the Charity Organization Society. Deeply embedded in the Victorian mind-set, it was taken up at the opening of the twentieth century by a new type of philanthropic organization epitomized by the guilds of help. Whereas the COS opposed much state intervention, the guilds saw themselves as partners of government, shaping a new civic consciousness which closed the gap between donor and recipient (Laybourn 1997). Their model was the German Elberfield system, in which unpaid workers administered relief and offered a casework service (Lewis 1995). In practice, however, the guilds were dominated by middle-class members whose attitudes and methods differed little from those of the COS (Cushlow 1997). The Nottingham District Cripples' Guild (NDCG) – my case study for the surveillance of disabled people – grew out of this tradition in 1908. We know of its existence from six surviving *Annual Reports* for the years 1914, 1915,

1924, 1939, 1950/1, and 1964, – all of which are lodged at the Local Studies Library in Nottingham. The piecemeal character of this evidence is typical of many organizations for and of disabled people, whose records are far less likely than those of statutory bodies and major charities to find safe repose in local libraries and record offices (Foster and Sheppard 1995), or national repositories like the Public Record Office (http://www.pro.gov.uk), the British Library (http://opac97.bl .uk), and the Wellcome Library for the History and Understanding of Medicine (http://library.wellcome.ac.uk). Even with few sources, however, it is possible to tease out a history of disability by situating the topic under investigation within its wider societal context.

The *Annual Reports* for the Nottingham District Cripples' Guild show that between 1914 and 1964 members were offered a recreational programme of entertainments and excursions. By the end of the period, this was all that was left. Prior to World War II, however, the guild was at the centre of a web of voluntary and statutory organizations, which included the Charity Organization Society, the National Society for the Prevention of Cruelty to Children, the Education Committee of the local authority, and the Poor Law guardians and their successors, the Public Assistance Committee (NDCG 1914). Within this network, the guild was responsible for a system of first moral and then medical surveillance. The *Annual Reports* for 1914 and 1915 split the city into fifteen districts. Each was serviced by a group of visitors who were headed by a 'captain': a title imported from Elberfield (Lewis 1995: 73). The visitor attached to every case was to 'be the cripple's trusted friend' and send in reports which spelt out 'any useful thing to be done' (NDCG 1915: 8). In 1913, the guild had adopted the COS's 'casepaper' system. Therefore, all applications were subjected to a robust scrutiny, which noted the employment record, patterns of income and expenditure, signs of thrift and recourse to poor relief (Kidd 1999). Requests for help were then processed by the weekly committees, whose members sought the causes of need, judged whether satisfying it was a proper use of funds, and tried to learn systematically from their experiences (NDCG 1914).

In reaching decisions, a stringent moral discourse was imposed. Like the COS and the new philanthropy in general, the NDCG believed that charitable assistance was not suitable where self-help was unlikely to result (NDCG 1914). In the *Annual Report* for 1915, two categories of miscreant were depicted: the ubiquitous adult male unwilling to take employment and the neglectful families of 'crippled' children.

A bright intelligent child with seriously deformed feet and appealing personality, living in unsatisfactory surroundings and receiving many pennies, was medically examined. It was clear that an operation would very greatly improve his condition. This the parents opposed in the first instance but eventually, largely owing to the intervention of the Inspector of the NSPCC, the operation was performed and gave every promise of success. A return from the hospital to the home would, it was feared, destroy the benefit of the treatment. Arrangements were made with the Education Authority to send the child away to a Sanatorium School until his cure had been completed. The cost was to be shared by the Education Authority and the Guild. The child however returned home, resumed the receipt of his pennies, his parents refused to take advantage of the arrangements suggested, deprived the child of months of benefit at the sea, and seriously lessened the success of the hospital treatment. (NDCG 1915: 6)

This vignette manifests a refusal to grasp the realities of poverty in early twentieth-century Britain (Vincent 1991). The diseases which 'crippled' many members of the guild – rickets, tuberculosis, infantile paralysis – were associated with economic and social deprivation. Yet the causes of such hardship in inadequate wages, parsimonious social security benefits and bad housing were never confronted. Nor were parents credited with a reluctance to decant their children into institutions which, for all the benevolent gloss, imposed a harsh, disciplinarian regime. Instead, disabled people and their families were subjected to moral condemnation through a surveillance network funded and managed by the voluntary sector. By the mid-1920s, however, the casework which dispensed these judgements was in retreat as a shift towards medical treatment after World War I seized the agenda (NDCG 1924).

Medical surveillance

The hagiographic tale of medicine's progress has now been debugged by sociologists and historians, and the celebration of great inventions, heroic doctors and benevolent institutions subdued by critical enquiry (Jordanova 1995). Particularly corrosive was Foucault's connection between knowledge and power. 'We should admit...that power produces knowledge,' he wrote; 'that power and knowledge directly imply one another; that there is no power relation without the correlative constitution of a field of knowledge, nor any knowledge that does not presuppose and constitute at the same time power relations' (1991: 27). The medical speciality of orthopaedics, closely associated with physical impairment at the start of the twentieth century, illustrates well the politicization of clinical knowledge. Early hospitals like the General Institution in Birmingham were largely preoccupied with deformities of the feet, and became ever more marginalized after 1850 'by the rise of "orthopaedic surgery" ... in general hospitals'. Simultaneously, there was a refinement of physiotherapeutic techniques (medical gymnastics, massage, electrotherapy, hydrotherapy) and the absorption of a holistic philosophy of diet, rest and fresh air. Nevertheless, a fatalistic attitude often prevailed. Many surgeons admitted 'to a large class of "stationary cripples" who, as a result of congenital malformations, accidents of childbirth, infantile paralysis or long-standing rickets, were beyond the surgical pale and were capable of help only through special educational and training facilities' (Cooter 1993: 18, 60).

Clinical interest rallied after 1900 primarily because of the prevalence of 'crippling' conditions thrown up by the increase in surgery at paediatric hospitals. As chronically impaired children blocked beds intended for acute, short-term cases, an alternative model of long-term treatment unfolded. It was exemplified by Agnes Hunt's charitable convalescent home at Baschurch near Oswestry in Shropshire, which, during the Edwardian period, pioneered an orthopaedic facility of international renown with a programme of surgery, open-air therapy and satellite after-care clinics. Between 1914 and 1918 World War I created additional clinical opportunities. Two-thirds of all casualties suffered locomotor injuries; and the treatment of fractures, gunshot wounds and nerve lesions all fell within the province of orthopaedics. Furthermore, the orthopaedic hospitals set up during the war for military patients generated a new power base which their medical occupants were anxious not to lose. So, on return to civilian work, orthopaedic surgeons promoted 'an ambitious scheme to recreate the power and glory of their military empire' through a national scheme for the cure of 'crippled' children. The influence of local authorities in medical planning made it impossible for the Ministry of Health to co-ordinate this scheme. Consequently, orthopaedics turned to the charitable sector in the form of the Central Council for the Care of Cripples (Cooter 1993: 153; Hunt 1924a, 1924b, 1924c).

The Central Council (eventually the Royal Association for Disability and Rehabilitation) was set up in 1919. Whereas pre-war charities had been divided between medicine, education and welfare, the Central Council brought together representation from these different constituencies. Based on the arrangements at Baschurch, the national scheme of which it became the sponsor advocated a network of central orthopaedic hospitals, allied to a series of affiliated local after-care clinics. The central orthopaedic hospital provided the 'crippled' child with skilled surgery and nursing, a good diet, education and 'the benefits of the sun and the open air ... for as long as his physical disability demands'. The local after-care clinics supplied a 'short-cut' to accurate diagnosis and hospital admission, enabled 'the surgeon to supervise his own handiwork ... and to realize the end results,' and offered him 'a wonderful school' in which to learn 'more and more all his life how best to help the crippled child' (Girdlestone 1924: 3).

The Nottingham District Cripples' Guild was a recognized enthusiast for this national scheme (Anderson 1969), and in 1923 a new honorary orthopaedic surgeon was appointed to implement the plan. Subsequently lauded as 'one of the pioneers of modern orthopaedic surgery', he played a key part in establishing both a central hospital and a constellation of after-care clinics (NDCG 1964: 6). When the Harlow Wood Orthopaedic Hospital opened in 1929 to serve Nottinghamshire and the East Midlands, the guild referred patients – more than forty a year by 1939. However, its role was fundamentally recast from the mid-1920s on, when direct responsibility was assumed for running the first of what became six after-care clinics. At these clinics, and at Harlow Wood, power resided primarily in the hands of the orthopaedic surgeons. But the guild reinforced this professional control by establishing a visiting sub-committee of 'ladies' whose job was to remain 'in touch with patients, especially those who are inclined to stay away from the Clinic and thereby risk undoing much of the good that the Hospital or out-patient treatment was intended to do for them' (NDGC 1939: 7). Charitable effort was being harnessed to medical surveillance.

By 1936 there were forty orthopaedic hospitals in the British Isles and 400 orthopaedic clinics (Anderson 1969). Their history demolishes any claim to an objective base for medical authority. Though the surge of interest in the 'crippled' child bore some relation to the trajectory of clinical knowledge, it was also embroiled in a quest for professional power. Orthopaedics was a poor relation within medicine. Long-term rehabilitation did use some technology, but the bone-setting that was its main craft fell short of the scientific paradigm. Tapping into contemporary concerns about child welfare not only boosted the profile of orthopaedics, but also unlocked charitable resources to expand the arenas of practice. Furthermore, it allowed the speciality to authenticate its expertise and build a platform from which to capitalize on the exigencies of World War I. The experience gained from military casualties then invested the reversion to 'crippled' children with a credibility which underwrote the development of an orthopaedic power base where the influence of the hospital radiated into the community.

Childhood impairments were declining during the inter-war period as the incidence of rickets and tuberculosis fell, and orthopaedic surgeons increasingly moved on to the management of fracture cases in order to advance their professional ambitions (Cooter 1993). However, the networks established with the collaboration of organizations like the Nottingham District Cripples' Guild were an important precursor of the 'surveillance medicine' which David Armstrong has dated from World War II. Though the national scheme lacked the resources to spread 'its gaze over the normal person to establish early detection . . . and enable the potentially abnormal to be adequately known' (Armstrong 1983: 9), its supervisory aspirations exposed many disabled people to painful and intrusive medical intervention. For by 1923 a minute to the Board of Education supporting a proposal for an orthopaedic hospital in Yorkshire was asserting that every disabled child required surgery (Bourke 1996).

The politics of resistance

The medicalization of physical impairment propelled by the national scheme was legitimated by recourse to economic rationality. As a representative of the Board of Education argued in 1920, the proper treatment of 'child cripples' was a 'sound investment', because it meant that 'thousands . . . who would otherwise grow up to be a burden on their relatives and the community will become useful, self-supporting citizens' (Girdlestone 1924: 21). This mission to rescue disabled people from idleness had eugenic undertones. Physical impairment was not necessarily viewed with the biological determinism of Darwin, but the impediments to reform were stressed in a way which resonated with the social evolutionism of Spencer (Freeden 1979; Harris 1995). Therefore, supporters of the national scheme warned that though slum clearance removed 'crippled' children from insanitary environments that bred disease, a new house did not 'bestow a new sense of the responsibilities of parenthood or civic life'. The 'malign influence of alcohol' was likewise unaffected (Watson 1930: 80–4). Long hospital stays protected against the 'defective' family who not only undermined the prescribed post-operative care but also inculcated financial dependency. And, by acquiring the functional ability to work, 'crippled' children were released from degeneracy and tooled for the full citizenship that was conditional upon economic activity (Parker 1998).

This connotation of impairment implies a profound disablism in British society, which undercuts the politics of resistance. Foucault was adamant that 'we can never be ensnared by power; we can always modify its grip' (1988: 123). However, the idea that recipients, perceived in eugenic terms, might resist assistance was alien to most early twentieth-century service providers; so, when clients – like those of the Nottingham District Cripples' Guild – forfeited help rather than knuckle down to the terms attached, their actions were construed as delinquent (NDGC, 1915). The expression of consumer opinion was also rendered redundant by the widespread assumption that the benevolent and the professional knew best. In the first issue of the *Cripples' Journal*, for instance, the editor claimed that its appeal was 'primarily ... to all institutions, medical men, nursing staffs and helpers' (Watson 1924). No reference was made to the patients whom we might deduce from the title were its audience.

There were signs of this convenient elision in the medical representation of the orthopaedic hospital as a happy, supportive environment for disabled children:

> As one approaches such a hospital one becomes aware of its presence by eye and by ear – an attractive sight and a most cheerful sound. One sees wards open to sun and wind, one hears happy shouts and laughter. Gaiety and fun seem to be distilled unendingly out of the children. (Girdlestone 1924: 30)

Few accounts of this hospitalization survive from patients' standpoints. However, we know from the 'memories' recorded in Maurice White's popular history of the Royal Orthopaedic Hospital in Birmingham that children were subjected to repeated surgical interventions over many years. Mr N. H. Field, for example, recalled how he was admitted at the age of three with spinal TB and immobilized on a spinal frame for six years. Similarly, Bobby James was admitted in 1928 with 'very serious deformities to both his legs'; only a few months old, he was to spend ten years 'on and off' in the hospital, where he underwent sixteen operations (White 1997: 196–7, 205).

Whilst neither Mr Field nor Bobby James complained about the treatment which they received, the study was a celebration of a revered local institution which was unlikely to elicit critical comment. Conversely, *Out of Sight* – the Channel 4 documentary on the experience of disability in the first half of the twentieth century – portrayed harrowing personal testimonies to excruciating surgery and harsh regimes in the institutions which accommodated 'crippled' children. Take Bill Elvy, born in 1918 with 'severely deformed hands and feet which prevented him from walking'. Admitted to an institution for 'crippled' children, he was periodically dispatched to hospital for surgery.

> They operated on me when I was still very young. It was so frightening. In and out of hospital all the time I was. You couldn't have any visitors and anyway my parents couldn't afford to come 'cos the hospital was in London. I used to have to live in the Shaftesbury Home to get ready for

them doing operations on me. But you got no real care there even though they must have known how bad the operations were and how much pain I was in. They were meant to prepare me, build me strength up kind of thing for carting me off for the next operation on me hands or me feet. But it was very harsh. You more than likely got a clout round the ear or a wallop rather than caring. It was like prison to us kids. All our letters were censored, in and out. You were there to do your chores, hard graft and try and keep your head down as far as I could see. Then the hospital would ring and say, 'Right, let's have him in for another op.' And off I'd be sent for some more torture at the hospital. (Humphries and Gordon 1992: 80–1)

Though this story, and the others in the collection, cannot be specifically bound to orthopaedic hospitals under the national scheme, they do cast doubt on the benign image of medicalization and long-term care. Even under such extreme circumstances there were acts of resistance: strikes against bad food or excessive punishment, raids on the kitchen or the orchard to supplement meagre diets, bids to escape (Humphries and Gordon 1992: 80–1). But if disabled people were able to show defiance, the structures within which they exercised that power were ultimately constraining. Institutional practices were not overturned as a result of their child inmates rebelling. Consequently, power was structured rather than free-floating, because, despite having some scope for resistance, all individuals and all social groups were not equally able to exert their influence.

Identity and history

In examining the transition from moral to medical surveillance, and the capacity of disabled people to resist, I have discarded the notion of a unitary state and teased out the dispersal of power through charity and medicine. The construction of identity is also swayed by this decentring. The social model of disability locates personal identity in the concrete experiences of discrimination. Critics of a cultural bent have pressed for the reinstatement of an individual dimension which acknowledges that pain, fatigue, depression and 'internalised oppression' may accompany impairment (Marks 1999: 25–6; see also Barnes and Mercer 1996). Dismissive of calls for the inclusion of social class, gender, ethnicity and age, this group refutes the relevance of structural characteristics. Identities, fluid through an ongoing process of engagement with a rapidly changing world (Sarup 1996), have to be reflexively fabricated by 'sustaining...coherent, yet continuously revised, biographical narratives'. As Anthony Giddens has elaborated:

Because of the 'openness' of social life today, the pluralization of contexts of action and diversity of 'authorities', life-style choice is increasingly important in the constitution of self-identity and daily activity. Reflexively organized life-planning, which normally presumes consideration of risks as filtered through contact with expert knowledge, becomes a central feature of structuring self-identity. (Giddens 1991: 5)

Disabled people's material disadvantages discredit the wholesale rejection of structural factors. Poverty excludes many from the prosperity which is essential for 'life-style choice', whilst the consumption of social policies inflicts professional control and damaging assumptions about dependency, which any expression of resistance may only partially alleviate (Hughes 2000; Marks 1999). Therefore, it is important to mine alternative reserves for positive identity.

The disabled people's movement is confident that direct political action will not only win policy changes, but also empower its participants and erode their negative self-images. The Disability Arts Movement has also attacked offensive and demeaning stereotypes in the media (Barnes et al. 1999). However, since identities are rooted in the past as well as the present, knowing where we have been helps us to know where we are and where we are going (Jenkins 1991; Sarup 1996). As a result, histories of disability are another, complementary route to individual and collective esteem. Whilst memory is a key factor in structuring fixed identities, it assumes greater significance when these become more transitory. With reminiscence, often used as a therapy for elderly people, personal narratives occupy a private space of little relevance beyond the settings in which they are told. History, on the other hand, offers a public space for reflexive interaction with the past, having proved its worth as part of a 'pedagogical political culture' which helps individuals and social groups to comprehend their 'place in local, national and international realities' (Sarup 1993: 186–7).

Disabled people's testimonies have an important role to play in this process. Of course, there is a risk that these narratives are privileged over other accounts and regarded as '*the* truth...[rather than] inevitably partial'. Furthermore, their '"confessional" stance may function as a form of self-subjugation, affirming a fixed "disabled" identity' that either represents all disabled people as '"triumphing over adversity" or ...as ...pathological objects available for voyeuristic gaze' (Marks 1999: 183). None the less, these stories – rich in detail and telling in their condemnation of past practices – may be liberating for those whose self-esteem has been battered by discrimination. In the words of one former inmate of a mental deficiency institution: 'I'd just like people to know so they can realize what it was we'd had to go through. It's not just what was written down! They did it just to keep us locked up, so that people would think we're mental' (Fido and Potts 1997: 45).

Placing such experiences within a wider historical context, and searching for their antecedents in previous centuries, increases their potency by supplying the story, or 'chain of events', with a 'discourse' or 'plot' that explicates what has happened (Sarup 1996: 17). Far from being a nostalgic quest for a cosy, comforting past, histories that combine intellectual rigour with the revelation of exploitation have the potential to raise personal and political consciousness. First, they may undermine the passive, tragic, medical assumptions of the individual model and shift the burden of responsibility to the economic, social and political organization of society. Second, they may demonstrate that attitudes and policies towards disability are culturally constructed, and hence open to change. Third, they may reach disabled people – for example, those with learning difficulties or the impairments of old age – who are not currently active in the disability movement. And finally, as the record of labour history and women's history testifies, they may encourage the inclusiveness necessary for effective political action, breaking down the artificial divisions between different types of impairment (Barnes et al. 1999; Tosh 1991). In these ways, an awareness of disability in the past nurtures more positive individual and collective identities.

Conclusion

This chapter has been organized around four main themes. First, I traced the neglect of the past in disability studies to incompatibilities between sociology and history. Second, the materialist histories developed in the social sciences have been evaluated from a cultural perspective. Third, a case study of moral and medical surveillance has been used to show that though power operates outside the unitary state, resistance is constrained by structural forces which articulate the work ethic. And, finally, history's most valuable contribution to disability studies has been seen as the encouragement of a critical reflexivity to feed personal and political identities. Confronting the past is no panacea. Though we might hope to learn from at least its worst mistakes, history never repeats itself exactly, so there are few problems today for which blueprint solutions can be extracted (Tosh 1991). Nor is historical research – like social research (Oliver 1996) – necessarily emancipatory for those who conduct and consume it. But if undertaken with a sensitivity towards the perspectives of disabled people, and if critically orientated towards the institutions of able-bodied society, history is capable of enhancing individual and collective consciousness. As Young and Quibell conclude for intellectual impairment in the twentieth century: 'When one can intertwine th[e] sense of a historical story with the autobiographies of real people, deeper and broader understanding becomes possible' (2000: 759).

REFERENCES

Anderson, J. 1969: *A Record of Fifty Years Service to the Disabled by the Central Council for the Disabled.* London: Central Council for the Disabled.

Armstrong, D. 1983: *Political Anatomy of the Body: Medical Knowledge in Britain in the Twentieth Century.* Cambridge: Cambridge University Press.

Barnes, C. 1996: Theories of disability and the origins of the oppression of disabled people in Western society. In L. Barton (ed.), *Disability and Society: Emerging Issues and Insights.* London: Longman, 43–60.

Barnes, C. and Mercer, G. (eds) 1996: *Exploring the Divide: Illness and Disability.* Leeds: Disability Press.

Barnes, C., Mercer, G. and Shakespeare, T. 1999: *Exploring Disability: A Sociological Introduction.* Cambridge: Polity.

Barns, I., Dudley, J., Harris, P. and Petersen, A. 1999: Introduction: themes, context and perspectives. In A. Petersen, I. Barns, J. Dudley and P. Harris, *Poststructuralism, Citizenship and Social Policy.* London: Routledge, 1–24.

Bellers, J. 1987: An essay towards the improvement of physick. In G. Clarke (ed.), *John Bellers: His Life, Times and Writings.* London: Routledge & Kegan Paul, 174–220.

Bentley, M. 1999: *Modern Historiography: An Introduction.* London: Routledge.

Borsay, A. 1998: Returning patients to the community: disability, medicine and economic rationality before the Industrial Revolution. *Disability and Society.* 13 (5), 645–63.

Borsay, A. 1999: *Medicine and Charity in Georgian Bath: A Social History of the General Infirmary c.1739–1830,* Aldershot: Ashgate.

Bourke, J. 1996: *Dismembering the Male: Men's Bodies, Britain and the Great War.* London: Reaktion Books.

Burke, P. 1992: *History and Social Theory.* Cambridge: Polity.

Burrow, J. W. 1966: *Evolution and Society: A Study in Victorian Social Theory.* Cambridge: Cambridge University Press.

Cholmeley, J. A. 1985: *History of the Royal National Orthopaedic Hospital.* London: Chapman and Hall.

Cooter, R. 1993: *Surgery and Society in Peace and War: Orthopaedics and the Organization of Modern Medicine 1880–1948.* Basingstoke: Macmillan.

Crowther, A. 1981: *The Workhouse System 1834–1929: The History of an English Social Institution.* London: Methuen.

Cushlow, F. 1997: Guilded help? In K. Laybourn (ed.), *Social Conditions, Status and Community 1860–c.1920.* Stroud: Sutton Publishing, 29–44.

Evans, E. J. 1983: *The Forging of the Modern State: Early Industrial Britain 1783–1870.* London: Longman.

Fido, R. and Potts, M. 1997: Using oral histories. In D. Atkinson, M. Jackson and J. Walmsley (eds), *Forgotten Lives: Exploring the History of Learning Disability.* Kidderminster: British Institute of Learning Disabilities, 34–46.

Finkelstein, V. 1980: *Attitudes and Disabled People.* New York: World Rehabilitation Fund.

Foster, J. and Sheppard, J. 1995: *British Archives: A Guide to Archive Resources in the United Kingdom.* 3rd edn. Basingstoke: Macmillan.

Foucault, M. 1988: Power and sex. In M. D. Kritzmann, (ed.), *Politics, Philosophy, Culture.* London: Routledge.

Foucault, M. 1991: *Discipline and Punish: The Birth of the Prison.* Harmondsworth: Penguin (originally published in 1977, Alan Sheridan).

Freeden, M. 1979: Eugenics and progressive thought: a study in ideological affinity. *Historical Journal.* 22 (3), 645–71.

Giddens, A. 1984: *The Constitution of Society: Outline of the Theory of Structuration.* Cambridge: Polity.

Giddens, A. 1991: *Modernity and Self-Identity: Self and Society in the Late Modern Age.* Cambridge: Polity.

Girdlestone, G. R. 1924: *The Care and Cure of Crippled Children.* Bristol and London: John Wright and Simpkin Marshall.

Gleeson, B. 1999: *Geographies of Disability.* London: Routledge.

Gray, R. 1996: *The Factory Question and Industrial England 1830–1860.* Cambridge: Cambridge University Press.

Hammond, J. L. and Hammond, B. 1934: *The Bleak Age.* West Drayton: Penguin.

Harris, J. 1995: Between civic virtue and social Darwinism: the concept of the residuum. In D. Englander and R. O'Day (eds), *Retrieved Riches: Social Investigation in Britain 1840–1914.* Aldershot: Scolar Press, 67–87.

Hughes, B. 2000: Medicine and the aesthetic invalidation of disabled people. *Disability and Society.* 15 (4), 555–68.

Humphries, S. and Gordon, P. 1992: *Out of Sight: The Experience of Disability 1900–1950.* Plymouth: Northcote House.

Hunt, A. G. 1924a: Baschurch and after: 1. The birth of a pioneer hospital. *Cripples' Journal.* 1(1), 18–23.

Hunt, A. G. 1924b: Baschurch and after: 2. Fourteen Years On. *Cripples' Journal.* 1(2), 86–94.

Hunt, A. G. 1924c: Baschurch and after: 3. During the war. *Cripples' Journal.* 1(3), 180–5.

Jenkins, K. 1991: *Rethinking History.* London: Routledge.

Jordanova, L. 1995: The social construction of medical knowledge. *Social History of Medicine.* 8 (3), 361–81.

Jordanova, L. 2000: *History in Practice.* London: Arnold.

Kidd, A. 1999: *State, Society and the Poor in Nineteenth-Century England.* Basingstoke: Macmillan.

Laybourn, K. 1997: The guild of help and the community response to poverty 1904–c.1914. In K. Laybourn (ed.), *Social Conditions, Status and Community 1860–c.1920.* Stroud: Sutton Publishing, 9–28.

Lewis, J. 1995: *The Voluntary Sector, the State and Social Work in Britain: The Charity Organization Society/Family Welfare Association since 1869.* Aldershot: Edward Elgar.

Lyon, D. 1994: *Postmodernity.* Buckingham: Open University Press.

Marks, D. 1999: *Disability: Controversial Debates and Psychosocial Perspectives.* London: Routledge.

Marwick, A. 1970: *The Nature of History.* London: Macmillan.

Marx, K. 1961: Preface to *A Contribution to the Critique of Political Economy.* In T. B. Bottomore and M. Rubel (eds), *Karl Marx: Selected Writings in Sociology and Social Philosophy.* Harmondsworth: Penguin, 67–9.

Nottingham District Cripples' Guild (NDCG) 1914: *Annual Report.*

NDCG 1915: *Annual Report.*

NDCG 1924: *Annual Report.*

NDCG 1939: *Annual Report.*

NDCG 1950/1: *Annual Report.*

NDCG 1964: *Annual Report.*

O'Brien, M. and Penna, S. 1998: *Theorising Welfare: Enlightenment and Modern Society.* London: Sage.

Oliver, M. 1990: *The Politics of Disablement.* Basingstoke: Macmillan.

Oliver, M. 1996: *Understanding Disability: From Theory to Practice.* Basingstoke: Macmillan.

Parker, J. 1965: *Local Health and Welfare Services.* London: George Allen and Unwin.

Parker, J. 1998: *Citizenship, Work and Welfare: Searching for the Good Society.* Basingstoke: Macmillan.

Paterson, K. and Hughes, B. 1999: Disability studies and phenomenology: the carnal politics of everyday life. *Disability and Society.* 14 (5), 597–610.

Prochaska, F. 1988: *The Voluntary Impulse: Philanthropy in Modern Britain.* London: Faber & Faber.

Sarup, M. 1993: *An Introductory Guide to Post-Structuralism and Postmodernism.* Hemel Hempstead: Harvester Wheatsheaf.

Sarup, M. 1996: *Identity, Culture and the Postmodern World.* Edinburgh: Edinburgh University Press.

Scull, A. 1993: *The Most Solitary of Afflictions: Madness and Society in Britain 1700–1900.* New Haven: Yale University Press.

Shore, C. and Wright, S. 1997: Policy: a new field of anthropology. In C. Shore and S. Wright (eds), *Anthropology of Policy: Critical Perspectives on Governance and Power,* London: Routledge, 3–39.

Thomas, K. 1966: The tools and the job. *Times Literary Supplement,* 275–6.

Thompson, E. 1963: *The Making of the English Working Class*. Harmondsworth: Penguin.

Thomson, M. 1998: *The Problem of Mental Deficiency: Eugenics, Democracy, and Social Policy in Britain* c.1870–1959. Oxford: Clarendon Press.

Topliss, E. 1975: *Provision for the Disabled*. Oxford and London: Basil Blackwell and Martin Robertson.

Tosh, J. 1991: *The Pursuit of History: Aims, Methods and New Directions in the Study of Modern History*. London: Longman.

Traill, H. D. and Mann, J. S. 1895: *Social England*. London: Cassell.

Trevelyan, G. M. 1973: *English Social History*. London: Longman.

Vincent, D. 1991: *Poor Citizens: The State and the Poor in Twentieth Century Britain*. London: Longman.

Warren, J. 1998: *The Past and Its Presenters: An Introduction to Issues in Historiography*. London: Hodder & Stoughton.

Watson, F. 1924: The gist of the matter. *Cripples' Journal*. 1 (1), editorial.

Watson, F. 1930: *Civilization and the Cripple*. London: John Bale.

White, M. 1997: *Years of Caring: The Royal Orthopaedic Hospital*. Studley: Brewin Books.

Wilson, A. 1993: A critical portrait of social history. In A. Wilson (ed.), *Rethinking Social History: English Society 1570–1920 and its Interpretation*. Manchester: Manchester University Press, 9–58.

Young, D. A. and Quibell, R. 2000: Why rights are never enough: rights, intellectual disability and understanding. *Disability and Society*, 15 (5), 747–64.

7

Work, Disability, Disabled People and European Social Theory

Paul Abberley

Introduction

In this chapter I consider how two forms of classic social theory, one generally classified as conservative, the other as radical, understand the relationship between work and social inclusion. I argue that, despite their differences, they converge insofar as they both imply the inevitability of the social exclusion of some impaired people in any possible society. I indicate where other kinds of social theory, particularly certain approaches within feminism, can provide a vision of a more inclusive society in which work is not regarded as the defining characteristic of full social inclusion. The practical implication of such a view is the advocacy of a dual strategy, of work facilitation for those who want it and can meaningfully take part in the labour process and the general valorization of non-working lives for those, including impaired people, who are unable to work. To achieve this, it is necessary to relate to the real changes occurring in European social and economic life.

If we are to look at disability as a form of oppression, we need to develop views of what a society would need to be like for impaired people not to be disabled, in order to develop effective policies to combat social exclusion. And this requires social theory, since, if we are to understand how we might overcome social exclusion, we must have some ideas about what it is that brings about social inclusion.

Disability and the discourse of citizenship

The notion of citizenship is frequently employed today at both national and European levels to deal with issues related to the social status of disabled people. 'The language of citizenship continues to lie at the heart of New Labour's project and in particular its proposals for welfare reform' (Dean 1999: 213). Equally, the European Commission has proposed the declaration of the year 2003 as the European Year of Disabled Citizens, with the objective of 'strengthening the concept of citizenship for people with disabilities' (European Commission 2000). Thus the concept of the enhancement of citizenship is used to focus on the social exclusion of disabled people from the mainstream of European social life.

Although ostensibly a purely descriptive term, the idea of social exclusion is theoretically laden, in that it seems to imply a majority who are 'included' in a relatively unproblematic manner and a problem minority whose 'outsiderness' can be remedied by what are essentially minor social adjustments. The term is thus essentially related to a sociological perspective which characterizes society as a substantive or potential unity, as proposed by for example Durkheim, rather than the fundamentally conflictual and contradictory entity posited by amongst others, Marx. Indeed, Silver (1994) argues that the origins of European Union (EU) discussion of social exclusion lie in the French, and by extension Durkheimian, concern primarily with moral and cultural integration, rather than the economic activity that in Durkheim's idealist social theory is presented as a mechanism for bringing about the former, ultimately desirable end (Durkheim 1964). Having said this, it is still useful to point out that the antithesis between exclusion and inclusion constitutes a relevant terrain even for those of us for whom the perspective it implies appears to be fundamentally mistaken about the nature of societies in general.

In particular, the attempt by some writers to construct a debate based upon an antithesis between exclusion and citizenship – 'social exclusion may.... be seen as the denial (or non-realisation) of the civil, political and social rights of citizenship' (Walker and Walker 1997: 8) – would seem to locate discussion in a useful framework for disabled people. It is thus probably not excessive to make the claim that citizenship can be regarded as 'one of the central organising features of Western political discourse' (Hindess 1993: 19), and thus a notion that disability theory must repeatedly address.

To talk of a 'discourse' is to say more than that new words are being used to convey old ideas. Rather, it means that a set of interrelated concepts are being employed to try to understand the social world and ultimately to govern paths of action which seem to be open to us. A discourse both opens up and closes down possibilities for action; it constitutes ways of acting in the world at the same time as it posits a description of it. 'Discourse' draws attention to the language of politics, not simply as a way of expressing its content, but as the very substance of it. In its idealist form the term is used to imply that language is everything, and that 'material' relations are the mere epiphenomenal product of discourse. In its more plausible, less self-obsessed usage, the notion of discourse points to the fact that the concepts through which we both understand and act in and upon the world affect these actions and thus the world itself, whilst still maintaining the materiality of the world and of social relations.

Dwyer argues that notions of citizenship can 'provide a bench-mark against which it is possible to assess the status of certain individuals or groups in relation to access to the agreed rights and resources that are generally available to all those who are regarded as citizens . . . also . . . the levels and causes of inequality within a society' (Dwyer 2000:3). In addition to this sociological aspect, as a political focus,

> citizenship is very much about relationships between individuals, groups, rights, duties and state institutions; it is about relative degrees of incorporation and empowerment . . . effective citizenship . . . means being included in the systems of rights and welfare provisions that are mediated or managed by state agencies, and having one's needs met through mainstream political intermediation. (Harrison 1995: 20–1)

Such discourses, crossing academic boundaries between the self-styled 'purely' descriptive and the political, are clearly of relevance to disabled people's struggle to reconceptualize and transform our situation.

Levitas, in her study of social exclusion and New Labour, makes a useful distinction between three ideal types of discourse of social exclusion:

> a redistributionist discourse (RED) developed in British critical social policy, whose prime concern is with poverty; a moral underclass discourse (MUD) which centres on the moral and behavioural delinquency of the excluded themselves; and a social integrationist discourse (SID) whose central focus is on paid work. (Levitas 1998: 7)

Each of these perspectives contains its own prescriptions for combating social exclusion – in particular, SID's emphasis on exclusion from paid work leads its proponents away from a broader view of social participation, and towards a concentration on 'work' as definitional of social membership. Thus a SID-type European Commission document, whilst ostensibly aimed at promoting the social integration of disabled people, looks only at training and help in entering the labour market; and on the 'key issue of improved access to means of transport and public buildings', states that the Commission should 'press for the adoption of the proposed Directive on the travel conditions of workers with motor disabilities' (European Commission 1994: 51–2). Since this document starts with a focus on employment, this partiality is not surprising in itself; but it does indicate some consequences of a work-based focus for the citizenship of disabled people in Europe as a whole.

That this is also the case in the specific conditions of the UK is evidenced by a consideration of the first five years of the Disability Discrimination Act (DDA) undertaken by the Royal National Institute for the Blind. The complexity and exorbitant cost of bringing cases in the county court for discrimination in the provision of goods, services, facilities and premises makes it virtually impossible for disabled people to enforce their rights in these areas, concludes *The Price of Justice* (Royal National Institute for the Blind 2000). Since the DDA came into force in 1996, more than 5,000 cases claiming discrimination at work have been taken to employment tribunals. In contrast, the RNIB knows of only twenty-five cases claiming discrimination in the provision of goods, services and facilities. Since there is no evidence that disabled people face more discrimination at work than in the rest of their lives, the report attributes the disparity to the different ways that parts of the DDA are enforced. Employment cases go to employment tribunals, where it costs nothing to bring a claim and the risks of having costs awarded against an applicant are negligible. In contrast, claims against a shop manager for verbally abusing a disabled person, or a company for failing to produce bills in Braille, would have to go through the county courts, an often complicated, costly process which is said by the RNIB to put most people off at the first hurdle.

Thus the adoption of a SID perspective by the state serves to define what is 'significant' discrimination, whose combating it will facilitate, and what, by implication, is of less importance. A recent study (Burchardt 2000) suggests that one in six of those in work who become disabled loses his or her job within twelve months. The research also indicates that disabled people find it hard holding on to a new job: one in three of those who get work is out of it again within a year, compared to one in five non-disabled people. The findings indicate that while we are supposedly surrounded by increasingly positive images of disabled people, like publicity surrounding British performers in the Paralympics and the government's awareness campaign aimed at disabled people capable of and wanting to work, they are still significantly disadvantaged. About 60 per cent of disabled people of working age do not have a job. ' "Disabled people make up half of all those who are not employed but would like to work and one third of those who are available to start in a fortnight" says the study' (Burchardt 2000: 13–14). Depending on how disability is defined, disabled people are currently calculated to make up 12–16 per cent of the working age population. The proportion is growing, with 3 per cent of those in work reporting each year that they have become 'limited in daily activities', and half of them reporting a continuing impairment twelve months later.

The report, based on analysis of official data, also shows that disabled people remain relatively poor despite social security changes since 1985: 'earnings differentials between disabled and non-disabled workers, controlling for differences in age, education and occupation, have increased. The disability "penalty" appears to be growing.' (Burchardt 2000: 14). Half of all disabled people live on incomes of less than half the national average, a level commonly taken to represent the poverty line. Of disabled adults with children, 60 per cent fall below this bench-mark. Burchardt says that benefit rules need to be made more flexible to help disabled people stay in work if they have fluctuating medical conditions. And benefit levels need to be reviewed to help those who are unemployed, who have non-working partners, or who have retired early.

> Those with more severe impairments are slipping behind the rest of the population, and will continue to do so while the benefits that make up a high proportion of their family income are up-rated only in line with inflation. Unless the link between national prosperity and benefit income is restored, the standards of living of those who have few opportunities for paid work will continue to diverge from those who are in employment. (Burchardt 2000: 53)

Functionalism and disability

What are the pre-conditions of social inclusion? The classical conservative viewpoint in social theory is embodied in the work of the founding father of functionalist sociology Emile Durkheim (1964). He posits a fundamental distinction between non- or pre-industrial societies and industrial ones. In the former social integration is characterized as based on the similarity of roles in the social division of labour, 'mechanical' solidarity. After industrialization, with a growing separateness and distinction of the individual from the group as the division of labour is increasingly specialized and individuated, a good society is one with strong bonds of 'organic' solidarity. These bonds are constituted through the recognition of the role of others in the complex division of labour that makes up that society. The venue where this solidarity is to be forged is the occupational associations. Thus, to be deprived of such a role is to be deprived of the possibility of full societal membership. Whilst some of his polemical writing, like the essay 'Individualism and the intellectuals' (Durkheim 1971), written as an intervention in the Dreyfus Affair, places great stress upon the necessity for the good society to recognize diversity, there is no suggestion that this extends to the incorporation of those unable to work into society.

Following this view, the modern English sociologist Eda Topliss came in 1982 to advance the following argument for the inevitability of discrimination against disabled people:

> While the particular type or degree of impairment which disables a person for full participation in society may change, it is inevitable that there will always be a line, somewhat indefinite but none the less real, between the able-bodied majority and a disabled minority whose interests are given less salience in the activities of society as a whole.
>
> Similarly the values which underpin society must be those which support the interests and activities of the majority, hence the emphasis on vigorous independence and competitive achievement, particularly in the occupational sphere, with the unfortunate spin-off that it encourages a stigmatising and negative view of the disabilities which handicap individuals in these valued aspects of life. Because of the centrality of such values in the formation of citizens of the type needed to sustain the social arrangements desired by the able-bodied majority, they will continue to be fostered by family upbringing, education and public esteem. By contrast, disablement which handicaps an individual in these areas will continue to be negatively valued, thus tending towards the imputation of general inferiority to the disabled individual, or stigmatisation. (Topliss 1982: 111–12)

For Topliss the inevitable disadvantage of disabled people, in any possible society, stems from our general inability to meet standards of performance in work. This can be compared to other perspectives like interactionism, where writers (e.g., Haber and Smith 1971) draw a similar conclusion, but suggest that the core 'deficiency' of disabled people is an aesthetic one. However, aesthetic judgements may themselves be related, albeit in a complex manner, to the requirements of production, so it seems unlikely that the aesthetic explanation, however attractive it may be in certain cases, possesses the irreducibility that its proponents ascribe to it.

The historical construction of disability

Topliss's analysis points to an important truth about the social exclusion of disabled people today: that it is intimately related to our exclusion from the world of work. And it seems fair to contrast this to pre-industrial societies, which, for all their negative features, 'did not preclude the great majority of disabled people from participating in the production process, and even where they could not participate fully, they were still able to make a contribution. In this era disabled people were regarded as individually unfortunate and not segregated from the rest of society' (Oliver 1990: 27). Indeed, certain important occupations like shoemaking and repair seem to have had a disproportionately large number of disabled practitioners, as disabled people or their relatives who could afford to do so bought in to suitably sedentary occupations. Now this is not the whole picture, and there are clearly many salient differences between feudal societies and our own, and this makes disability today a very different thing from disability in the past (Gleeson 1999; Bredberg 1999). Historically, then, disability can be understood as a changing social experience arising from the specific ways in which society organizes its fundamental activities like work transport, leisure, education and domestic life as they relate to the impaired individual; so disability differs not only between historical eras but also within eras and between societies. It is above all a relationship, between impaired people and society. It follows that changes in society as a whole, which may not be directed at disabled people at all, can have profound implications for disability. This certainly seems to have been what happened in Britain in the nineteenth century, as the juggernaut of industrialization crushed all previous social arrangements that resisted its progression. To examine this, I turn to what is often regarded as the polar opposite of conservative social theory, Marxism.

Marxism, industrialization and impairment

In *The Condition of the Working Class in England*, written in 1844/5, Engels argues that the Industrial Revolution created the proletariat in a gigantic process of concentration, polarization and urbanization, and with it, despite expansion of the whole economy and an increased demand for labour, a 'surplus population', which Marxists were later to refer to as the 'reserve army of labour'. He was concerned to explore the conditions of life and the collective and individual behaviour that this process produced, and the greater part of the book is devoted to the description and analysis of these material conditions. His account is based on first-hand observations, informants and printed evidence, such as commission reports and contemporary journals and periodicals. 'Cripples' are cited as evidence of injurious working practices: 'The Commissioners mention a crowd of cripples who appeared before them, who clearly owed their distortion to the long-working hours' (Engels 1969: 180). He cites the evidence of a number of doctors who relate particular kinds of malformation and deformity to working practices, as an 'aspect of the physiological results of the factory system' (Engels 1969: 181) He continues: 'I have seldom traversed Manchester without meeting three or four of them, suffering from precisely the same distortions of the spinal columns and legs as that described...It is evident, at a glance, whence the distortions of these cripples come; they all look exactly alike' (Engels 1969: 182). He continues for some pages to relate particular forms of impairment to factory working conditions, and to condemn 'a state of things which permits so many deformities and mutilations for the benefit of a single class, and plunges so many industrious working-people into want and starvation by reason of injuries undergone in the service and through the fault of the bourgeoisie' (Engels 1969: 194). He concludes his description of 'the English manufacturing proletariat' thus: 'In all directions, whithersoever we may turn, we find want and disease permanent or temporary...slow but sure undermining, and final destruction of the human being physically as well as mentally' (Engels 1969: 238).

A hundred years later Wal Hannington, leader of the Unemployed Workers Movement, used a similar analysis and sources of evidence, this time to condemn not factory work, but the lack of it: 'These youths...meet problems which render them increasingly conscious of the way in which their lives have been stunted and their young hopes frustrated and of the results of the physical impairment which they have suffered through the unemployment and poverty of their parents' (Hannington 1937: 78). Doyal (1979) refined this general thesis, and documented a relationship between 'capitalism' and impairment on a wide variety of fronts, adding consumption, industrial pollution, stress and imperialism to the labour-centred concerns of Engels and Hannington.

Now I in no way wish to dispute the general accuracy and pertinence of these studies. My point is rather that such an analysis, linking impairment to capitalism as a very apparent symptom of its inhumanity and irrationality, is of little use in the struggle against the disablement of impaired people. All it implies is that the number of impaired people is seen as declining in a society progressively abolishing the injurious consequences of production for profit. But there are two crucial objections to the notion of the problem of disability ending up in the dustbin of history. First, whilst socially produced impairments of the kind outlined by Doyal and others may decrease in number, it is inconceivable that the rate of impairment should ever be reduced to zero. Secondly, and of significance for disabled people today, it is an issue whether such a situation, even could it occur, would be desirable.

If Marxist analyses are exclusively concerned with the prevention and cure of impairment, this emphasis is no accidental consequence of the marginality of disabled people to Marxism's primary concern with production relations under capitalism; rather, it is deeply grounded in Marxist notions of humanity as intrinsically involving labour (Abberley 1996). But, in addition to this, it may also be that important elements of social inclusion may be overlooked in theoretical perspectives which place excessive emphasis upon ensuring material well-being.

Respect

What social utopias that aim at eliminating deprivation often fail to deal with are assaults on human dignity: 'social utopias are oriented predominantly toward the elimination of human misery, natural law predominantly towards the elimination of human degradation' (Bloch 1986: 234). Degrading or insulting behaviour is injurious because it restricts people in their positive appraisal of self, depriving them of what Hegel called 'recognition', and what Otis Redding and Aretha Franklin have sung of as 'respect'. Honneth (1995a, 1995b) argues that social struggles motivated by the experience of being denied conditions for identity formation – which he calls 'disrespect' – establish necessary conditions for self-realization as an autonomous individual. His accounts of self-confidence, self-respect and self-esteem involve dynamic processes whereby individuals come to experience themselves in certain ways, ways that necessarily involve recognition from others. They are thus inter-subjective and ultimately social processes, which are not an abstract property, but an emergent, developing result of the experience of others' attitudes to the subject.

Whereas Thompson (1963) and Barrington Moore (1978) had previously argued that motives for revolt and resistance can be identified in the destruction of traditional ways of life, Honneth wants to argue that such motivation can also occur when established ways of living have become intolerable. It may be the case that the experience of disempowering 'care', and the threat of the institution being offered as a 'promise' in the golden age of welfare, allows disabled people as a group for the first time to identify 'respect', rather than physical survival, as a collective objective.

The violation of self-confidence, self-respect and self-esteem can be seen as providing the pre-theoretical basis for social critique, and once it becomes clear that these are experiences shared by many others, the potential emerges for collective action aimed at expanding social patterns of recognition. The importance of the establishment of a pre-theoretical experience of oppression is that it establishes a basis for theories of oppression, independent of the intellectuals who formulate them. Oppression is thus seen as an objective condition 'exposed' by theory, not a purely intellectual construct arising solely out of 'oppression' discourse. This leads to the debates engendered by the Anglophone adoptions of a variety of elements from the work of Foucault. For Foucauldians of a philosophical idealist turn, the notion of pre-theorized oppression is a fundamentally incoherent one; nothing can exist prior to discourse 'about' it, which is seen as, in truth, giving rise to it. It may be that such notions hold a particular appeal in relation to the theorizing of learning difficulty, or of deafness.

Others, however, may find it useful to take from Foucault a notion of power, more subtle and more supple than the traditional hierarchical structure found in the work of Weberian organization theorists, and try to apply this to developing a sense of the multiple levels at which the relations between impaired people and those they interact with construct the web of disablement. I have argued in an exploratory analysis of the discourse of occupational therapists (Abberley 1995) that the development of mechanisms to meet the 'obvious' need for the work of 'professionals' to be evaluated is itself sufficient to give rise to a work process that disempowers clients. There is, I think, considerable benefit to be gained from a Foucauldian emphasis on how and where power circulates in our understanding of the process of disablement.

For Honneth, 'trust in oneself' involves the capacity to express needs and desires without fear of being abandoned as a result. For his general theory, it is usually only when extreme experiences of physical violation, such as rape or torture, occur that one's ability to freely identify and express one's needs without anxiety is thrown into question. But in the autobiographies of disabled people we repeatedly encounter instances of such fundamental experiences of insecurity produced by medical, rehabilitative, family or general public interactions. This notion of bodily integrity, Honneth argues, captures something that cuts across historical and cultural differences to a far greater degree than do the two other elements of respect and esteem, which are essentially historical artefacts.

Self-respect is about viewing oneself as entitled to the same status and treatment as anyone else, and is organized in terms of legal rights. This aspect has changed historically, and Honneth indicates a change in both the proportion of the population who have been regarded as full citizens and the content of citizen rights, particularly political and welfare rights which indicate what capacities and opportunities must be present for the exercise of legal capacities to be feasible. Self-respect, then, is constituted through interactive experiences which legitimate claims to citizenship. Finally, self-esteem addresses what it is that makes the individual special, unique, different and of value. There must therefore be something positive in this aspect of identity, something 'valuable'.

Honneth disputes Mead's claim that individuality involves what 'we do better than others' (Mead 1934: 205), since modern divisions of labour and evaluations of non-productive roles give rise to a socially produced hierarchy ranging from esteem to insignificance. Rather, he claims that a good society is one in which common values would match the concerns of individuals in such a way that no member would be denied the possibility to earn esteem for her or his contribution – 'to the extent to which every member of a society is in a position to esteem himself or herself, one can speak of a state of societal solidarity' (Honneth 1995b: 129).

Work and disability theory today

Claus Offe, among others, has suggested that the changing patterns of work within Europe suggest the need for social policy in the EU as a whole to break from work-based entitlement to a citizenship entitlement of basic income or social dividend (Offe 2000). Yet both the British government and European programmes put entry to the work-force at the core of their strategies to combat social exclusion.

Research (Lunt and Thornton 1994) has surveyed some of the issues involved in implementing employment policies in terms of a social model of disablement. Direct discrimination and lack of suitable educational and training opportunities have been and continue to be a barrier. Just as importantly, the structure of employment has implications for disabled people. Jobs designed around the capacity, stamina and resources of the average worker, nine-to-five, five day a week employment, which have been termed 'job-shaped jobs', are incompatible with the needs of a wide variety of citizens. This first became apparent in relation to women, but is equally relevant to disabled people, whatever their gender. In Great Britain unemployment is at a twenty-year low (at the time of writing), but it is dubious that this is the result of more long-term job-shaped jobs. With accelerating technological change and the globalization of markets, for the less skilled, future prospects of stable employment look bleak, whereas for those possessing qualifications three or four career changes in forty years do not seem unlikely. Both these tendencies make the prospects of inclusion in the permanent labour force, and consequent citizenship status, more problematic for disabled people. As technological advances and increased globalization combine to make permanent full-time employment an increasingly rare phenomenon for the majority of the work-force, disabled people will continue to be in the forefront of those groups who cannot provide the versatility and work rates demanded by the labour market.

Beyond this, though, is an underlying problem: even in a society which *did* make profound, genuine attempts, well supported by financial provision, to integrate impaired people into the world of work, some would be excluded. Whatever efforts are made, some will not be capable of producing goods or services of social value – that is, 'participating in the creation of social wealth'. This is so because in any society, certain, though varying, products are of value and others are not, regardless of the effort that goes into their production.

To explore the possible nature of the situation of disabled people in Europe in the future, it is necessary to locate the possibilities of disability practice and policy in the context of future developments in social and economic tendencies at present only nascent. In particular, there are two significant trends in the analysis of work. The first foresees a dramatic decline in demand for labour as a result of technological advances. Thus Bauman writes:

> For the first time in human history, the poor, so to speak have lost their social uses. They are not the vehicles of social repentance and salvation; they are not the hewers of wood and drawers of water, who feed and defend; they are not the 'reserve army of labour', nor the flesh and bones of military power either; and most certainly they are not the consumers who will provide the effective 'market clearing' demand and start up recovery. The new poor are fully and truly useless and redundant, and thus become burdensome 'others' who have outstayed their welcome. (1997: 4–5)

Rifkin (1995) and Forrester (1999) similarly envisage the rapid erosion of any need for surplus labour other than that which the global economy can supply cheaply, ready trained and without social rights from beyond national and continental boundaries. On another view, with its basis in the analysis of demographic trends, the ratio of employed to retired requires migrant labour to support the non-productive and maintain, even at a constrained level, the welfare state. In neither case are the mass of disabled people likely to figure in the list of requirements, since, even as consumers, they are not likely to generate a large market. This point probably requires a distinction between poor disabled people and the minority of pension-rich 'normal age impaired' people whose needs will increasingly lead to the expansion of the Saga holiday / mobility aid / stairlift market and concomitant personal services. One of the more wide-ranging and detailed of these analyses can be found in the work of Ulrich Beck. In his recent book (2000) he argues that the work society is irrevocably gone, and that sources of identity will in future reside in the 'self-active civil society' characteristic of 'second modernity'.

The nature of the welfare state

The expansion of welfare states in the post-World War II period was an outcome of the strength of the working class, which forced the bourgeoisie to provide services, resources and interventions. However, the fact that the bourgeoisie remained, and remains, the dominant class should be looked to for an explanation of why these services, in addition to being useful, have at the same time a controlling function. The dual function of the welfare state, which takes place within a set of class (and other) forces continuously in struggle, consists in services provided with an inextricably dominating character and function. This applies across the whole range of welfare provision, but varies in relation to the relative sectional powers of consumers, providers and the overarching class relations. This is not a consequence of any class or social group 'lying'; rather, it results from the dominant group's vision of reality being presented as universal and valid for all groups. What happens is not, though, the simple outcome of what the ruling class wants – the dominance of the state takes place within a set of power relationships of which the bourgeoisie is only one player, albeit at present the dominant one. The nature of welfare is the outcome of a struggle which takes place between classes and other social groups in a situation of power relations dominated by the bourgeoisie. Welfare is a social relation in contradiction, not an instrument that can be split into different parts. Thus contention over the frontier of control, in relation to welfare as much as to production, has a historically transformative effect, even though it does not address the relations which constitute the most profound determinants of the social formation. Scientific knowledge is itself produced and reproduced not in the abstract, but through activities that embody power relations, though this is not to imply that knowledge does not have a certain autonomy. But this autonomy exists within a set of power relations that determine not only how knowledge is used, but what and how knowledge is produced.

Feminist analyses and social status

One area where the analysis of oppression has become rich enough to deal with this issue is feminist theory. Feminists have pointed out that Marxism is deeply marked by the maleness of its originators – and never more so than in the key role assumed by work in the constitution of human social identity. It is argued that the apparent gender neutrality of Marxist theoretical categories is in reality a gender bias which legitimizes Marxism's excessive focus on the 'masculine sphere' of commodity production. Whilst some approaches in feminist sociology have reproduced the concern with work as definitional of social inclusion (Abberley 1996), others have more profoundly disputed labour-dependent conceptions of humanity.

Lister's work on feminism and citizenship (1997) is identified by Fawcett (2000) as developing a viewpoint which recognizes that the notion does not need to have an identical and homogeneous meaning for all members of society. Fawcett praises Lister for highlighting gendered assumptions and formulating a reappropriation of citizenship that acknowledges the effects of structural constraint on women whilst at the same time emphasizing individual agency. Viewing citizenship as a dynamic process, Lister is seen as developing an approach which does not involve a hierarchical framework, but rather looks to both universalism and diversity. Lister argues for a concept of citizenship as differentiated universalism 'which embodies the creative tension between universalism and particularity or difference' (Lister 1997: 197).

However, whilst her theoretical formulations place 'work' as only one aspect of citizenship qualification, the proposal that 'policy needs to create the conditions in which the citizen – the earner/carer and carer/earner – can flourish' (Lister 1997: 201) seems to be more involved with the redefinition of 'work' than that of the conditions of citizenship. Whilst enhancing the social status of the not inconsiderable number of disabled people who are also carers, such a formulation does nothing to benefit those who do not participate in this now expanded category. However, this move of Lister's is not a simple advocacy of the equation of 'care work' with 'work-shaped work'. Rather, she cites the work of Tronto (1993), who both de-genders the notion of care and makes it 'both a moral value and a political basis for the political achievement of a good society' (1993: 9).

Such a world, 'where the daily caring of people for each other is a valued premise of human existence' (Lister 1997: p. x), is to be distinguished from the 'compulsory altruism' (Land and Rose 1985) which deprives both care-givers and recipients of choices as to how needs are met and reinforces enforced dependence. This detracts from the citizenship of both care-givers and care-recipients. Lister points out that in the public sphere 'the obstacles to women's citizenship...are to be found in the labour market, the (welfare) state and the polis' (Lister 1997: 202).

This diagnosis is equally applicable to major aspects of the determinants of the social status of disabled people, female or male. Equally extendable to *some* disabled people is the conclusion that 'the strengthening of... labour market position is important also for...social citizenship rights' (Lister 1997: 202). Indeed, it may be that for all disabled people, the improved labour market position of some visibly disabled people may be advantageous, if the status-enhancing effects of improved status of others 'rubs off' on us all. But the opposite effect can equally occur, and as more disabled people become 'work-normalized', those who are not may find their exclusion, isolation and stigmatization exacerbated. An inclusion which is dependent upon employment is by no means advantageous to all disabled people, since it is not likely in modern labour markets that all disabled people could find or reliably retain employment. Those disabled people further from the ideal type of the 'normal' worker will remain socially excluded on the SID model, whilst those of us whose capacities to conform decline with advancing impairment and changing demands of labour markets will find exclusion creeping up on us at an accelerated pace.

It is thus probably more in our interests to pursue and emphasize the aspects of citizenship less tied to economic function. But I suspect that we cannot concern ourselves with economics only with regard to specific financial compensations for the extra costs of disablement either on an individual (disabled living allowance) or collective (cost of making public places accessible) basis. Such measures, however well they are carried out, will not produce a world in which we have equality of earning power.

Conclusion

The theoretical perspectives I have considered above seem to me to imply an important distinction between disablement and other forms of oppression. Whilst the latter involve steps in which freedom can possibly be seen as coming through full integration into the world of work, for impaired people the overcoming of disablement, whilst immensely liberative, would still leave an uneradicated residue of disadvantage in relation to power over the material world. This in turn restricts our ability to be fully integrated into the world of work in any possible society. One implication that can be drawn from this, which finds most support in classical sociological perspectives, with their emphasis on the role of work in social membership, is that it would be undesirable to be an impaired person in any possible society, and thus that the abolition of disablement also involves as far as possible the abolition of impairment. The dominant strand of both national and European policy on the social inclusion of disabled people stresses the significance of incorporation in the global, flexible labour force. This work-based model of social membership and identity is integrally linked to the prevention/cure-orientated perspective of allopathic medicine and to the specific instrumental logic of genetic engineering, abortion and euthanasia. Ultimately it involves a value-judgement upon the undesirability of impaired modes of being. However, this logic allows for the integration of perhaps a substantial proportion of any existing impaired population into the work process, but only in so far as there is a happy conjunction between an individual's impairment, technology and socially valued activity. Thus the abolition of an individual's disablement is ultimately dependent upon, and subordinate to, the logic of productivity.

An alternative kind of theory can be seen as offering another future in so far as it rejects work as crucially definitional of social membership and is sceptical about some of the progressive imperatives implicit in modern science. This is by no means to deny that the origins of our oppression, even for those with jobs, lie in our historical exclusion as a group from access to work; nor is it to oppose campaigns for increasing access to employment. It is, however, to point out that a consistently liberative analysis of disablement today must recognize that full integration of impaired people in social production can never constitute the future to which all disabled people can aspire. If we must look elsewhere than to a paradise of labour for the concrete utopia that informs the development of theories of our oppression, it is not on the basis of classical analyses of social labour that our thinking will be further developed. Rather, it involves a break with such analyses, and an explicit recognition that the aspirations and demands of disabled people involve the development of values and ideas which run profoundly counter to the dominant cultural problematic of both left and right. This is not a matter of choice, but of the future survival of alternative, impaired modes of being. One practical implication of this view is to caution against the over-enthusiastic espousal of work-based programmes for overcoming the exclusion of disabled people which leave welfare systems unchanged or, worse still, depleted. They must be maintained, enhanced and above all democratized if dis- abled people as a whole are to experience any degree of emancipation. At a more general level, systems of basic income (Offe 2000), unconnected to individual labour, in addition to realistic compensatory benefits on the model of the British mobility allowances, would seem to allow for fuller social integration for disabled people in the context of the likely coming world of work (Beck 2000). I am thus arguing that we need to develop theoretical perspectives that express the standpoint of disabled people, whose interests are not necessarily served by the standpoints of other social groups, dominant or themselves oppressed, of which disabled people are also members. Such sociology involves the empowerment of disabled people because knowledge is itself an aspect of power. Disabled people have inhabited a cultural, political and intellectual world from whose making they have been excluded, and in which they have been relevant only as problems. Scientific knowledge, including sociology, has been used to reinforce and justify this exclusion. The new sociology of disablement needs to challenge this 'objectivity' and 'truth', and replace it with knowledge that arises from the position of the oppressed and seeks to understand that oppression. It requires an intimate involvement with the real historical movement of disabled people if it is to be of use. Equally, such developments have significance for the mainstream of social theory, in that they provide a testing ground for the adequacy of theoretical perspectives that claim to account for the experiences of all a society's members.

REFERENCES

Abberley, P. 1995: Disabling ideology in health and welfare – the case of occupa- tional therapy. *Disability and Society* 10 (2), 221–32.
Abberley, P. 1996: Work, utopia and impairment. In L. Barton (ed.) *Disability and Society: Emerging Issues and Insights*. London, Longman, 61–79.
Barrington Moore, J. 1978: *Injustice: The Social Bases of Obedience and Revolt.* New York: M. E. Sharpe.
Bauman, Z. 1997: No way back to bliss: how to cope with the restless chaos of modernity. *Times Literary Supplement*, 24 January.
Beck, U. 2000: *The Brave New World of Work.* Cambridge: Polity.
Bloch, E. 1986: *Natural Law and Human Dignity.* Cambridge, MA: MIT Press.
Bredberg, E. 1999: Writing disability history: problems, perspectives and sources. *Disability and Society*, 14 (2), 189–202.

Burchardt, T. 2000: *Enduring Economic Exclusion – Disabled People, Income and Work.* York: Joseph Rowntree Foundation.

Dean, H. 1999: Citizenship. In M. Powell (ed.), *New Labour, New Welfare State? The 'Third Way' in British Social Policy,* Bristol: Policy Press, 213–33.

Doyal, L. 1979: *The Political Economy of Health.* London: Pluto Press.

Durkheim, E. 1964: *The Division of Labour in Society.* Glencoe, IL: Free Press.

Durkheim, E. 1971: Individualism and the intellectuals, tr. S. and J. Lukes. *Political Studies,* 17, 14–30.

Dwyer, P. 2000: *Welfare Rights and Responsibilities: Contesting Social Citizenship,* Bristol: Policy Press.

Engels, F. 1969[1844/5]: *The Condition of the Working Class in England.* St Albans: Granada Publishing.

European Commission 1994: *European Social Policy: A Way Forward for the Union.* Brussels: European Commission.

European Commission 2000: Towards a barrier free Europe for people with disabilities. 12 May COM (2000) 284 final, Brussels, European Commission.

Fawcett, B. 2000: *Feminist Perspectives on Disability.* Harlow: Prentice-Hall.

Forrester, V. 1999: *The Economic Horror.* Cambridge: Polity.

Gleeson, B. 1999: *Geographies of Disability.* London: Routledge.

Haber, L. and Smith, T. 1971: Disability and deviance. *American Sociological Review,* 36, 82–95.

Hannington, W. 1937: *The Problem of the Distressed Areas.* London: Gollancz / Left Book Club.

Harrison, M. L. 1995: *Housing, 'Race', Social Policy and Empowerment.* Aldershot: Avebury Press.

Hindess, B. 1993: Citizenship in the modern west. In B. Turner (ed.), *Citizenship and Social Rights,* London: Sage.

Honneth, A. 1995a: *The Fragmented World of the Social: Essays in Social and Political Philosophy.* Albany, NY: SUNY Press.

Honneth, A. 1995b: *The Struggle for Recognition – The Moral Grammar of Social Conflicts.* Cambridge: Polity.

Land, H. and Rose, H. 1985: Compulsory altruism for some or an altruistic society for all? In P. Bean, J. Ferris and D. Whynes (eds), *In Defense of Welfare,* London: Tavistock.

Levitas, R. 1998: *The Inclusive Society? Social Exclusion and New Labour.* London: Macmillan.

Lister, R. 1997: *Citizenship: Feminist Perspectives.* New York: New York University Press.

Lunt, N. and Thornton, P. 1994: Disability and employment: towards an understanding of discourse and policy. *Disability and Society,* 9 (2) 223–38.

Mead, G. H. 1934: *Mind, Self and Society from the Standpoint of a Social Behaviourist.* Chicago: University of Chicago Press.

Offe, C. 2000: Pathways from here. *Boston Review,* October / November.

Oliver, M. 1990: *The Politics of Disablement.* London: Macmillan.

Rifkin, J. 1995: *The End of Work.* New York: Putnam.

Royal National Institute for the Blind 2000: *The Price of Justice*. London: RNIB.

Silver, H. 1994: Social exclusion and social solidarity: three paradigms. *International Labour Review*, 133 (5–6) 133–63.

Thompson, E. P. 1963: *The Making of the English Working Class*. London: Gollancz.

Topliss, E. 1982: *Social Responses to Handicap*. London: Longman.

Tronto, J. 1993: *Moral Boundaries*. New York: Routledge.

Walker, A. and Walker, C. (eds) 1997: *Britain Divided: The Growth of Exclusion in the 1980s and 1990s*. London: Child Poverty Action Group.

8

Shooting for the Moon: Politics and Disability at the Beginning of the Twenty-First Century

Phil Lee

Introduction

Most of the writing about disability and politics has been generated by activists within or around the disability movement itself, broadly conceived. I will suggest that these writings tend – understandably perhaps – toward a rather 'romanticized' view of the relationship between these two concepts. Recent developments in state policy – notably the Disability Discrimination Act (DDA) of 1995 and the introduction of the Disability Rights Commission in 2000 – have revealed considerable disagreements amongst disabled activists about how closely involved they should be with such developments. I will suggest that certain paradoxes face the British disability movement, and that these have to be comprehended in *realpolitik* terms. It is insufficient to claim simply that civil rights for disabled people will only be realized by continuous radical struggle outside the arena of the state's apparati (see Barnes et al. 1996: 115). The central issue is over which issues and through which strategies (how) such struggles should take place – *in* and around the state. There is evidence that such strategic thinking is taking place, but it is underdeveloped. Whilst the present conjuncture appears to be most unfavourable for disabled people to make significant political gains, there are a number of real potential opportunities if an effective politics of coalition can be built.

The constituency of 'the disabled'

A key issue when attempting to politically mobilize any group is under-standing their precise nature and numbers. Just who are 'the disabled' and how, and who, might best advance, and define, their interests? We will see below just how pertinent these questions are. On whom, and concerning what issues, should the demands of the movement be based?

The Disability Rights Commission's Disability Briefing (November 2000) Labour Force Survey, drawing on the government's Labour Force Survey (Summer 2000), indicates that there are over 6.6 million disabled people of working age – 20 per cent of the working age population. Yet, as Barnes et al. observe, many people of working age 'defined as "dis-abled" in national surveys . . . do not see themselves in this way, and even fewer actively engage in political activities with the disabled people's movement' (1999: 174). Moreover, in 1991 there were just over 10 million people in Britain over the age of 60. At the beginning of the new millennium people over 85 years old make up about 11 per cent of the elderly population. The social needs, due to increasing incapacity, of this growing and disparate group are vast (see Zarb 1993).

It is instructive to note also that the disability movement recognizes that it has 'been relatively unsuccessful in reaching out to the disabled population as a whole' (Barnes et al. 1999: 179). Significantly, the movement has been dominated, and fuelled, by the successes achieved for a very particular constituency, notably 'those with physical and sensory impairments, who are both relatively active and relatively young' (Barnes at al. 1999: 179). This fact has had considerable impact on the present structure of British disability politics.

It is also not mischievous to acknowledge that able-bodied people do not readily think much about disability, other than, of course, when members of their own families are affected. Taylor-Gooby (1985) has argued, more generally, that the electorate will support only those wel-fare policies that they perceive to be in their own 'felt' interests. The able-bodied may be 'forced' to think about 'disability' by television charity programmes, or 'accidental' meetings with disabled people in shops or wherever. In these instances, though, *their gaze* will be one of the *charit-able impulse*. We will all die, but we do not like to think much about the fact. The majority of the able-bodied will, equally, get frailer, and become – dis-abled. We are all in this sense *'tabs'* (see Rae 1989 for the first usage of this term) – only temporarily able-bodied. Disability, like death though, is something we do not care to think about too much – in contemporary argot 'we do not want to go there'. This fact, too, has significant effects on the present structure of British disability politics.

The present political conjuncture

Less than twenty years ago, many of us lived through the *maelstrom* that was Thatcherism! Yet, electorally the political party that delivered those enormous transformations to our body politic and social structure appears now to be, for all practicable purposes, unelectable. Thatcherism had a very clear, and well-documented strategy (Hall and Jacques 1989), to shift the terrain of British politics considerably to the right. Many commentators on the left perceive the present New Labour government as a product – prisoner? – of that earlier period. For Hall, the Blair project, in its assumptions and overall goals, is still 'essentially framed by, and moving on terrain established by Thatcherism' (1998: 14).

Whatever else, New Labour politics are dominated by *style* – a form of hyper-politics, in which politics is exclusively preoccupied with itself. Politics reduced to the language – or sound bite – of politics (for a most insightful discussion, see Fairclough 2000). There is little of an *intellectual* project marked out by New Labour. Certain measures are, on occasion, described as influenced by communitarianism and / or ethical socialism. If any overarching intellectual description is employed, it is that of the Third Way (Blair 1998; Giddens 1998, 2000, 2002) – allegedly a new political project carefully picking its way between the untrammelled excesses of the private market and the dead hand of state control.

It is difficult not to have sympathy with Hall's severe judgements on the Third Way – he light-heartedly quotes Francis Wheen's wry observation in his *Guardian* column – about it occupying some 'vacant space between the Fourth dimension and the Second Coming' (Hall 1998: 10). On a more serious note, it is difficult to detect real intellectual sustenance, or the seeds of a convincing political strategy in Giddens's or any other New Labour supporter's writings (see Mouffe 1998; Rustin 1999; Westergaard 1999). To paraphrase Giddens's contributions (1998, 2000, 2002), perhaps overly cynically, we live in a global marketplace – this is a fact of life – and the principal political task must be to adapt society and its members to the needs of this global economy. There is, as with New Labour generally, some genuine concern with 'social exclusion' – noting that it is not simply economic factors that relegate some groups to the margins of society. There is no mention of disabilities in any of this. In fact, we might add that there is very little writing about disabilities in any mainstream commentaries on recent political developments, or within the discourses of sociology.

Hall appears correct also in noting that New Labour's principal audience appears to be a mythologized 'Middle England' – 'a profoundly traditionalist and backward looking cultural investment' (Hall 1998: 13). He goes on to argue that:

> [T]he framing strategy of New Labour's economic repertoire remains essentially the neo-liberal one: the de-regulation of markets, the wholesale refashioning of the public sector by the New Managerialism, the continued privatisation of public assets, low taxation, breaking the 'inhibitions' to market flexibility, institutionalising the culture of private provision and personal risk, and privileging in its moral discourse the values of self-sufficiency, competitiveness and entrepreneurial dynamism. (Hall 1998: 11)

Not a particularly pleasing prospect, but there are, nevertheless, this author wants to stress, 'spaces' for political gains (see Mulgan 1998). They are, of course, limited, and their successful realization will require detailed comprehension of the political terrain, alongside carefully designed and orchestrated strategies and campaigns.

The majority of the electorate, meanwhile, appear to remain disengaged from active politics – busy trying to be enterprising subjects, standing, as much as possible, on their own two feet. Above all, wise 'consumers' – in the retail parks and on matters of their own welfare – judging 'what they can spend now' with less and less concern for the public sphere and the idea of a common citizenship. Some aspects of the disability movement's trajectory could be construed to gel with this – notably, the emphasis on ownership and choice in benefits and on getting disabled people into work. New Labour continues to strenuously 'buy into' the idea that direct taxation should remain static, however much social exclusion apparently requires tackling.

It is undoubtedly true, as Oliver and Barnes (1998) have argued, that the costs of excluding disabled people from the work-force are considerable. The Treasury could make significant savings in benefits by introducing policies that accommodate disabled people's employment needs within the work-place. Equally, though, activists need to recognize, in my opinion, that any important political advances for disabled people will require significant costs to 'business', notably with significant restructuring of work environments – see below. Money saved by the Treasury will not automatically be passed to employers. Such advances will also require a significant sea change in British political culture, involving, among other things, fundamental shifts in the *mind-set* of the electorate. For that *mind-set* to be shifted, campaigns must tap into *existing* possibilities. It is worth reflecting, for example, on one of the products of the new post-Thatcherite, consumption-orientated culture: the growing number of television and newspaper advertisements that focus on private 'risks', particularly in the sphere of pensions, health and life insurance. The undoubted retreat of British public welfare – with its assumption of collective response to risk (see Taylor-Gooby 2000) – might superficially induce deep pessimism into welfare activists concerned with extending public provision and civil rights for disabled people. Yet these advertisements are undoubtedly designed to puncture the complacency – indeed, the above-noted amnesia – the general public may feel towards their own frailty – bringing them face to face with their 'tab' status. In this sense, there may be real, if somewhat ironic, opportunities for political advancement.

Before we leave this brief overview of the conjuncture, it would be most remiss not to note that disability issues, as conceptualized by the disability movement, were not very salient in the last general election. This fact was discussed most perceptively on a recent Radio Four programme *Sunday Best – Why People Hate Prejudice against Disability* (August 2001). We also need to recognize what Barnes et al. (1999: 154–5) have documented: the actual and potential exclusions of many disabled people from participation in the electoral process.

The politicization of disability – a new social movement?

Within such a conjuncture it is hardly surprising that the broadly defined left have found much comfort in the progressive efforts of groups other than the traditionally defined, male trade union-led working class, and considerable energy has been spent on analysing the nature of so-called new social movements (NSMs). For many progressive intellectuals the 'crisis of Marxism' in the 1980s was a 'watershed' – a symbolic confirmation that the European working class had compromised its revolutionary potential by allowing itself to be co-opted into the management of welfare capitalism. These developments provoked a search for alternative 'agencies' of 'revolutionary change'. Of particular note were the women's movement, the anti-nuclear movement and the green movement. Some of this material smacks of considerable optimism – romanticism? By romanticism I mean an overly optimistic assessment of the achievements and prospects for radical change.

It is not the intention of this article to overview the many arcane arguments that surround NSMs – notably how to characterize them, whether they are really 'new' or not, and their potential for progressive change. This has been done extensively elsewhere (see Bagguley 1992; Fagan and Lee 1997; Martin 2001). For our purposes we need simply to note three substantive points.

First, commentators such as Habermas (1987) and Melucci (1989) emphasized the cultural and symbolic nature of these new movements, arguing that NSMs could resist the further encroachments of bureaucratized systems into everyday life. Habermas (1981: 36–7) suggests that these self-help organizations will develop in such ways as to challenge the organized political party system through their emphasis on expressive politics and more direct forms of democracy.

Second, and most important for our purposes, there are a number of significant contributors who have characterized the disability movement as an NSM. Oliver (1990) was the first, arguing that the disability movement ought to be characterized as an NSM, as it is *internationalist*, aims at *empowerment* and *consciousness raising*, offers a *critical evaluation* of society, and lies at the *periphery of the conventional political system*. Further, it is such a movement because it can be seen to focus on the *quality of life* of a particular section of society, and as such must be seen as *post-materialist*. For our purposes, whether this characterization is correct or not is less important than the content of Oliver's descriptors and the implicit judgements contained therein. There is a celebration of the rejection of conventional political forms and a strong belief in the inherently progressive nature of the enterprise that a clearly identifiable disability movement has embarked upon.

Third, it is clear from many commentators that NSMs should be viewed as complex, flexible movements needing to adapt in form and content to the environment around them. Whilst, in one sense, this may be regarded as a potential strength, it also signifies a certain temporality and fragility (Bartholomew and Mayer 1992). Giddens (1991: 155) indicates significantly that NSMs will only be able to capitalize on this adaptability if they can connect with 'institutionally immanent possibilities'. For Giddens, and I would concur, this must indicate an ability to engage with the wider, conventional political system.

Influence of postmodern analysis

Increasingly, disability activists have argued that it is necessary to engage with developments in postmodern theory (Shakespeare and Watson 1997) if they are to properly conceptualize their project. Mullard and

Spicker (1998: 130) offer a useful summary of the essence of the 'postmodern' contribution:

> In the postmodern period .... society has become more fragmented, more diverse, more full of differences. . . . Postmodernity can be described as the process which seeks to replace the values of homogeneity and universalism with those of . . . pluralism, variety and ambivalence.

As Bauman (1992: p. ix) states, postmodernist theory braces people 'for a life without truths, standards and ideals . . . . for sniffing a knife of unfreedom under any cloak of saintly righteousness'. At first glance, then, not a very likely ally for either critical welfare theory or a radical politics wishing to champion precisely issues such as equality and rights, and disclose 'truths' about the extent of continuing inequalities and injustices! (see Mann 1998: 82).

This clear emphasis within postmodernism on *diversity, fragmentation* and, above all, *difference* was welcomed by many radical scholars wrestling with the precise ways in which 'class' issues and identities related to other forms of 'difference' – sexualities, age, gender and, of course, impairments. It allows for a certain *legitimacy* to be attached to *privileging* the political interests of separate groups. We can see that such contributions are possible, without any postmodernist vogue, by assessing the powerful and influential contribution made by Lister (1997). She argued that the term 'citizenship' conveyed a 'false universalism' that failed to recognize the significant *differences* between the genders.

It is one thing to recognize that diversity and difference must be accommodated by radical activists, altogether another to know how to do this, and to what extent. The starting point must be comprehending fully the complexities of the social and structural relationships between such variables as age, race, gender, sexuality and impairment. Some very insightful work has been done, and is documented perceptively by Williams (1994: 207).

Building from such work, the second stage involves appreciating the optimum ways to make significant political gains. For it is vital to recognize that an unproblematic emphasis on 'difference' in the present conjuncture could be politically problematic, if not dangerous. As Taylor-Gooby (1994) indicates, emphasizing diversity, pluralism and choice might easily be used as a smokescreen for the promotion of forms of selectivism, and the further residualization of welfare. Further, the use of discretionary benefits could easily be deepened; sectional groups could be played off against each other; those caring for certain groups may be overlooked, or disadvantaged; precarious short-term projects could be relying on insecure and vulnerable grant aid; new inequalities could emerge, either intentionally or unintentionally.

Moreover, the political strategies that flow from these 'additions' are not always clear. Consider, for example, albeit briefly and simplistically, the contrast between 'liberal' (or 'rights-based') feminists, who adopt a universal position advocating sexual equality, and those 'difference' feminists who would claim that such equalities are inevitably tailored to suit the needs of men (Pateman 1988). We must be careful not to throw out the universalistic bathwater in the rush to marinade provision with various groups' diverse, and multi-faceted, identifiable needs. The notion of citizenship envisaged in the post-war settlement, whilst fundamentally flawed, did at least recognize the importance of social rights. Is it possible to reconcile universalism with a proper political commitment to recognizing, and accommodating, diversity?

Difference and particularistic universalism

In a most stimulating paper Thompson and Hoggett (1996) suggest that it is. They offer a defence of what they describe as a 'sophisticated universalism' that, whilst committed to equality, is able to be sensitive to diversity by 'incorporating significant elements of both selectivism and particularism' (1996: 21). By this latter term, they are describing a process whereby 'different standards are appropriate to different circumstances for different individuals and groups' (1996: 22). The core of their argument is contained in the following passage:

> If the particularistic critic of universalism condemns it for failing to notice and thus allow for difference, then the moral force of that condemnation must be derived from a commitment to a normative principle holding that differences (or at least *certain* differences) should be respected. But what is this norm of respect if not some kind of universalist principle? (Thompson and Hoggett 1996: 34)

They reinforce the point in a more accessible manner: 'any universalism that makes serious attempts to be sensitive to the differences between particular cases, and any particularism with the moral force to adjudicate between differences, are in fact the same theories looked at from opposite points of view' (1996: 35). More specifically, and meeting Taylor-Gooby's charge above, they are clear that 'the demand to protect rights, meet needs, or reward desert, can in practice enjoin very different treatments for particular individuals or groups' (1996: 35). This has been a useful, if somewhat abstract, sortie that has allowed us to recognize that any successful *politics of diversity* must be ultimately guided – justified – by egalitarian, or universal, principle(s).

Self-organization

Oliver's description of the disability movement as an NSM implied a freshness, a certain 'romanticism', about its politics; a clear rejection of reformism and conventional political forms of activity. There is also a celebration of the fact that these activities lie at the *periphery of the conventional political system*. These activists have also established *a critical evaluation of society*, principally through a *clear critique* of models that imply that the primary way to treat disabled people is to get them to *adapt* to the world as they find it. Grounding their practice firmly in what has become known as the *'social model'* – effectively a structural sociological model – they have indicted the inaccessible environment they find themselves stuck in. Inaccessible buildings, transport designed to exclude wheelchairs, housing that cannot accommodate those with mobility problems, become objects for unequivocal political challenge. Such activism has begun to critique the conventional ways in which disabled people have been regarded and treated, as well as to challenge the exceptional levels of discrimination that they face (Barnes 1991). In essence, the culmination of such activity has been the demand for equal rights and treatment.

Much of the progress of the disability movement is due to such uncompromising national and *international* political organization and activity. There is now British, as well as American, legislation that does directly outlaw some, albeit limited, forms of discrimination against disabled people – see below. But the political context into which such demands were being made, as we shall see, was also significant. Asking the 'impossible', demanding that people adopt completely new *mind-sets – shooting for the moon* – has advanced the collective interests of disabled people in Britain and the USA in significant ways. Is it, however, sufficient? And are there certain dangers within such an approach?

More than a new social movement?

More often than not when academic commentators refer to the politics of disability, it is the emergence of the self-conscious movement described above to which they refer (Campbell and Oliver 1996; Reynolds in John-stone 1998: ch. 6). The emergence of articulate, organized and effective disability activists is seen, quite correctly, as crucial – *putting the politics into disability*. However, as already indicated, this article suggests that this is a limiting, and limited, way to understand the interrelationship between politics and disability, focusing too exclusively on the political activists, their actions and desires. I wish to *stretch* the linkages between these terms – 'politics' and 'disability'.

Returning to our discussion of NSMs, some political progressive – largely social democratic – commentators were much less pessimistic about the conjuncture described above, and argued that the labour movement had made, and consolidated, considerable gains in citizenship rights during the post-war period (Therborn 1986; Esping-Andersen 1985; Giddens 1991). Gains that had helped to create new opportunities for political participation, whilst increasing the economic security of previously marginalized sections of the population. For these commen-tators – and I am in considerable agreement with their position – NSMs needed to be seen as a direct, material development within this new phase of politics.

At issue here is the extent to which activists wish their activities to be seen as 'reformist' activities *within* the existing state machinery, or as unsullied, uncompromised activities *outside* such a framework. The ori-ginal NSM concept applied to the disability movement in the early 1990s was undoubtedly motivated by sensitivity towards the latter position. However, over the years a number of commentators have acknowledged that the disability movement is concerned centrally with issues of *con-tinuing and deep material inequality*. Shakespeare (1993: 258–9) pre-serves the unsullied discourse by arguing that the movement has to focus on issues to do with 'liberation' rather than simply developing post-material values. Fagan and Lee (1997) put it more bluntly when insisting that so-called new social movements are every bit as much concerned with *distribution issues* and *resource allocation* as any other previous movements have been. Their point is that, at the end of the day, politics is about such *perennial* concerns.

The social model – conceptually strong, politically problematic

The disability movement also offered a very clear *critical evaluation* of society, emphasizing the importance of *consciousness raising*. The central vehicle for this *critique* was, of course, *the social model of disability*. My argument will be that some over-simplistic applications of this model can promote an underdeveloped – indeed fundamentalist – politics which inhibits the development of realistic strategies.

Producing evidence of this inaccessible, segregated and exclusionary world is relatively straightforward. Yet how far is the 'able-bodied' majority prepared to go in reconstructing 'its' social order so that 'it' can accommodate a far wider spectrum of abilities? What *political*, adaptational choices are this majority prepared to make; or rather, as disability activists would see it, can they be forced into making?

The social model developed from subjecting the time-honoured manner of conceptualizing disability since the end of the nineteenth century – the *medical model* – to a comprehensive critique (Oliver 1996; Priestley 1999). This original model, as an ideal type, defines people as disabled as a result of conditions necessitating medical intervention and diagnosis. Despite the clear limiting effects of this model on the way that disabled people are conceptualized, the extraordinary 'successes' of Western medicine has had far-reaching impact.

The medical model, despite the growing impact of the social model on the political activity of some disabled people and the practices of some professionals, still holds enormous sway. This is partly, of course, due to the fact that medical diagnoses and interventions are so extremely important for the management and maintenance of some disabling conditions. It must be appreciated that we cannot simply dispense with medicine (see Doyal and Doyal 1984). Radicals still have to be able to conceptualize *individual* actions and *individualized* interventions; they cannot simply be 'magic-ed' away. Nor can individual action simply be reduced to structural determinations. There has to be a *politics* of *individual actions and interventions*, and in the case of disability politics, this *must* recognize the saliency, and vital necessity, of medical interventions.

In spite of this observation, it is not surprising that a thoroughly structural sociological view – the social model – has had such an enormous ideological impact over the last two decades. Non-disabled people can relatively easily accept the idea *conceptually* that 'disabled' people are hugely constrained by an environment that is 'disabling'. Its attractiveness is enhanced also by the fact that the model has been so clearly constructed out of the 'experiences' of disabled people, and disseminated by them.

Yet we must be cautious. Left-leaning intellectuals equally accurately explain poverty or unemployment as *systemic failures*, not individual ones. Of course, in a simple intellectual sense that would be true – many can theoretically appreciate that capitalist society structurally generates poverty. But it would be phenomenally *simplistic politics* that merely stated that we eradicate poverty by systemically overthrowing capitalism. It would be equally naïve not to recognize that the behaviour of certain individuals does compound their poverty, in the same way that individuals' smoking jeopardizes their health status.

The social model, despite its conceptual insights, has clear limitations – not least, the potential simplistic and uncompromising, indeed *fundamentalist*, politics that it might generate (see Lee and Raban 1988). In the last decade there has been considerable criticism of the social model from both within and outside the disabled movement. Barnes (2000: 443) observes that it is simply misinterpretation by some disability activists that has led these criticisms to flourish. The simple fact is that to avoid such 'misinterpretations' requires a clear modification of the *political* drift of the model.

Many disabled people themselves are unconvinced that the model sufficiently allows for issues of *personal identity*. Following this theme, Hughes and Paterson (1997) comment on the social model's *theoretical* basis for an emancipatory politics, but are unconvinced that this model could encapsulate *an emancipatory politics of identity*. Swain and French develop this point:

> Non-disabled people can generally accept that a wheelchair user cannot enter a building because of steps. Non-disabled people are much more threatened and challenged by the notion that a wheelchair user could be pleased and proud to be the person he or she is. (2000: 570)

They construct an *affirmative* model, largely derived from work in the Disability Arts Movement, which asserts positive personal identities, both *individual* and collective, that combat the personal tragedy view. Finkelstein (2002), on the other hand, suggests that any attempt to incorporate personal experiences detracts from the effectiveness of the social model. Shakespeare and Watson defend the model whilst warning, insufficiently in my opinion, that to base it too firmly on a Marxist world-view might lead a 'universalising and monolithic rationality' (1997: 299). They take up the theme explored above, and one increasingly popular across the British left, that the model has to develop 'a more nuanced world-view drawing on feminist and postmodern accounts' (1997: 299).

Limitations of identity politics

One final observation demands comment, and it derives from the emphasis placed on *experiential* understanding within the model; only the 'disabled' being able to have *the* proper political insights. As Branfield so graphically puts it 'Non-disabled people cannot possibly know..... their experience, their history, their culture is our oppression' (1998: 143). If the model does not incorporate sufficient understanding of personal identity, its employment by activists within the movement most certainly does!

Such activists appear to want to exclude those without impairments from any front-line political involvement. This position can only, in the long run, *marginalize* the politics of disability, leading eventually to splits and recriminations about who can 'know' what about which conditions. An interesting debate has ensued, within the movement, about the 'visibility' of various conditions and the impediments to political progress imposed by such fundamentalism (see Drake 1997; Humphrey 1999, 2000).

Any politics based purely on 'identity' is likely to face major problems, not least due to the fact that such socially constructed identities are *contestable* and subject to change; sub- and splinter groups emerge, as different aspects of the identities are prioritized. What of non-visible impairments – learning or mental health ones? Or deaf people 'who are classified as disabled.... but who repudiate the disabled identity on the grounds they constitute a distinct linguistic and cultural minority?' (Humphrey 2000: 65). Would it be acceptable for an obese woman to call herself disabled?

It is instructive to note how the social model became operationalized within the UNISON group researched by Humphrey. She argues that it 'both reified the disability identity and reduced it to particular kinds of impairments – physical, immutable, tangible and "severe" ones – in a way which can deter many people from adopting a disabled identity and participating in a disability community' (2000: 69). Humphrey goes on to suggest that an *inclusive model* of disability needs to be constructed. Her work dramatically poses the question of what disabled activists mean by their 'community'. However – another note of caution – it is all too easy to privilege the term 'community' as much communitarian discourse does, reifying it in such a way as to disguise considerable differences within it (see Young 1990). When referring, for example, to the Muslim community of Leicester, to whom are we referring – the community leaders (*sic*), the community of Muslim men, or whom? What of gender, age, etc.? Humphrey (2000) is precisely drawing attention to the considerable *diversity* of conditions that can be described as 'disabled', and the vital political need for clear *coalitions of interest* to be established between them. It is worth noting that 'disability' is a difficult category to both politically organize and respond to, given the wide disparities in the political demands which those different constituent parts make – from 'independence' through to improvement in conditions of 'dependency'.

Putting rights on the agenda

Barnes et al. (1999) are clear that a 'civil rights' agenda was generated by the international actions of the disability movement. They document why anti-discrimination legislation (ADL) became the most favoured option for such political activists. We must, however, be cautious not to exaggerate this point. Other salient political factors must also be considered in a British context. First, control of Parliament by Thatcherite radical conservatism produced an extremely difficult situation for many British 'welfare' pressure groups concerned with lobbying. In this situation, Harlow and Rawlings (1992: 298) suggest that legal processes were increasingly asked to assume the function of the surrogate political system. Second, community activism had blossomed in the 1970s, and out of such activity had developed the law centre movement. At a local level, radicals were able to see concrete gains from *legal* interventions. Third, pressure groups such as the Child Poverty Action Group and Mind were increasingly using public interest law to secure political change, the former by employing legal test cases, the latter through rights enforcement.

Gooding (1994) and Barnes et al. (1999) document the campaigns, and the resultant limited successes, of the first extensive piece of ADL: the 1990 Americans with Disabilities Act (ADA). Subsequently, Australia, New Zealand, France and Britain introduced such civil rights-orientated legislation. The struggle for the 1995 British Disability Discrimination Act (DDA) is also well documented by Barnes et al. (1999).

Of significant interest for our concerns is the political judgement they make about the passing of this legislation. They suggest that it reopened internal divisions and brought to an end the uneasy coalition between organizations *of* and organizations *for* disabled people. These are the divisions referred to by Williams (1994) as struggles from *below* (of) and from *above* (for). Barnes et al. (1999) employ the more conventional distinction between 'reformist' organizations and 'radical' ones. With clear 'radical' sympathies, they are clearly worried that their members' interests will be diluted by too proximate involvement with the formal political system, and in particular the state's administrative machinery. In an earlier contribution Barnes and Oliver (1996) depict this particular dilemma most graphically:

> To get too close to the government is to risk incorporation and end up carrying out their proposals rather than ours. To move too far away is to risk marginalisation and eventual demise.... To remain aloof risks

appearing unrealistic and/or unreasonable, and denies possible access to much-needed resources. (1996: 115)

There is, therefore, an understandable ambivalence in Barnes et al.'s (1999) descriptions of both the experiences of campaigns for British civil rights and the nature of their achievement. On the one hand, 'the disabled peoples' movement can claim to have made significant advance in convincing the general public of the merits of ADL'. On the other, one must be very sceptical of such legislation, and its implementation 'must be coupled with the spread of user-led initiatives' (Barnes et al. 1999: 172). Even with such initiatives, there is 'no guarantee that these measures will be implemented as intended, or that their outcomes will necessarily be as anticipated' (1999: 173). Such intellectual ambivalence was matched politically by the refusal of 'radical' disability groups – *of* not for – to get involved with the consultation for the DDA. It was regarded as too weak and, in any case, unenforceable. Of course, non-compliance could have been a useful strategy to try to strengthen this piece of legislation. If it was so, it did not work. The DDA was, by any standards, an insufficient instrument.

State action

The Disability Discrimination Act (1995) makes discrimination against disabled people illegal in the areas of employment, services and the sale and rental of property. However, there are substantial limits on the scope of both the employment and services provision. Employment discrimination only applies to employers with more than fifteen employees in total, and does not apply to certain categories: for example the armed forces, police officers, barristers and fire-fighters. The prohibition against discrimination in the provision of goods and services expressly does not apply to education and transport. Gooding in an insightful overview of the act's operations and development has argued that the DDA suffered from fundamental design faults: notably, 'its restrictive and complex definition of disability; the broad scope for "justifying" potential discrimination, particularly with regard to services; its failure to tackle indirect and direct discrimination' (Gooding 2000: 542). Moreover, the DDA failed to include any strategic enforcement agency such as the Equal Opportunities Commission or Commission for Racial Equality.

The DDA defines discrimination in two ways. The first is 'less favourable treatment': where an employer or service provider treats a disabled person less favourably for a reason to do with that person's disability, and cannot demonstrate justification for it. The second is if an employer or service provider discriminates against a disabled person by failing to provide such reasonable adjustment to the environment as required by the act. Much revolves around the concept of 'less favourable': less favourable than whom? We are back with disability and 'difference'; and I will return to it below.

It is instructive to note that much of the legalistic controversy revolves around disputation about medical categorization, and/or other forms of individualized actions. There is little emphasis on collective, proactive measures. British anti-discriminatory laws principally operate by seeking to create *disincentives* against discrimination. As Gooding indicates:

> This disincentive effect might be postulated to depend on the perceived likelihood of successful legal action being taken to counter discrimination and the estimated costs (in terms of financial compensation and adverse publicity) to an employer or service provider of losing such cases. (Gooding 2000: 543)

The Labour Party was critical of the DDA whilst in opposition, and entered government in 1997 with a manifesto commitment to secure civil rights for disabled people. Towards this end a Disabled Rights Taskforce was set up. Its report *From Exclusion to Inclusion* (Disability Rights Taskforce 1999) made a significant number of recommendations. In particular, the DDA's right of non-discrimination should be extended to small employers, prison and police officers, and, in modified forms to take account of the particular nature of such services, to education and transport. New Labour also rectified the lack of an enforcement agency by creating the Disability Rights Commission (DRC) in April 2000.

My concern is not with the minutiae of these legal enactments and the procedures they invoke, but rather with the *principles* at work, and at stake, in their operations. Freedman (1999) argues that if the deep-seated prejudices experienced by certain groups are to be tackled effectively, it is essential that the ambiguous and restrictive goal of 'equal opportunities' is transcended (see Drake 2001). This means adopting the political goal of 'substantive equality', involving the use of social policy instruments such as education, training and family friendly measures. Effectively this could shift emphasis away from individualized instances of 'unfair' or 'unequal' treatment on to more proactive actions promoting equal opportunities (affirmative action programmes) and encouraging employers into 'good' practices (contract compliance).

This is *not* to argue that combating discrimination should be seen, as it is in European Community measures, as exclusively a welfare matter.

A 'rights strategy' is a necessary, but not a sufficient, strategy. In particular, with regard to disabled people, there needs to be an assertion of positive rights to supplement the right to equal treatment, even when the latter guarantees the valuing of differences and diversities. A strong welfare element must be central – collective provision of transport, caring and health services, and education – for those who cannot meet their needs within the labour market.

Politics, 'difference' and work

It is essential to examine what we mean when we argue that disabled people are 'different'. Some people are born 'disabled', and, as we have seen, the social construction of 'disability', and in particular the structure of the social environment, compound and reinforce those initial 'disabilities'. Others – many others – *become disabled* during the life course – a fact of huge political significance. There are three other further vital issues that require noting. The first is that the disabled people considered within the social constructions to be the least able-bodied – the least able to live 'normal' lives – have been responded to politically. It has long been an established principle that some disabled people should be, and are, treated *differently* – an obvious example being that whilst all children's needs are covered between the ages of three and sixteen, children with special educational needs may receive more resources. Second, financial support for disabled persons differentiates not only between the able-bodied and the disabled, but also in accordance with the assessed severity of the impairment. Third, much of this provision may, and often does, contain elements of severe discrimination against disabled people (Barnes 1991).

Yet this new postmodern emphasis on 'difference' appears to mean for disabled people, at first glance and somewhat ironically, *forget* your differences. Simply adapt the environment. Simply restructure the environment, and those 'differences' – in terms of our ability to contribute and be productive – will simply melt away. As Branfield (1999: 401) puts it, 'the disability movement, at its most basic level, is fighting for our right not to be disabled...there is.... nothing inevitable about disability.' Stated thus, this is a politically dangerous idea, for it minimizes, and potentially trivializes, the necessary social care and accommodations that many disabled people require.

At a common-sense level, and within the present political conjuncture as described above, there would also be considerable resistance to taking this idea, as Branfield does, to its logical conclusion. The social model simplistically applies to all impairments. I can hear people now – 'Of course, there are barriers to certain people, disabled people, doing certain jobs – brain surgeon (learning difficulties) or electrician (partially sighted).' Indeed, I can hear some of my own students in seminars. In the United States a legal category of 'insurmountable barriers' can be invoked in anti-discrimination discourse, barriers related to an impairment that would cause, even with appropriate modification, insuperable problems in accessing and carrying out certain types of work.

Such intellectual resistance would involve a severe, but – and this is also an important point – understandable misunderstanding. Of course, there are certain jobs that no amount of modification of the environment will enable people with certain impairments to perform. Such people would simply not be able to meet a basic job specification: that is, they would not be qualified for the job – in the same way as I was never able, sadly, to play for Manchester United or asked to accompany Miles Davis! So such common-sense arguments should not be the starting point of *resistance* to change, and they can be combated. In *realpolitik* terms, the major source of resistance will always be, as noted earlier, the costs to the employer of carrying out the necessary restructuring.

The world of work is, in any case, changing rapidly; undergoing constant, and necessary, restructuring. Employers have to introduce major changes in their infrastructure and practices merely to keep up with competitive pressures. Castells (1996) assesses the recent changes in the productive forces – informationalization, shifts away from manufacturing to service industries; the general effects of globalization, etc. – as of greater significance than the original transformations wreaked by early industrialization. Barnes (2000) suggests that these developments offer a major strategic opportunity for major political advances by disabled people. Certainly computerized technology does appear to open up considerable possibilities for employment for *certain* categories of disabled people, and one that complements New Labour's objective of returning people to work and taking them off benefits. Vast savings could be made of social security budgets by increasing disabled peoples' access to work.

Without disagreeing with Barnes, I must add some notes of political caution. First, as Barnes (2000: 446) recognizes, these flexible production techniques may be enabling to some, but will increase the social isolation of others. Second, potential beneficiaries are much more likely to be those disabled people whom we noted above are in the vanguard of the disability movement. The increased social isolation and marginalization are likely to affect people with learning difficulties, the mentally distressed and older workers.

It would be unproductive to try to politically organize to force all large employers to adapt their environments in the short, or even medium, term for every variety of impairment. The costs would be massive and, as such, would be a constant, and successful, cause of employer resistance. However, within localities, agreements could be brokered that facilitated, through government quota schemes, the adoption of certain environments for certain impairments, including learning difficulties. This would reduce *choice* of work for disabled people, and some sections of the movement might oppose it on these grounds, but it could achieve significant political gains for many. Government departments could be charged with initial quotas, alongside other public bodies such as local authorities and universities. The political brokering could also involve shifting the control of grants to disabled people from certain voluntary and privatized organizations to organizations of disabled people (Barnes 2000).

The politics of coalition – a conclusion

This chapter has established a number of key things about the relationship of disability and politics. First, there remain major barriers within the electorate to recognizing that disabled people are entitled to full, and equal citizenship, or civil rights, and can make productive contributions to society, particularly in the world of work. Second, there is an irony to this, as many working people and older people will *become* disabled themselves. Third, and reflecting the above two points, the disability movement manages only to engage with a narrow constituency of the disabled. There are considerable 'absences', such as older persons with severe physical impairments and people with learning difficulties. Fourth, campaigns based on the social model of disability will, and have, produced some significant gains, but over-reliance on it can also produce a simplistic and fundamentalist politics incapable of difficult political calculations. For example, it is very difficult to privilege the *choices* of disabled people – which may, and will, differ – at the same time as winning the arguments with the electorate about the fact that disabled people should be allowed such choices. Moreover, what has to be worked out is how to make it impossible for governments to ignore carefully orchestrated demands and campaigns.

Difficult, sensitive political calculations will have to be made in the next few years of struggle. Politics is not just about powerful ideologies and direct action; it is also about smoke-filled rooms, balancing interests and, often, making only slow and painful gains. It is about the nature of the opposition and why it inhibits, or defeats, progress. So political judgements have to be brought to bear on day-to-day developments. What should be prioritized then?

First, there is great potential, in my opinion, in campaigns that stress that *all* people are 'tabs' – temporarily 'able-bodied'. As indicated above, advertising campaigns for pensions and life insurance already 'tap' into this. This would create a considerably more empathetic environment in which more specific demands could be made. An analogy would be with men's health issues. For years, governments argued that men simply would not be interested in campaigns about their health. Yet, campaigns in Australia (see Lupton 1995: ch. 4) have had a huge impact, and the recent British television advertisement involving Robbie Williams highlighting the need to check for testicular cancer has been much discussed.

Second, of course, carefully selected campaigns highlighting the inadequacies of the DDA legislation must be designed and carried out, chosen to highlight the worse 'absences' in coverage. These external campaigns, however, should not be allowed to prevent engagement with the present state machinery. We should also not underestimate that these campaigns may struggle to engage all disabled people *in situ* – for example, in educational establishments without effective access.

Third, heavy emphasis should be placed on the politics of coalition, in which 'identities may be supplanted by issues, as substantive campaigns around housing, health, welfare, education, employment, immigration, reproduction and media representations' combat 'the multidimensional oppression matrix' (Humphrey 2000: 75). There is, in my opinion, much potential for campaigns that link up with older people – for example, for better pensions and guaranteed rights to health care treatment. We will all age, and, as stated above, this could be heavily stressed in such campaigning. Fourth, major efforts have to be made to engage those parts of the disabled constituency that the movement itself accepts that it ill serves.

REFERENCES

Bagguley, P. 1992: Social change, the middle class and the emergence of 'new social movements': a critical analysis. *Sociological Review*, 40 (1), 26–48.
Barnes, C. 1991: *Disabled People in Britain and Discrimination: A Case for Anti-Discrimination Legislation*. London: Hurst.
Barnes, C. 2000: A working social model. *Critical Social Policy*, 20 (4), 441–57.
Barnes, C. and Oliver, M. 1996: Disability rights: rhetoric and reality in the UK. *Disability and Society*, 10 (1), 111–16.
Barnes, C., Mercer, G. and Shakespeare, T. 1999: *Exploring Disability: A Sociological Introduction*. Cambridge: Polity.

Bartholomew, A. and Mayer, M. 1992: Nomads of the present: Melucci's contribution to 'new social movement' theory. *Theory, Culture and Society*, 9 (4), 141–59.

Bauman, Z. 1992: *Intimation of Postmodernity*. London: Routledge.

Blair, T. 1998: *The Third Way*. London: Fabian Society.

Branfield, F. 1998: What are you doing here? 'Non-disabled' people and the disability movement: a response to Robert F. Drake. *Disability and Society*, 13 (1), 143–4.

Branfield, F. 1999: The disability movement: a movement of disabled people – a response to Paul S. Duckett. *Disability and Society*, 14 (3), 399–403.

Campbell, J. and Oliver, M. 1996: *Disability Politics: Understanding Our Past, Changing Our Future*. London: Routledge.

Castells, M. 1996: *The Information Age: Economy, Society and Culture*, vol. 1: *The Rise of the Network Society*, Molden, MA: Blackwell.

Disability Rights Taskforce 1999: *From Exclusion to Inclusion*. London: Department for Education and Employment.

Doyal, L. and Doyal, L. 1984: Western scientific medicine: a philosophical and political prognosis. In L. Birke and J. Silvertown (eds), *More than the Parts: The Politics of Biology*. London: Pluto Press.

Drake, R. F. 1997: What am I doing here? 'Non disabled' people and the disability movement. *Disability and Society*, 12 (4), 643–5.

Drake, R. F. 2001: *The Principles of Social Policy*. Basingstoke: Palgrave.

Esping-Andersen, G. 1985: *Politics against Markets – the Social Democratic Road to Power*. Cambridge, MA: Harvard University Press.

Fagan, T. and Lee, P. 1997: 'New' social movements and social policy: a case study of the disability movement. In M. Lavelette and A. Pratt (eds), *Social Policy: A Conceptual and Theoretical Introduction*. London: Sage, 140–60.

Fairclough, N. 2000: *New Labour, New Language?* London: Routledge.

Finkelstein, V. 2002: The social model of disability repossessed. *Coalition* (February): Greater Manchester Coalition of Disabled People, 10–17.

Freedman, S. 1999: *A Critical Review of the Concept of Equality in UK Anti-Discrimination Laws*. Cambridge: University of Cambridge Centre for Public Law.

Giddens, A. 1991: *The Consequences of Modernity*. Cambridge: Polity.

Giddens, A. 1998: *The Third Way: The Renewal of Social Democracy*. Cambridge: Polity.

Giddens, A. 2000: *The Third Way and its Critics*. Cambridge: Polity.

Giddens, A. 2002: *Where Now For New Labour?* Cambridge: Polity.

Gooding, C. 1994: *Disabling Laws, Enabling Acts: Disability Rights in Britain and America*. London: Pluto Press.

Gooding, C, 2000: Disability Discrimination Act: from statute to practice. *Critical Social Policy*, 20 (4), 533–49.

Habermas, J. 1981: New social movements. *Telos*, 49, 33–7.

Habermas, J. 1987: *The Theory of Communicative Action*, vol. 2. Cambridge: Polity.

Hall, S. 1998: The great moving nowhere show. *Marxism Today*, November/December, 9–14.

Hall, S. and Jacques, M. 1989: *New Times*. London: Lawrence and Wisehart.

Harlow, C. and Rawlings, R. 1992: *Pressure through the Law*. London: Routledge.

Humphrey, J. C. 1999: Disabled people and the politics of difference. *Disability and Society*, 14 (2), 173–88.

Humphrey, J. C. 2000: Researching disability politics, or some problems with the social model in practice. *Disability and Society*, 15 (1), 63–85.

Hughes, B. and Paterson, K. 1997: The social model of disability and the disappearing body: towards a sociology of impairment. *Disability and Society*, 12, 325–40.

Johnstone, D. 1998: *An Introduction to Disability Studies*. London: Fulton.

Lee, P. and Raban, C. 1988: *Welfare Theory and Social Policy: Reform or Revolution*. London: Sage.

Lister, R. 1997: *Citizenship: Feminist Perspectives*. London: Macmillan.

Lupton, D. 1995: *The Imperative of Health*. London: Sage.

Mann, K. 1998: Lamppost modernism: traditional and critical social policy? *Critical Social Policy*, 18 (1), 77–102.

Martin, G. 2001: Social movements, welfare and social policy: a critical analysis. *Critical Social Policy*, 21 (3), 361–83.

Melucci, A. 1989: *Nomads of the Present: Social Movements and Individual Needs in Contemporary Society*. London: Hutchinson Radius.

Mouffe, C. 1998: The radical centre: politics without adversaries. *Soundings*, 9, 11–23.

Mulgan, G. 1998: Whinge and a prayer. *Marxism Today*, November/December, 15–16.

Mullard, M. and Spicker, P. 1998: *Social Policy in a Changing Society*. London: Routledge.

Oliver, M. 1990: *The Politics of Disablement*. Basingstoke: Macmillan.

Oliver, M. 1996: *Understanding Disability: From Theory to Practice*. Basingstoke: Macmillan.

Oliver, M. and Barnes, C. 1998: *From Exclusion to Inclusion: Social Policy and Disabled People*. London: Longman.

Pateman, C. 1988: *The Sexual Contract*. Cambridge: Polity.

Priestley, M. 1999: *Disability Politics and Community Care*. London: Jessica Kingsley.

Rae, A. 1989: What's in a name? *International Rehabilitation Review*, 8.

Rustin, M. 1999: A Third Way with teeth. *Soundings*, 11, 7–21.

Shakespeare, T. 1993: Disabled people's self-organisation: a new social movement? *Disability, Handicap and Society*, 8 (3), 249–64.

Shakespeare, T. and Watson, N. 1997: Defending the social model. *Disability and Society*, 12 (2), 293–300.

Swain, J. and French, S. 2000: Towards an affirmation view of disability. *Disability and Society*, 15 (4), 569–82.

Taylor-Gooby, P. 1985: *Public Opinion, Ideology and State Welfare*. London: Routledge & Kegan Paul.

Taylor-Gooby, P. (ed.) 1994: Postmodernism and social policy: a great leap backwards? *Journal of Social Policy*, 23 (3), 385–404.

Taylor-Gooby, P. (ed.) 2000: *Risk, Trust and Welfare*. Basingstoke: Macmillan.

Therborn, G. 1986: *Why Some People are More Unemployed than Others*. London: Verso.

Thompson, S. and Hoggett, P. 1996: Universalism, selectivism and particularism: towards a postmodern social policy. *Critical Social Policy*, 16 (1), 21–43.

Westergaard, J. 1999: Where does the third way lead? *New Political Economy*, 4, November.

Williams, F. 1994: Somewhere over the rainbow: universality and diversity in social policy. In N. Manning and R. Page (eds), *Social Policy Review*, vol. 4, London: Social Policy Association, 200–19.

Young, I. 1990: The ideal of community and the politics of difference. In L. Nicholson (ed.) *Feminism / Postmodernism*. London: Routledge, 300–23.

Zarb, G. 1993: The dual experience of ageing with a disability. In J. Swain, V. Finkelstein, S. French and M. Oliver (eds), *Disabling Barriers – Enabling Environments*, London: Sage, 186–95.

9

Academic Debates and Political Advocacy: The US Disability Movement

Harlan Hahn

Introduction

The issue of disability in the USA and elsewhere has reflected widely divergent orientations as well as radical shifts in public policy during the twentieth century. Contrary to popular belief, efforts to improve the status of disabled citizens have been marked by significant changes. Much of the variation can be explained by the fact that so-called experts and professionals have never been able to reach agreement on policies concerning the struggles of disabled people. Four issues in these developments seem especially important. First, most political changes have been preceded by an intense conflict among researchers and professionals about the most appropriate framework for studying disability. Second, despite the seemingly abstract – or even esoteric – nature of these debates, the outcome of the arguments has been shaped, at the end of the day, by social and political considerations rather than by the alleged success or failure of plans based on any of these studies. Third, even the limited or begrudging acceptance of a new approach ordinarily did not occur because an earlier paradigm was vanquished. Instead, prior theoretical constructs ordinarily have survived alongside the latest plans. Finally, at

This study was supported in part by a Mary Switzer Distinguished Rehabilitation Research Fellowship from the National Institute on Disability and Rehabilitation Research (NIDRR).

least until recently, disabled people themselves have seldom been invited to participate in such discussions.

Obviously these tendencies have had many different effects. One consequence has become particularly evident when the remedies implied by established paradigms have not been successful in achieving the results they initially appeared to promise. In such circumstances, researchers and policy makers have frequently been provoked to begin a renewed search for innovative ideas and creative solutions. Unfortunately, many of the individuals who formulated earlier measures have already invested so much intellectual energy and resources in existing plans that they are reluctant to advance new proposals. The capacity of politicians or professors to change their minds or to relinquish reputations based on previous work in order to pursue alternative solutions is rare.

The purpose of this analysis is to examine several different concepts that have previously been adopted as a basis for improving the status of disabled people and to explore new thoughts and proposals that might achieve this objective in coming years. Although an effort is made to include comparative data, this investigation focuses primarily on a case study of changes in US disability laws and programmes. The first section contains a brief history of disability policy, including the problems created by judicial resistance to anti-discrimination statutes such as the Americans with Disabilities Act. An attempt will be made to assess the strengths and weakness of proposals that stem from the emerging social model for research and advocacy on behalf of disabled people. The second portion assesses the threat to the lives of disabled citizens posed by plans such as rationing health care, assisted suicide and other medical interventions founded, in part, on quasi-utilitarian constructs and on cost–value analysis. The final part investigates several possible innovations implied by the principle of empowerment. In particular, emphasis is devoted here to the possibility of enhancing the strength of disabled citizens through permanent, systemic and institutional change in the policy-making process.

A brief history of disability policy

One dominant issue in early controversies surrounding disabled people and society has revolved about competing claims concerning the association between disability and work. Prior to the transition from feudalism to capitalism, many disabled individuals working in families supported by peasant farms and small shops made important contributions to household economies. Yet, policies dating from the early English Poor

Laws, which defined disabled people as almost the only group worthy of receiving so-called outdoor relief that did not require them to live in dreaded almshouses or workhouses, also seemed to be founded on the supposition that disability signified an inability to work. The first major disability policy adopted in the United States, for example, was designed to aid officers of the Revolutionary army who 'became so disabled as to prevent their... getting their livelihood, and may stand in need of relief' (quoted in Liachowitz 1988: 22). Such programmes were also designed exclusively for military officers, rather than enlisted personnel; money for the first such benefits was not appropriated by Congress until long after most eligible recipients had died. In the nineteenth century, the so-called Arrears Act of 1879 was enacted seemingly on the premiss that veterans who had survived for more than twenty years after the Civil War had become eligible through disability or other means to receive benefits that a Republican Congress wanted to dispense to former members of the Union army (Skocpol 1992). None the less, the keystone of US welfare policy, the Social Security Act, enacted during the administration of a powerful disabled president, was designed to provide government benefits only on the basis of age, not disability. During World War II, extensive provisions were made for the medical rehabilitation of veterans with disabilities. However, direct payments to unemployed disabled persons were not provided in the USA until a post-war compromise defining disability as an inability to engage in 'substantial gainful activity' was finally adopted by Congress (Erlanger and Roth 1985).

As Western nations emerged from the transition from feudalism to capitalism, as well as the separation of home and work, the economic value of disabled workers became a growing concern. Despite the prior resistance of the Supreme Court to almost any form of government regulation of the US economy, state workers' compensation laws were passed in the early twentieth century to protect labourers from serious injury or disability due to accidents in operating crude machinery (Erlanger and Roth 1985). Perhaps the principal public response to the growing problem of joblessness and begging among disabled citizens, however, was the introduction of vocational rehabilitation programmes. These plans were first adopted for disabled veterans of World War I, and they were broadened in 1920 to include unemployed disabled civilians (Obermann 1965). As predicted by Marx's concept of an 'industrial reserve army', when the demand for labour in defence industries increased during World War II due to the absence of young, non-disabled, heterosexual and predominantly white males serving in the military abroad, disabled workers, along with other oppressed groups such as ageing individuals, gays and lesbians, African-Americans, Latinos and housewives, were temporarily admitted to the work-force. Disabled adults, who compiled favourable work records during these years, were granted the opportunity to hold jobs primarily through the waiver of requirements that all employees pass a medical examination. But, with the massive return of non-disabled veterans after the war, these requirements were frequently reinstated; and unemployment among disabled workers continued to soar. The ubiquitous questions about disability on job applications and admission forms became a device primarily to sort out an excessive number of candidates during a period of high demand for employment and, thereby, to simplify the complex decisions that must be made in the hiring process. Despite the boasts of rehabilitation counsellors who claimed extraordinary success in job placements to impress gullible politicians, the incredible unemployment rate that plagued disabled persons in the USA and other industrialized countries remained at the level of approximately two-thirds (Bowe 1978; Hahn 1984). The major theme of rehabilitation research in the post-war years was an emphasis on so-called psychological adjustment (Abberley 1993), which in the USA could mean either a relentless struggle to 'overcome' an impairment or a passive acceptance of supposed limitations during extended periods of unemployment.

By the final quarter of the twentieth century, there was a growing search for new programmatic approaches to the social and economic problems that confronted disabled people everywhere in the world. In both developing and industrialized nations, disabled citizens have been compelled to encounter extraordinary levels of poverty; massive unemployment, formidable barriers to housing, transportation and freedom of movement, as well as exclusion or segregation in education and public accommodations. At least part of the source of these developments could be traced to extraordinarily high rates of unemployment; vocational programmes primarily for the most co-operative, middle-class and least impaired clients; as well as the lack of effective services for significantly impaired individuals. Hence, the initial objectives of the US Rehabilitation Act of 1973, which was finally passed by Congress over President Nixon's veto, included plans to conduct a study of environmental barriers, to reverse the priority in rehabilitation programmes that had previously favoured their least impaired clients, and to establish plans to aid disabled individuals for whom employment did not appear to be a 'feasible' economic goal. Perhaps the most crucial component to this measure, however, was an anti-discrimination clause known as Section 504, copied almost verbatim from the Civil Rights Act of 1964, that applied to institutions receiving 'substantial Federal financial assistance'. This clause was inserted in the rehabilitation bill by Congressional staff members almost as an afterthought (Scotch 1984). In accordance with conventional procedures, the Department of Health, Education and Welfare (HEW) was designated as the lead agency to draft administrative rules to implement this portion of the legislation. Despite attempts by disabled citizens to persuade government officials to sign the regulations, no action had been taken during three presidential administrations.

The first national law to protect disabled Americans from the effects of pernicious discrimination, therefore, was not enacted after an intense legislative controversy, a relentless struggle to gain broad political support, or massive public protests and demonstrations. Moreover, most of the members of Congress who voted for the final version of the Rehabilitation Act had little understanding of the content or meaning of Section 504. When HEW lawyers began to comprehend the sweeping implications – and the potential costs – of this legal requirement, top administrators responded by attempting – in a word that would eventually become an infamous part of the Washington lexicon – to 'stonewall' the issue, simply by not taking any action on it. Despite repeated efforts to persuade government officials to sign regulations drafted by attorneys, nothing had been done about the matter when President Jimmy Carter entered office in 1977. The unenviable task of choosing between the claims of disabled people and political worries about budgetary concerns as well as broad legal precedents, therefore, fell to Carter's new Secretary of Health, Education and Welfare, Joseph A. Califano, Jr. For a while Califano continued to stall, but the imperative to sign the regulations became almost inescapable when a group of disabled people organized sit-ins and protests at HEW offices and elsewhere. These demonstrations have been described as exemplary models of political protest (Johnson 1999; Shaw 1996). Another event that may have contributed to Califano's decision to sign the regulations on 28 April 1977 happened twenty-five days earlier. While disabled protesters were picketing his home, Califano suddenly realized that his dog was not in the house. Califano (1981: 260) allowed his imagined fears to influence his judgement. Later he said, 'I saw the television pictures and the newspaper headlines: CALIFANO DOG ATTACKS CRIPPLED WOMAN...CALIFANO DOG BITES BLIND MAN.'

The perception of rigid cultural norms that moulded Califano's behaviour certainly seemed to permit less discretion than the attitudes that shaped Sheriff Bull Connor's decision to use police dogs and fire hoses against a group of demonstrators led by the Rev. Martin Luther King, Jr., almost fifteen years earlier in Birmingham, Alabama. Califano's action may reveal the faint residue of paternalistic sentiments that had moulded non-disabled beliefs about disabled people for centuries; but the signing of the regulations signalled a victory that would open up opportunities for many new developments in the interpretation of disability rights.

Suddenly aware that the signing of the Section 504 regulations had actually been caused by these protests, the disabled segment of US society, which had been almost politically dormant even when a prominent disabled leader was elected President, began to stir slightly. Several new developments began to indicate that many disabled people were prepared to claim a direct role in decisions affecting their fate. At the University of Illinois and the University of California, Berkeley, for example, disabled college students demanded to leave hospitals and nursing homes in order to live on their own. This defiance of professional authority led to the emergence of the concept of independent living which was, at first, so closely intertwined with the struggle for equal rights that they were frequently described as the 'independent living/disability rights movement'. Other goals were sought in the courts by disabled individuals who initiated litigation (Olson 1984) before the formation of groups such as the Disability Rights Education and Defense Fund (DREDF). The trend marked by protests, demonstrations and acts of civil disobedience, of course, was also pursued in local incidents such as the one-day stoppage of bus traffic in Denver, Colorado, by 'the gang of nineteen' and the Rev. Wade Blank, one of the founders of a group known initially as Americans Disabled for Accessible Public Transportation (ADAPT).

Some of the changes that occurred in the disability rights movement are illustrated by transitions within ADAPT in the final quarter of the twentieth century. For several years, ADAPT focused on attempts to persuade the American Public Transit Association (APTA) to pass a resolution calling upon its membership, which consists primarily of municipal transportation bureaus, to provide full access to disabled passengers on public vehicles. Blocking the sightseeing buses of APTA delegates after their business meetings, wheelchair users frequently revived another theme from the civil rights movement by demanding 'access to the bus, even if it is the back of the bus'. APTA often called the police to arrest the demonstrators, and ADAPT leaders later held news conferences to disseminate information about the inaccessibility of local gaols.

While government policy on the accessibility of public buildings and transportation evolved at a glacial pace (Katzmann 1986), the conflict between ADAPT and APTA was constantly re-enacted throughout the 1980s. In the last decade of the century, however, several factors, including the death of the Rev. Blank, caused ADAPT to concentrate on efforts to get disabled men and women out of nursing homes and enabling them to gain the support needed to live in their own homes. ADAPT wanted to allocate a fraction of the funds designated for nursing homes and grant them directly to disabled individuals so that they could hire their own personal assistants and defray other costs of living independently. By replacing the American Public Transit Association with the nursing home industry, ADAPT challenged a formidable adversary. The issue, however, embodied numerous themes – including de-institutionalization, attendant or assistive services, and personal autonomy – that had been a significant part of the disability movement for years. Moreover, these acts of civil disobedience may have contributed to the growth of a new sense of personal and political identity among disabled citizens. A survey of ADAPT demonstrators, for example, found that more than half would not take a 'magic pill' to become cured; and these feelings were most closely related to a positive rather than a negative orientation toward their experience as disabled people (Hahn and Beaulaurier, in press).

Meanwhile, the instability stirred by the growing influence of disabled Americans was also reflected by a mounting debate among academicians engaged in the study of disability. While some members of the non-disabled public seemed willing to accept at least some of the objectives implied by the concept of independent living, researchers as well as ordinary citizens appeared to resist the goal of equal rights. During the last quarter-century, a group of university professors, many of whom were disabled themselves, began to dismantle the conventional paradigm that had long dominated investigations of disability. Oliver (1990) performed a crucial task by dissecting 'the sense of personal tragedy' that permeated perceptions of disability in Western culture. In addition, increasing controversy began to revolve around the definition of disability (Liachowitz 1988; Higgins 1992; Bickenbach 1993; Swain et al. 1993). Much of this debate also focused on a socio-political concept, which defined disability as the product of interactions between individuals and the surrounding environment (Hahn 1982, 1985a, 1985b, 1986b, 1987a, 1993a, 1993b). From this perspective, of course, disability can be perceived as the product of a disabling environment instead of organic impairments, defects or deficiencies. This understanding provided an agenda for the examination of topics such as personal identity, architectural or communications barriers, accessible transportation and public accommodations, and unfair practices in employment, education and government programmes. In addition, it formed the foundation for legal and political arguments about the principle of equality. Most disabled people simply wanted 'to level the playing field'. They did not seek special favours. They wished to gain the same rights and privileges that had been granted to non-disabled citizens. They sought only to be treated equally.

Many disabled Americans identified discrimination as the principal problem that they confronted in everyday life. This perception was founded on several sources of information. First, a large proportion recalled specific encounters in their lives when non-disabled persons had displayed unsophisticated and blatantly prejudicial attitudes. Because they had been told that they lived in a world where such opinions were virtually non-existent, these incidents were especially salient and hurtful. The assumptions that shaped their behaviour had been suddenly destroyed. They frequently felt vulnerable and defenceless. Similarly, some disabled people analysed factors such as circumstances and non-verbal behaviour to form an interpretation in which their disabilities represented the only possible explanation for rejection or animosity. The expectation of a few activists that the prohibition of discrimination would yield equal or impartial treatment for disabled people, however, was soon shattered. Finally, there is definitive empirical evidence of unfavourable attitudes towards disabled people in the research literature of the social sciences. While the dominance of a medical model of disability – as well as the absence of survey questions about visible or labelled traits that might elicit prejudicial reactions – precluded further analyses of this issue, the early psychological experiments by Kleck (1966) and the sociological studies concluded by Richardson (1970) and by Richardson and his colleagues (1968) provided strong and incisive data about attitudes toward disabled people that could be cited to build a persuasive case against bias and discrimination (Hahn 1996).

The quest for equality aroused intense covert resistance from the non-disabled majority. Some opponents simply felt that disabled people were biologically inferior. According to this belief, since disabled citizens did not possess the same abilities as their non-disabled counterparts, critics were not prepared to recognize that the alleged inequality of disabled persons was spawned primarily by a disabling environment instead of bodily impairments. While few so-called 'experts' seemed willing to claim publicly that disabled people were biologically inferior, the lack of a definitive refutation of this allegation fuelled lingering suspicions.

Part of the hidden opposition to the goals of disabled people also reflected a dawning realization that, if major features of the architectural and communications environment were no longer regarded as fixed or unalterable, the granting of equal status to disabled citizens would entail major expenditures. Unlike changes that had been achieved by other minority groups, the agenda of the disability rights movement carried a high price tag. In order to fulfil the promise of equal rights for all persons, the inclusion of disabled citizens in many facets of society required a sizeable allocation of economic resources. Both social institutions and physical structures would need to be changed permanently. Many entrenched interests recognized that spending increased funds to gain equal rights for disabled citizens necessarily meant that less money would be available for other purposes.

Most of the organizations that were secretly opposed to the objectives of disabled people, however, did not proclaim their resistance either in legislative chambers or in corridors haunted by lobbyists. They were probably influenced by the phenomenon of paternalism, which prevented non-disabled professionals and others from calling attention to the advantages they enjoyed as the alleged protectors of disabled people (Hahn 1983). Because of historical traditions that had defined disabled people as the 'deserving poor', the disability movement was enmeshed in a legacy of charity. Most non-disabled observers claimed that they were sympathetic to disabled people, even if they did not actively support their objectives. Paternalism implies that benefits for disabled people are motivated by private philanthropy instead of government decision making. Prevailing assumptions about charitable sentiments placed disabled people in an unequal and subordinate position, where they could expect support only from personal benefactors, not from the government or from themselves. Paternalism also prevented the emergence of opportunities for compromise or a healthy debate concerning disability policies. Since everyone appeared to favour increased rights for disabled people, the relative absence of conflicting opinions about solutions to the problem stemming from disability reduced the prominence of these issues. Politicians were reluctant to admit to their constituents that they had voted against rights for disabled people. Most of the bills endorsed by the disability rights movement were passed without major opposition and by overwhelming legislative majorities. Instead, as evidenced by the failure to sign the regulation for Section 504, most of the hidden disagreements about disability rights were revealed by official inaction concerning the implementation and enforcement of these laws. Decades after the acceptance both of the legislative provisions and of administrative rules that later accompanied them, observable evidence reveals pervasive non-compliance in many US communities with legal mandates to provide accessible facilities and programmes for persons with sensory and mobility impairments.

The prevalence of paternalistic sentiments, however, produced a situation in which many members of Congress were prepared to extend and expand legal rights. Disabled people were finally granted protection against discrimination in the private sector as well as within entities receiving 'substantial Federal financial assistance' that were covered by Section 504. Under the leadership of Senator Tom Harkin from Iowa, the Americans with Disabilities Act (ADA) was passed and signed by the President in 1990. The approval of this statute, which was the only measure to be endorsed by a conservative administration, seemed remarkable in many respects. The legislative history of the bill suggested that Congressional representatives who voted for the law also appeared to understand the social model of disability and the need to combat the discrimination imposed by a disabling environment. Most legal and other commentators anticipated that the principal controversy regarding the ADA would revolve around the clause requiring 'reasonable accommodations' in employment, public accommodations and other areas of everyday life (Hahn 1993a). This was the first legal provision to impose an affirmative obligation upon members of the dominant majority in order to bestow equal rights on a disadvantaged group.

Despite the potential threat that such mandates could be subverted either by inaction or by escalating opposition, many activists in the disability movement felt that they had achieved another unqualified victory. The path to securing equal rights for disabled Americans was amply buttressed by available literature in disability studies. Extending the arguments implied by the socio-political definition and the concept of a disabling environment, for example, I (Hahn 1987a, 1993a, 1994, 1996, 1997a) proposed a 'minority-group model' for the study of disability. From this perspective, the problems faced by disabled citizens are essentially similar to the difficulties encountered by other minorities. The basic issues are prejudice and discrimination evoked by visible or labelled human differences (Hahn 1988). Like other physical traits indicating age, race or ethnicity, and gender, the principle features differentiating disabled and non-disabled persons are frequently obvious and perceptible to others. In addition, visible characteristics signifying a disability usually are devalued. On other occasions, evidence of a so-called 'hidden disability' may be found only in dossiers, files and other sources containing information from medical records, employment applications, insurance forms and similar sources. Non-disabled people, of course, often react to both visible and labelled attributes of disabled individuals. These phenomena have prevented an explicit test of the 'minority-group model'. Nevertheless, there are strong reasons to believe that adverse reactions by non-disabled persons comprise the basic source of the problems of disabled people. As a result, like other minorities, disabled citizens have been plagued by social inequalities such as extraordinarily high rates of unemployment, poverty and welfare dependency; school segregation; inadequate housing and transportation; and exclusion from many public facilities that appear to be reserved exclusively for the non-disabled majority (Bowe 1978). Moreover, laws prohibiting discrimination on the basis of disability appeared to be the primary remedy for these obstacles.

One of the last remaining obstacles to the quest by disabled people for equal rights entailed the interpretation of anti-discrimination laws by the judicial branch of government. The first Supreme Court controversy involving Section 504 of the Rehabilitation Act of 1973 appeared to be a harbinger of future events. In 1979, by refusing to reverse the decision of a community college to deny admission to a nursing student because of her hearing impairment, the judges concluded that accommodations for disabled people could not 'fundamentally alter' the nature of a public programme (*Southeastern Community College v. Davis*, 442 U.S. 397). In *Cleburne v. Cleburne Living Center* (473 U.S. 432), a 5–4 decision by the justices held that discrimination against disabled Americans would not be struck down unless the acts violated the minimal constitutional standard of 'reasonableness'. Although this 1985 case invalidated a municipal ordinance banning 'group homes' for persons with developmental disabilities in residential neighbourhoods on the grounds that it was 'unreasonable', the finding seemed to imply that only the most blatant acts of bigotry and irrationality would be invalidated by the courts. Under the leadership of Chief Justice William Rehnquist, the Supreme Court also nullified a Bill of Rights for developmentally disabled people in 1981 (*Pennhurst v. Halderman*, 451 U.S. 1) and equal educational opportunities for disabled students in 1982 (*Rowley v. Hudson Central Board of Education*, 458 U.S. 176).

Perhaps more importantly, most appellate courts continue to subscribe to a 'functional limitations' rather than a 'minority group' model of disability. The crucial parts of Section 504 and the ADA which prohibit discrimination against 'otherwise qualified' disabled individuals were interpreted in a highly restrictive manner by US courts. The judges appeared to think that if plaintiffs alleging discrimination were disabled, they could not be 'otherwise qualified'. Conversely, of course, if they were 'otherwise qualified,' they could not be disabled. By the end of the twentieth century, the misunderstanding of disability in American law was so grievous that some disabled researchers began to urge the movement to abandon a strategy based solely on lawsuits and to explore other means of seeking political objectives (Hahn in press). After nearly forty years of litigation, the courts seemed reluctant to heed the plea of Jacobus tenBroek (1966) to grant disabled people 'the right to live in the world'.

The pursuit of political and conceptual alternatives

Increasing disillusionment with the legal process prompted many disabled researchers and activists in the USA to pursue alternative means of fulfilling their aspirations. In addition to litigation, another major objective of the disability movement has revolved about strategies to enhance the political influence of disabled citizens. Eventually, a significant proportion of disabled people appeared to begin to consider the struggle to improve their status in society as a more significant aspiration than their own personal rehabilitation. The first national survey of disabled Americans disclosed in 1986 that the largest percentage felt that disabled persons are 'a minority group in the same sense as are Blacks and Hispanics' (Harris 1986: 114). The fundamental goals of the disability movement are nearly identical to the aim of other minorities. They are striving to improve their status in society. They want to achieve genuine equality, or parity between the privileges afforded disabled and non-disabled citizens. In addition, the tactics adopted by disadvantaged groups, which range from community organizing to non-violent civil disobedience, are essentially similar. Perhaps the primary differences between the experience of disabled people and other minorities are reflected in the residual effects of medical concepts that have been inherited from earlier studies of disability.

Quality of life

In many respects, the search outside the court-room for methods of improving the status of disabled people seemed to converge with a growing interest in the consequences of health care. Increasingly, doctors became discontented with a continual – and almost exclusive – emphasis on refining their procedures and forms of treatment. In a period of growing medical costs and fiscal stringency, the emphasis on the effects of professional intervention promoted intensified attempts to measure health care outcomes. This trend coincided with a mounting demand to scrutinize the conduct of professionals (Haug and Sussman 1969). In addition, legal restrictions prompted by the exposure of grave violations of ethical principles compelled health professionals to secure the consent of the client before embarking on most interventions (Rothman 1991). The first attempts to assess the satisfaction or dissatisfaction of patients or clients were, of course, denounced as too subjective by medical researchers. Thus, scientists began to search for other methods of analysing the consequences of their practices.

The barriers to the study of health care outcomes for disabled people seem to be especially formidable. By definition, of course, impairments are usually permanent. The purpose of medical rehabilitation is not to eradicate a functional problem. Despite the desire of many physicians to 'fix' what they view as unacceptable bodily anomalies, often the most that can be expected from a lengthy process of rehabilitation is the arrest of a steady deterioration of physical or mental attributes. 'Cure', or even the amelioration of chronic conditions, is usually not a viable prospect. Researchers cannot easily measure improvements in such characteristics. Although some studies have attempted to appraise personal improvements, a great deal of research on outcomes has consisted of investigations within separate diagnostic categories. From the perspective of disability studies, however, diagnostic classifications may be of limited value. While they may help to identify useful information about the aetiology or cause of impairments for planning prevention strategies, they provide little data either about the functional status of a disabled individual or about the presence of traits that may spawn prejudice and discrimination. Finally, the standards posed by 'quality of life' have often been invoked to the detriment of disabled people. One of the first versions of the notion of 'quality of life', for example, appeared in the 'bioethical' formula: $QL = NE \times (H + S)$, where NE is natural endowment, H is home, and S is society (Shaw 1977). However, within the same society, S drops out of the equation, so $QL = NE \times H$. In other words, where people in society are treated similarly, 'quality of life' is determined by 'natural endowment' times the influence of the 'home'. And the 'home' variable generally reflects the inheritance from parents and opportunities shaped by socio-economic status. To put it simply – and, some might claim, crudely – non-disabled rich people enjoy a higher 'quality of life' than persons who are poor and disabled. The 'formula', therefore, merely becomes a tautology. Nourishment and water have sometimes been withheld from disabled infants and adults, who are 'allowed' to die because the prospects for their lives do not meet the expectations of medical practitioners.

In addition, relatively few studies have focused on the social participation of disabled people after they leave hospitals or rehabilitation facilities. In fact, an investigation employing the Craig Handicap Assessment and Reporting Technique (CHART) discovered no relation between the community reintegration sub-scale and other predictors of rehabilitation effectiveness. The Harris survey (1986: 37–41) found that disabled people were much less likely than their non-disabled counterparts to engage in everyday activities such as shopping at supermarkets, eating at restaurants, attending concerts or seeing films, and visiting neighbours or friends. In fact, much of the isolation and exclusion of disabled people can be attributed to the prevalence of architectural and communications barriers, even where they are prohibited by law, that frequently prevent them from leaving their own dwellings or 'back bedrooms'.

The increasing realization that disabled people might sometimes need to move beyond their homes and enter the outside world gradually encouraged the development of measurements that departed from strictly clinical assessments by encompassing the external environment. One of the first significant steps in this direction was taken when the *International Classification of Impairments, Disabilities, and Handicaps* (*ICIDH*) was published by the World Health Organization (1980). This classification scheme included a separate category called 'Handicap', for 'a disadvantage...resulting from an impairment or a disability, that limits or prevents the fulfillment of a role that is normal (depending on age, sex, and social and culture factors) for that individual' (WHO 1980: 183). While some disabled leaders viewed this category as an opportunity to collect important data about environmental accessibility, others felt that the *ICIDH* signified the first wave of a renewed eugenics movement (Pfeiffer 1998). One valuable by-product of the *ICIDH*, however, was a model that incorporated environmental dimensions in plans for research on disability (Fougeyrollas et al. 1998). Finally, environmental components of research on disability were featured prominently in an important Institute of Medicine (1997) report on rehabilitation science and engineering. Despite these indications of gradual progress toward the acceptance of measures that would incorporate environmental as well as intra-personal variables in assessing health care outcomes, most medical rehabilitation professionals preferred to engage in arduous and often futile attempts to operationalize a concept such as 'quality of life' that allegedly could be related in a more direct manner to clinical evaluations of individual functioning. A review of articles containing 'quality-of-life' instruments disclosed troubling inconsistencies. Within a relatively short period of time, however, research and publications on measures of Health-Related Quality of Life (HRQOL) expanded profusely. Many of these conceptualizations were promoted by international scientists such as the WHOQOL Group, the EuroQOL Group, REAVES (the International Network on Health Expectancy and the Disability Process), and similar informal as well as formal organizations. Reiser (1993) noted that interest in the perceptions of the so-called 'patient' and the appraisal of 'quality of life' eventually converged.

Another major impetus for the increasing popularity of so-called quality of life measures emerged, ironically, from trends in the social sciences. Prominent researchers in the 1960s who witnessed dramatic outbreaks of ghetto violence prompted by long-standing grievances began to dream about the possibility of conducting periodic surveys to gather data on 'social indicators' similar to the economic indicators that had been used so successfully as a basis for fiscal policy. Drawing upon Cantril's (1965) studies of 'self-anchoring scales', in which respondents were asked to indicate their position on a ten-rung ladder representing the best (top) and worst (bottom) life they could lead, social scientists sought to fashion instruments that could be used longitudinally in frequent surveys (Campbell et al. 1976). Along with employment and family life, health was consistently rated throughout the world as one of three principal human concerns. Perhaps the major drawbacks to the 'social indicators' movement, however, entailed both the difficulty of applying them in a deterministic manner to complex phenomena such as urban uprisings and the inability to find a funding source willing to invest as much in social problems as it spends on economic forecasts.

The proliferation of the so-called health-related quality of life measures, however, seemed destined to continue unabated. Biomedical scientists appeared to stumble over themselves in a frantic rush to discover a composite indicator of health outcomes, both to satisfy the demands of administrators who sought to end escalating costs and to attract a consensus among professional colleagues that could yield personal rewards for the inventor of such an instrument. The inappropriateness of the use of such scales in the study of disability is indicated by evidence revealing that disabled people tend to rate the quality of their lives higher than most non-disabled individuals (Albrecht and Devlieger 1999). A significantly disabled psychotherapist reported that many of her clients who were almost comatose derived pleasure from 'the sensuous touch of the sheets on the skin'. Most HRQOL assessments, however, were based on clinical definitions that restrict the measure of observable differences in outcomes to organic conditions within the human body. Implicit within these measures is the incorrect and unspoken assumption that 'quality of life' is a direct, unmediated reflection of physiological traits, and that impaired people must, therefore, experience a lower quality of life than individuals without bodily impairments. Despite the supposed familiarity of health professionals with the controversy about the so-called handicap dimension of the *International Classification of Impairments, Disabilities, and Handicaps*, these scientists were reluctant either to extend their research beyond the physiological boundaries of the body or to admit researchers from other disciplinary traditions into the exclusive province of medical investigations. As a result, social or environmental measures were neither accepted as a supplement nor appended to the clinical or biomedical model.

Continual reliance on the clinical approach in nearly all branches of the health sciences imposes additional restraints on the progress of such investigations. The well-established standards of 'universal design' or an accessible environment for disabled people were never added to the 'medical model'. For many disabled persons who actually know that their organic conditions cannot be ameliorated and for health practitioners who realize that they cannot 'fix' or repair such impairments, changes that make the surrounding environment more accessible may represent the only feasible means of improving major facets of life, including their mobility, navigational skills, community participation and opportunities for social interactions with families, neighbours and friends. Without an accessible environment and public or private transportation, many disabled people are condemned to live indefinitely either in institutions or in their own domiciles and 'back bedrooms', where they remain virtually incarcerated without any real chance to interact with other human beings. Disabled people are seldom confined to wheelchairs, but often they are confined to nursing homes, residential institutions, houses or apartments. They are frequently barred from obtaining needed health care or social services simply because architectural or communication barriers prevent them from 'getting from here to there'. The persistent adherence to a clinical perspective that has excluded the accessibility of the environment from analysts of 'health-related quality of life' has prevented researchers from exploring many significant issues. Obviously, the most important advances in human mortality have resulted from environmental rather than clinical changes, through improved sanitation and related policies adopted in nineteenth-century cities. As organized medicine acquired increasing power in the twentieth century, however, the dominant emphasis in health affairs shifted from the analysis of public policies that affect large numbers of people to the refinement of clinical techniques performed on individuals. As a result, the major unit of analysis in health-related research reflected a corresponding tendency to move from aggregate entities such as governmental jurisdiction to the free-standing individual.

This trend has had the unfortunate consequence of inhibiting the development of adequate measures for rigorous examination of the impact of government policy on public health. Analyses of such policies and programmes have not been fully or effectively integrated into the study of health services. At least, this research literature has not provided political leaders with clear guidance about the best means of improving public health. These lacunae have had a detrimental impact on disabled people. In particular, the absence of such investigations has impeded the ability of researchers to answer many crucial questions.

Do disabled residents of communities that strictly enforce laws requiring accessible public accommodations, for example, enjoy increased social interaction and participation in comparison with counterparts who live in localities that have not fully implemented such statutes? Such an investigation would clearly seem consistent with the 'assessment' function of public health. Does the reduced social isolation and confinement that may presumably result from such legislation have a positive effect on personal health or longevity?

The use of traditional methods to examine 'health-related quality of life', however has also confronted two other obstacles. What is 'health'? What is 'quality'? The first issue, of course, revived debate about the WHO definition of health as a state of complete physical, mental and social well-being, rather than simply the absence of disease. This formulation has frequently been attacked as too idealistic. For many years, few, if any, prominent scholars devoted their work exclusively to the search for a more practical meaning. Most theoreticians and practitioners seemed content to allow health to be defined by an individual need which represented a deficiency from a condition that was often approximated by a bell-shaped curve or some notion of 'normality'. Such a conceptualization appeared to work reasonably well in a period dominated by acute problems, in which the subjective appraisal of signs or symptoms represented need, and a cure was the desired outcome. In this paradigm, of course, disabled people were usually perceived as individuals with deficiencies from a customary norm, or as 'outliers' on a bell-shaped curve, who could not be helped by conventional techniques. Gradually, as predominant health concerns shifted from acute to chronic difficulties, 'cure' no longer represented a feasible outcome. In fact, disabled participants in civil disobedience who tended to express favourable attitudes about many of their experiences with disability also stated that they would reject a 'cure', even if it were offered to them (Hahn and Beaulaurier, in press). The change from predominantly 'acute' to 'chronic' health problems meant that researchers had to redefine both 'need' and outcomes as practicable objectives.

People with chronic conditions frequently seek health care for secondary conditions, but may seldom 'need' medical treatment because of permanent impairments. Often the most that doctors can do for disabled individuals is to treat ordinary health problems or to monitor increases or decreases in functional capabilities. Full cognizance of the implications of these circumstances may require a significant redefinition of common medical objectives. For many years, such goals have revolved around the implications of morbidity *and* mortality. In the modern era, however, chronic limitations cannot be eliminated. Even though people with chronic health problems can survive, the full restoration of 'normal' functioning is usually not a viable prospect. A crucial question that appears to emerge from these trends, therefore, might be stated as follows: If 'cure' is not an appropriate goal of medical intervention in chronic health problems, what can disabled people reasonably expect from health professionals? What should health professionals expect of themselves? How can their efforts be measured? What are the criteria for success or failure?

Possible answers to such questions have not yet reached the level of extensive public discussion. Some disabled people have urged that rigid evaluations need to be applied to professional conduct in order to prevent further damage, and a few have even proposed that the goal of 'fixing' impairments be abandoned so that physicians and scientists can concentrate exclusively on the aim of extending life. Most non-disabled people still appear to believe that they must consult medical experts when a disabling incident occurs or, at least, that few other service providers can effectively engage in these activities. And the demand for norms or criteria regarding the performance of these duties seems almost inevitable.

Even more fundamentally, there seems to be a pressing need to revamp the theoretical framework in which the standard of 'quality of life' initially emerged. The basic precepts of the principles of utilitarianism are, of course, guided by the familiar maxim about 'the greatest good for the greatest number'. Almost by definition, since disabled people are probably destined to remain a minority for several decades, they are not likely to benefit from the application of judgements based on such logic. Utilitarianism appears to fit most comfortably in a legal context of individualistic choice based on the concept of liberty rather than the standard of equality. In addition, choice often implies a trade-off between people or goods of greater or lesser value. Thus, health care practices that yield the most benefit for the largest number of people ordinarily can be expected to provide rewards primarily for the non-disabled segment of the population that fits in the area under the 'normal' curve within a fraction of a standard deviation from the mean.

Perhaps even more fundamentally, utilitarian concepts have been adopted as a foundation for 'cost–benefit' or 'cost–value' calculations, yielding an outcome that justifies neglect of the needs and interests of disabled citizens. The clearest example is the concept of DALYs, literally Disability Adjusted Life Years. This formulation, which emerged from a project sponsored by the World Bank, seemed to combine indices of mortality, or death, and morbidity, or 'a diseased state' of some kind, into a single measure of 'health'. Disability is defined exclusively both as a negative factor that detracts from a healthy life and as a form of ill health that imposes a substantial 'burden' on society as well as the individual. Part of the fallacy of this concept appears to reflect confusion about the concepts of disability, sickness or illness, disease and impairment. Disability is neither a disease, a term that often stands for diagnostic classifications, nor a sickness, a word that usually implies an acute health problem from which a person can be expected to recover fully. Nor does it result exclusively from bodily impairments; in fact, disability is produced primarily by the effects of a disabling environment. Disability may be, in part, a chronic or persistent condition; but, since environmental configurations are seldom unalterable, it can be mitigated or ameliorated especially through improvements in the architectural and communications milieux. It is entirely possible to have a significant disability and to be perfectly 'healthy', in the conventional meaning of the term, simultaneously. DALYs not only signify an outdated notion; this measure also seems oddly incongruent in an era in which growing numbers of disabled people are beginning to consider disability as a positive source of personal and political identity, as well as an experience from which many valuable perspectives can be derived (Groce et al. 1999; Hahn 1997a).

Perhaps most importantly, DALYs pose a substantial danger to the lives and well-being of disabled people. As Nord (1999: 123) concluded, this threat 'is a heritage from utilitarian thinking in the QUALY approach, in which...the equal valuation of life for disabled people was not recognized as a salient societal concern'. The widespread use of DALYs and the increasing costs of medical treatment could promote numerous life-threatening plans, including a revival of the eugenics movement, the rationing of health care, and the legalization of euthanasia. For many disabled people, breathing an atmosphere fostered by ideas that characterize 'a healthy life' as 'living without a disability' has been permeated by the stale, sweet taste of death. Many disabled people have privately expressed the fear that the paternalistic attitudes displayed by the non-disabled may actually conceal unacceptable feelings of hostility and repugnance that, if they were ever to become exposed, might be related to a repressed desire even to kill disabled people. Obviously, women would feel justifiably threatened by the prevalence of measures that weight life as a female as only a fraction of the value of the life of males. Yet, for reasons which have not been fully uncovered and which comprise a pressing mandate for future scholars in disability studies, the general public does not display similar reactions when this formula is applied to disabled people. Although the World Bank has claimed that the DALYs score of a particular country will not be used as a basis for decisions about the extension or foreclosure of loans, there is nothing to prevent other agencies from using the statistic in this manner. Many nations might curtail social services to disabled people in the belief that fewer services might mean fewer disabled citizens, which would reduce costs and contribute to a higher DALYs measure, to convey the impression of a healthy and productive work-force. One example of the application of these concepts to contemporary American policy was provided by efforts of the state of Oregon to obtain a waiver from Federal Medicaid standards by rationing health care on the basis of discriminatory priorities from a public opinion survey that were deemed inconsistent with the ADA (US Department of Health and Human Services 1992). Eventually, other political leaders may find it difficult, if not impossible, to resist the temptation to invoke such medical excuses, which were used during the Holocaust to exterminate millions of disabled people.

Obviously there is a pressing need for an alternative method of measuring advances toward the goals of the disability movement. Experience in the United States has demonstrated that the principles of civil rights embodied in laws such as Section 504 and the ADA have been subverted by the reliance of the courts upon an antiquated functional understanding of disability that has prevented disabled people from fulfilling the aspirations implied by this legislation. Moreover, the utilitarian suppositions embedded in 'quality of life' measures have redounded to the disadvantage – and even to the life-threatening detriment – of disabled people. Consequently, a high priority must be assigned in coming years to the search for objectives and strategies to replace concepts that have been exposed as antithetical to the interests of the disability rights movement. In fact, without a new agenda and priorities, there is a danger that the movement could flounder and lose its sense of purpose.

Empowerment: an alternative remedy

Perhaps one of the most popular recent strategies for social change has revolved around the concept of empowerment. Unlike quasi-utilitarian notions that emphasize principles of liberty and free choice almost to the exclusion of other values, empowerment seems to imply at least an opportunity to consider the standard of equality. A fundamental goal of empowerment is to increase the influence of relatively powerless sectors of society. Since disabled people comprise a group that has been significantly disadvantaged by the environment surrounding them, empowerment would mean that they could eventually be elevated to a level commensurate with the benefits traditionally enjoyed by their non-disabled counterparts. The first stage of the agenda, therefore, might be achieved merely by 'leveling the playing field'. Part of this task would require that criteria take into account the so-called taken-for-granted environment that confers major privileges upon non-disabled persons and corresponding disadvantages upon disabled people (Hahn 2000). The disability movement cannot become a full participant in decisions about the distribution of resources until this initial goal is accomplished.

There is, however, still considerable debate about whether the struggle by disabled people for equal rights is a zero-sum game. From one vantage point, resources may appear to be so plentiful that the interests of a minority such as disabled Americans can be accommodated without disturbing the rewards that have previously been allocated to other segments of the population. By contrast, some analysts may contend that granting the demands of disabled citizens would entail redistribution of resources that could require political leaders to take privileges away from groups that traditionally have enjoyed them. The latter prospect obviously entails more political difficulties than the former scenario. Even when dominant interests display a supposedly sympathetic or paternalistic attitude toward disabled people, there is still a strong likelihood that powerful groups will not voluntarily surrender their traditional advantages for altruistic reasons.

Since disabled people seem destined to remain a minority at least until longevity extends beyond existing parameters, it is also unlikely that they can fulfil all their aspirations within the confines of a political system based on the rule of the majority. Certainly, there are some strategies that disabled people can pursue to enhance their influence. Perhaps one of the most important of these is the effort to redefine disability as a positive source of identity instead of a trait enveloped by feelings of shame or inferiority. This way of expanding the constituency of disabled people admittedly rests upon the shaky premiss that votes count in free elections, that the verdict of the electorate exerts some influence on the selection of government representatives, and that political institutions are capable of shaping the behaviour of financial élites. Many Americans believe that all these myths were shattered by the presidential elections of 2000. But, in a supposedly democratic country, politics appears to remain the only possible means by which ordinary people can seek to shape the policies that affect their lives. The mobilization of alienated citizens has not *yet* seemed to emerge as a viable option. In addition, leaders of the disability rights movement must always be mindful of the possibility of improving the status of disabled people through sweeping changes in the economic system. Capitalism is undoubtedly a root cause of the oppression of disabled people, and any act that diminishes the stranglehold of this form of control on human behaviour must be counted as an achievement for the movement.

Perhaps one of the most effective means of securing empowerment for disabled people, however, involves permanent systematic alterations in the decision-making process. Some local governments in the USA have attempted to augment the legislative strength of racial or ethnic minorities through devices such as proportional representation, which permits the weighting of votes and sometimes the recounting of ballots based on second or third choices after winners with a specified number of first choices have been selected. Other localities have experimented with cumulative voting, which allows the electorate to distribute votes for candidates in various combinations in order to maximize the strength of their preferences (Guinier 1994). Yet these measures were frequently repealed after their consequences were revealed, and they have seldom achieved the desired results. Unless the strivings of disabled people have a continuing effect on the political and economic institutions of a nation or the globe, they may never exert an impact that extends beyond a temporary and constantly shifting score-card of wins and losses. Animus toward disabled people seems to be an endemic and deep-seated characteristic of most cultures of the world. Thus, the battles of the disability movement cannot be waged solely within the confines of the existing political process; they must also seek to impose an imprint on the structure of society. In addition, and perhaps most importantly, the empowerment of disabled people must be permanent. In a legacy within social work that has been perpetuated by early works about community organizing, empowerment is frequently equated with a temporary intervention into a neighbourhood or locality that is intended to have lasting and sustained effects. Ironically, political science, as a discipline that is supposed to be concerned with the issues of power, minority rights and majority rule, has devoted relatively little attention to the concept of empowerment. Studies by Browning, Marshall and Tabb (1984) have suggested that local ethnic groups are often able to satisfy their political goals through governing coalitions; but another investigation indicated that the empowerment of disadvantaged groups may be relatively short-lived after the election of a minority candidate to high public office (Gillam 1998).

Perhaps the principal countries in which disabled people have been granted the greatest opportunity to participate in government decision making, however, are Uganda and South Africa. Although Western lawmakers may be unwilling ordinarily to accept recommendations born in developing nations, increased attention might be devoted to justifications for the creation of seats on local councils that are reserved for representatives of disadvantaged groups, including disabled people. Democratic government must be concerned not only about majoritarian rule; it must also discover mechanisms by which groups such as mentally and physically disabled people, ex-convicts and others who have been almost permanently excluded from the political process may be able to secure official recognition of their needs and interests. Details of this proposal, such as decisions about the citizens who would participate in the selection of representatives, as well as the qualifications of office-holders who would occupy these seats, could be negotiated after governments endorse the principles of the plan. By seeking a voice on local councils, disabled people would not be asking for pity or charity. Instead, they would be seeking to become full participants in political decision making on an equal basis with the non-disabled portion of society. As a result, establishing seats to represent disadvantaged and marginalized groups should also be regarded, at least in the USA, as an effort to fulfil a frequently neglected commitment to diversity and inclusion.

Conclusion

Disabled people, like other minorities, have followed a long and somewhat tortuous path toward full inclusion in social, economic and political structures. They have been told that they must complete long and seemingly senseless rehabilitation programmes in order to work; and later they were granted public benefits for *not* working. Many disability policies in the nineteenth and early twentieth centuries were designed to support groups such as Republican Congressmen, who sought to reinforce the loyalties of Civil War veterans with specious assumptions about the link between ageing and disability almost twenty years after the war. Similarly, the conflict between labourers and business interests that were willing to support workers' compensation laws to protect themselves from the dangers of crude machinery and the potential liability that could result from a shift in prevailing legal doctrines about employer responsibilities. Rehabilitation measures, of course, were introduced after World War I in part to avoid the embarrassment of unemployed disabled veterans begging on city streets. Subsequently, however, employers were permitted to continue the discriminatory practice of using questions on employment applications or visible evidence from interviews to sort out – and to reject – disabled workers seeking jobs; and the unemployment rate for disabled workers has held consistently at approximately two-thirds. Only during World War II, when most young non-disabled males were in military service, were disabled people admitted to the labour force, ordinarily through the waiver of medical requirements. After this war, disabled veterans were offered medical rehabilitation to 'fix' their impairments; and disabled civilians in vocational rehabilitation were told by psychiatrists and administrators that their inability to find jobs could be ascribed to a lack of psychological 'adjustment'. In addition, Congress finally enacted social welfare policies to provide SSI and SSDI payments to disabled people who were declared to be 'unable to engage in substantial gainful activity'.

The relatively abrupt shift to civil rights remedies began with the adoption, almost as an afterthought, of Section 504 of the Rehabilitation Act of 1973. Perhaps even more importantly, the failure of several administrations to sign regulations to implement the law, prompted a series of sit-ins and protests that contributed significantly to the birth of the disability movement in the USA. Early indications of unremitting judicial attempts to undercut such laws were revealed by an initial Supreme Court case in which a hearing-impaired nurse was denied acceptance by a community college programme on the grounds that her admission would result in a 'fundamental alteration' of the curriculum. Despite such forewarnings, Congress continued to pass even more stringent bans against disability discrimination, including the Individuals with Disabilities Education Act (IDEA), the Civil Rights Restoration Act and the Americans with Disabilities Act (ADA). In subsequent litigation, however, the Court decided that disabled people were not entitled to a strong defence against discrimination under the 'equal protection' clause of the Fourteenth Amendment to the US Constitution; that a deaf student who was merely passed by her teachers was receiving an 'appropriate' education, even though she may not have been able to learn what was being said in the classroom; that disabled people in institutions may not claim 'habilitation' or other minimal forms of training; and that a Bill of Rights for developmentally disabled people was not really a 'bill of rights' after all. Plaintiffs were frequently caught in a dilemma by judicial interpretations of statutes prohibiting discrimination against 'otherwise qualified' disabled individuals and, if they were 'otherwise qualified', they could not be disabled. Similarly, numerous appellate courts have refused to apply the ADA against employers who fired personnel suspected of having AIDS merely because they did not have the symptoms of the disease. Many of these results could be attributed to judicial understandings of the functional thrust of the definition of disability in ADA. Although this clause also prohibited discrimination against persons who are 'regarded as' having a disability or who have a 'history' of disability, courts have viewed medical evidence of a functional impairment as an essential pre-condition for legal findings about disability. Perhaps at least part of the explanation for this interpretation can be ascribed to the absence of data based on the visible or labelled characteristics of a disability. Visibility and labelling can be operationalized, and information about these attributes would not be difficult to collect; but neither the government nor private foundations have exhibited much interest in funding the surveys. Once again, public policies can be traced to the availability of research findings and to the theoretical or conceptual orientations that guide such investigations.

The strong popular interest in quasi-utilitarian concepts of 'quality of life' that emerged during the latter part of the twentieth century, along with a mounting concern for measuring the costs and outcomes of health care, prompted a relatively detailed analysis of the effects of this approach on disabled people. Thinly concealed within this perspective, for example, are majoritarian assumptions that tend to treat disabled people as 'outliers' or deviants from the norms prescribed by a bell-shaped curve. Perhaps even more significantly, utilitarianism seems to be an inappropriate source of measurements related to disability or chronic health conditions. Emerging from an era in which the signs or symptoms of acute sickness indicated a need for medical treatment, the difficulty of measuring outcomes has been exacerbated by the prevalence of chronic problems which denote the absence of such a 'cure' and the persistence of the condition. Perhaps the most dangerous aspect of 'quality of life' measures involves their use in 'cost–benefit' or 'cost–value' calculations, in which the worth of disabled people is purposely diminished in relation to non-disabled persons. Another manifestation of the inordinate stress on 'quality of life' is revealed by the invention of so-called DALYs, which purport to measure 'health' by subtracting the number of years lived with a disability from the longevity of individuals. Such concepts have provoked a major fear among disabled people about a possible resurgence of eugenics, euthanasia and the rationing of health.

The defects of existing conceptualizations have sparked a new search for a replacement for prior methods of assessing the status of disabled people. In this analysis, the principle of 'empowerment' is proposed as an excellent potential replacement for earlier measures. Unlike utilitarian notions that emphasize choice almost to the exclusion of other values, empowerment also encompasses an opportunity to examine the issue of equality. In fact, empowerment is often characterized by an increase in the social, economic and political influence of disadvantaged groups in relation to privileged segments of society. In fields such as social work, empowerment has tended to revolve around temporary interventions that are supposed to produce enduring effects. Experiments with proportional representation, cumulative voting and 'gerrymandering' have seldom produced the results desired by their originators. But the prospects for disabled people being able to satisfy their aspirations without systemic and permanent modifications of the decision-making process are slight. The high levels of political participation displayed by disabled people in Uganda and South Africa may provide a foundation for a debate about new arrangements such as the representation of disabled and other disadvantaged people through reserved seats in local councils. Both the dissatisfaction aroused by prior approaches and the promise indicated by untried plans demonstrate the need for a lively debate about the future of disabled people framed by innovative approaches to the controversy.

REFERENCES

Abberley, P. 1993: Disabled people and 'normality'. In J. Swain, V. Finkelstein, S. French and M. Oliver (eds), *Disabling Barriers – Enabling Environments*, London: Sage, 107–15.
Albrecht, G. L. and Devliger, P. 1999: The disability paradox: high quality of life against all odds. *Social Science and Medicine*, 48, 977–88.
Bickenbach, J. E. 1993: *Physical Disability and Social Policy*. Toronto: University of Toronto Press.
Bickenbach, J. E., Chattedi, S., Badley, E. and Ustun, T. B. 1999: Models of disablement, universalism, and the international classification of impairments, disabilities, and handicaps. *Social Science and Medicine*, 48, 1173–87.
Bowe, F. 1978: *Handicapping America: Barriers to Disabled People*. New York: Harper & Row.
tenBroek, J. 1966: The right to live in the world: the disabled in the law of torts. *California Law Review*, 54, 841–64.
Browning, R. P., Marshall, D. R., and Tabb, D. H. 1984: *Protest is not Enough: The Struggle of Blacks and Hispanics for Equality in Urban Politics*. Berkeley: University of California Press.
Califano, J. 1981: *Governing America: An Insider's Report from the White House and the Cabinet*. New York: Simon & Schuster.
Campbell, A., Converse, P. and Rodgers, W. L. 1976: *The Quality of American Life: Perceptions, Evaluations, and Satisfactions*. New York: Russell Sage Foundation.
Cantril, H. 1965: *The Pattern of Human Concerns*. New Brunswick, NJ: Rutgers University Press.
Dijkers, M. P. J. M., Whiteneck, G. and El-Jaroudi, R. 2000: Measures of social outcomes in disability research. *Archives of Physical Medicine and Rehabilitation*, 81, supp. 2, S63–80.
Erlanger, H. S. and Roth, W. 1985: Disability policy: the parts and the whole. *American Behavioral Scientist*, 28 (3), 319–45.

Fougeyrollas, P., Noreau, L., Bergeron, H., Cloutier, R., Dion, S. A., and St Michel, G. 1998: Social consequences of long-term impairments and disabilities: conceptual approach and assessment of handicap. *International Journal of Rehabilitation Research*, 21 (1), 127–41.

Gillam, K. L. 1998: Is there an empowerment life cycle? *Urban Affairs Review*, 33, 741–66.

Groce, N., Chamie, M., and Me, A. 1998: Measuring the quality of life: rethinking the World Bank's disability adjusted life years. *International Rehabilitation Research Review*, 4, 12–16.

Guinier, L. 1994: *The Tyranny of the Majority: Fundamental Fairness in Representative Democracy*. New York: Free Press.

Hahn, H. 1982: Disability and rehabilitation policy: is paternalistic neglect really benign? *Public Administration Review*, 43. 385–9.

Hahn, H. 1983: Paternalism and public policy. *Society*, 20, 36–46.

Hahn, H. 1984: *The Issue of Equality: European Perceptions of Employment Policy for Disabled Persons*. New York: World Rehabilitation Fund.

Hahn, H. 1985a: Changing perceptions of disability and the future of rehabilitation. In L. G. Perlman and G. F. Austin, (eds), *Societal Influences on Rehabilitation Planning: A Blueprint for the Twenty-first Century*, Alexandria, VA: National Rehabilitation Association, 53–64.

Hahn, H. 1985b: Disability and the problem of discrimination. *American Behavioral Scientist*, 28 (3), 293–318.

Hahn, H. 1986b: Public support for rehabilitation: the analysis of U.S. disability policy, *Disability, Handicap, and Society*, 1 (2), 121–37.

Hahn, H. 1987a: Adapting the environment to people with disabilities: constitutional issues in Canada. *International Journal of Rehabilitation Research*, 10 (4), 363–72.

Hahn, H. 1988: The politics of physical differences. *Journal of Social Issues*, 44, 39–43.

Hahn, H. 1993a: Equality and the environment: the interpretation of 'reasonable accommodations' in the Americans with Disabilities Act. *Journal of Rehabilitation Administration*, 17, 101–6.

Hahn, H. 1993b: The political implications of disability definitions and data. *Journal of Disability Policy Studies*, 4 (2), 41–52.

Hahn, H. 1994: The minority group model of disability: implications for medical sociology. In R. Wetz and J. J. Kronenfeld (eds), *Research in the Sociology of Health Care*, vol. 11, Greenwich, CT: JAI Press, 3–24.

Hahn, H. 1996: Antidiscrimination laws and social research on disability: the minority group perspective. *Behavioral Sciences and the Law*, 14, 1–19.

Hahn, H, 1997a: An agenda for citizens with disabilities: pursuing identity and empowerment. *Journal of Vocational Rehabilitation*, 9 (1), 31–7.

Hahn, H. 2000: Accommodations and the ADA: biased reasoning or unreasonable bias? *Berkeley Journal of Employment and Labor Law*, 21 (1), 166–92.

Hahn, H. (In press) Adjudication or empowerment: contrasting experiences with the social model of disability. In L. Barton, (ed.), *Society and Disability*.

Hahn, H. and Beaulaurier, R. (In press): ADAPT or perish: a research on interviews with participants in nonviolent protests. *Journal of Disability Policy Studies*.

Harris, L. 1986: *The ICD Survey of Disabled Americans: Bringing Disabled Americans into the Mainstream*. New York: Louis Harris and Associates.

Haug, S. and Sussman, M. 1969: Revolt of the clients. *Social Problems*, 13, 108–14.

Higgins, P. C. 1992: *Making Disability: Exploring the Social Transformation of Human Variation*. Springfield, IL: Charles C. Thomas.

Johnson, V. 1999: Mobilizing the disabled. In J. Freeman and V. Johnson (eds), *Waves of Protest: Social Movements since the Sixties*, Lanham, MD: Rowman and Littlefield.

Katzmann, R. 1986: *Institutional Disability: The Saga of Transportation Policy for the Disabled*. Washington, DC: Brookings Institution.

Kleck, R. 1966: Emotional arousal in interactions with stigmatized persons. *Psychological Reports*, 19 (3), 1226.

Liachowitz, C. H. 1988: *Disability as a Social Construct: Legislative Roots*. Philadelphia: University of Pennsylvania Press.

Nord, E. 1999: *Cost–Value Analysis in Health Care: Making Sense out of QUALYs*. New York: Cambridge University Press.

Obermann, T. E. 1965: *A History of Vocational Rehabilitation*. Minneapolis: T. S. Denison Co.

Oliver, M. 1990: *The Politics of Disablement*. Basingstoke: Macmillan.

Olson, S. M. 1984: *Clients and Lawyers: Securing the Rights of Disabled Persons*. Westport, CT: Greenwood Press.

Pfeiffer, D. 1998: The *ICIDH* and its need for revision. *Disability and Society*, 13 (4), 503–23.

Richardson, S. A. 1970: Age and sex differences in values toward physical handicaps. *Journal of Health and Social Behavior*, 11 (3), 207–14.

Richardson, S. A. and Royce, J. 1968: Race and handicap in children's preferences for other children. *Child Development*, 39, 457–80.

Rothman, D. 1991: *Strangers at the Bedside: A History of How Law and Bioethics Transformed Medical Making*. New York: Basic Books.

Scotch, R. K. 1984: *From Good Will to Civil Rights: Transforming Federal Disability Policy*. Philadelphia: Temple University Press.

Shaw, A. 1977: A short formula for quality of life. *Hastings Center Report*, 5 (1), 37–43.

Shaw, R. 1996: *The Activist's Handbook*. Berkeley: University of California Press.

Skocpol, T. 1992: *Protecting Soldiers and Mothers: The Political Origin of Social Policy in the United States*. Cambridge, MA: Harvard University Press.

Swain, J., Finkelstein, V., French, S. and Oliver, M. (eds) 1993: *Disabling Barriers – Enabling Environments*. London: Sage.

US Department of Health and Human Services 1992: Press release, 3 August.

World Health Organization 1980: *International Classification of Impairments, Disabilities, and Handicaps*. Geneva: World Health Organization.

10

Globalization and Disability

Chris Holden and Peter Beresford

Our aim has been to build the global economy that leaves no one behind.
(President Clinton, Warwick University, 14 December 2000)

The gap between rich and poor has grown greater over the eight years of his presidency... Now 100 million more people are in absolute poverty than when he became president.
Barry Coates, Director, World Development Movement, Channel 4 News, UK, 14 December 2000

Introduction

In an extremely short space of time, the idea of 'globalization' has become a key issue in national and international politics and policy. It has also become a central topic of debate in a range of social science disciplines. In many of these it has become the key topic of debate, and for some the central explanatory paradigm in understanding contemporary social change. This chapter discusses what relevance debates about globalization in the social sciences may have for disabled people, how they are impacting upon policy affecting disabled people, and the implications this may have for disabled people and their organizations. We focus on the political economy aspects of globalization, and debates within the discipline of social policy about the impact of changes in the world market on the welfare state.

So far there has been relatively limited discussion of globalization either in relation to, or by, disabled people. As we have argued elsewhere, there has been little attempt to relate the discourses of globalization and of disabled people to each other (Beresford and Holden 2000). Yet, as we shall see, globalization clearly impacts powerfully on the lives of disabled people; increasingly there are globalized responses to disability (Stone 1999: 7–9), and disabled people and their organizations can be expected to challenge the narrowly economistic way in which globalization has often tended to be presented. Just as disabled people made sense of disability in the twentieth century through their analysis of industrial capitalism, so we may expect that an understanding of 'post-industrial' capitalism, including globalization, will help make sense of disability in the twenty-first century.

The chapter begins with a brief summary of some of the economic changes which have been associated with globalization and the different positions which have been taken on the significance of these within the political economy literature. We put these in context with earlier economic developments and their implications for disability globally. We then move on to a discussion of the alleged effects of the changes relating to globalization upon welfare states and consider, in particular, the significance of these debates for disabled people. Finally, we discuss changes in the nature of long-term care for older people and other disabled people, stemming from the growth of private provision and the increasing internationalization of that provision.

The political economy of globalization

'Globalization' has now become a household term. The political economy aspects of globalization are associated with the increasing integration of the world economy. This has manifested itself through international trade (which has been growing at a faster rate than world output for most of the post-war period), foreign direct investment (FDI, which has been growing at an even faster rate than trade since the 1980s), and world financial flows (where international dealing in currencies, shares and complex financial instruments has grown to unprecedented levels). However, commentators differ as to the significance of these developments. The different positions taken by the various writers have been grouped by Held et al. (1999) into three categories: the 'hyperglobalizers', the 'sceptics' and the 'transformationalists'.

Hyperglobalizers tend to emphasize the extent of economic integration, arguing that the increased mobility of capital has led to the supplanting of national economies by a genuinely single global market. Multinational, or 'transnational', corporations can move across the globe with ease, searching out the most efficient outlets for investment and creating an international division of labour in the process. These corporations have no allegiance to nation-states, and are not subject to control by them. Hyperglobalizers may be either neo-liberals celebrating the triumph of unfettered capitalism or Marxists who oppose the exploitation and inequality which results from this. For neo-liberals such as Ohmae (1990), globalization renders the nation-state effectively redundant, a relic of a bygone age.

Sceptics, however, question many of the assumptions of the hyperglobalizers. First, sceptics tend to argue that recent changes in the world economy represent a deepening of internationalization, rather than a qualitative shift towards a genuinely 'global' economy where borders are irrelevant. Ruigrok and van Tulder (1995), for example, convincingly demonstrate that the majority of the world's largest firms retain a clear national base, despite significant overseas sales. Secondly, sceptics argue that the extent of internationalization in the contemporary world economy is no more than, and probably less than, that which existed in the period of the classical gold standard from the 1870s up to World War I (Hirst and Thompson 1999). Thirdly, sceptics point out that the pattern of international investment is not evenly distributed, with most of it flowing from advanced capitalist economies to other advanced capitalist economies. Moreover, most of this investment is regionally based, with the world split into three main blocs around the USA, Europe and Japan (Hirst and Thompson 1999; Ruigrok and van Tulder 1995). Finally, sceptics reject the notion that nation-states have become powerless or irrelevant, a particularly important argument for social policy.

The transformationalist thesis accepts that contemporary processes of globalization are unprecedented, but argues that these processes are contradictory and 'open-ended' (Held et al. 1999). Transformationalists reject teleological notions of globalization, whether they be the utopian ones of neo-liberals or the dystopian ones of some Marxists. Rather, globalization is seen as reflexive and contested: 'globalisation today reflects the varied and self-conscious political or economic projects of national elites and transnational social forces pursuing often conflicting visions of world order' (Held et al. 1999: 430). For transformationalists, globalization presents nation-states with new challenges which they must take account of and adapt to. However, it does not rob them of power, since states may proactively shape processes of globalization. State power is thus transformed, rather than diminished. According to Held et al., states in advanced capitalist societies (SIACS) are undergoing a profound transformation as their powers, roles and functions are rearticulated, reconstituted and re-embedded at the intersection of globalising and regionalising networks and systems. The metaphors of the loss, diminution or erosion of state power can misrepresent this reconfiguration or transformation.... For while globalisation is engendering a reconfiguration of state-market relations in the economic domain, SIACS and multilateral agencies are deeply implicated in that very process. (Held et al. 1999: 440)

This chapter takes a 'transformationalist' approach, in so far as it is accepted that the world market is becoming more integrated, but sees 'globalization' as a contested process or set of processes, not a fully realized end point. Furthermore, whilst nation-states may have to adapt to new circumstances, rather than losing power, their power is being transformed. Indeed, the most powerful capitalist states are active agents in shaping processes of globalization. In social policy this means that the state is not withdrawing, but that the form of its intervention is changing in some areas.

Disability: from industrialization to globalization

Our focus is on the globalization of the late twentieth and early twenty-first centuries. But this needs to be put in the context of preceding economic developments. The disabled people's movement has analysed the way in which nineteenth-century industrialization created dominant modern understandings of disability. As Mike Oliver has written:

> Whatever the fate of disabled people before the advent of capitalist society... with its coming they suffered economic and social exclusion. As a consequence of this exclusion, disability was produced in a particular form; as an individual problem requiring medical treatment. Old age (and I would suggest, madness and distress) suffered a similar fate. (Oliver 1996: 127)

Critiques of industrialization by disabled commentators have highlighted its role in the creation of impairment and the construction of disability (Abberley 1996, 1997; Finkelstein 1981). Its association with environmental pollution, unhealthy and dangerous industrial conditions and accidents, as well as poverty, linked with low wages and exclusion from the labour market, have been key factors in generating impairment and chronic disease. Disability has been inextricably associated with poverty in the West since industrialization. This has been centrally related to the *disemployment* of disabled people in capitalist and capitalist-driven economies. In a statement presented to the United Nations World Summit on Social Development in 1995 on behalf of Disabled People's International, Lisa Kaupinen, General Secretary of the World Federation of the Deaf, said: 'We are the poorest of the poor in most societies .... Two thirds of disabled people are estimated to be without employment. Social exclusion and isolation are the day-to-day experience of disabled people' (Kaupinen 1995).

It is generally accepted that the majority of disabled people live in 'developing' countries (Beresford 1996). People with impairments in the developing world are more likely to be poor (Stone 1999: 4). Disability Awareness in Action has stated: 'In the developing world, the extremely high percentage of unemployment among disabled people means they are forced to beg to survive' (1995: 1).

Western industrial conceptualizations of disability and impairment were rapidly applied to the rest of the world and imposed upon societies in the Southern hemisphere without regard to their particular histories, cultures, traditions, circumstances or preferences (Coleridge 1993; Ingstad and Reynolds-Whyte 1996; Stone 1999). As Mike Oliver has said, just as industrialized societies created their own particular category of disability, so they generated an industry to service it (and then exported it to the developing world). This industry was based on a medicalized individual model of disability and was associated with the medicalized 'rehabilitation', segregation, exclusion and institutionalization of disabled people (Oliver 1996: 127).

We can expect globalization to continue to play a central role in the social construction of disability and impairment, like nineteenth-century industrialization before it, even if the resulting dominant paradigms differ from those of the past. We can also expect that many of the key features of globalization, like the deregulation of capital, the labour market and employment conditions, will have similar effects to earlier industrialization in terms of maintaining exclusions and the link between poverty and disability. The removal of disabling physical and social structures is unlikely to be prioritized within the imperatives of a globalized economy.

However, one key difference between early industrialization and globalization can be identified. The process of industrialization which happened in the UK in the nineteenth century is currently taking place in the developing world. Many of the companies which are leading this development are multinationals based in the developed nations. The increased mobility of capital has led to a shift in unskilled and semi-skilled manufacture to developing nations. The impairment-creating and disabling conditions associated with Western industrial economies in the nineteenth centuries are now being replicated by globalization in the Third World.

Globalization, social policy and disabled people

Debates within the discipline of social policy have reflected those within the wider political economy literature. Thus, some writers view globalization as having profound, irresistible effects on the capacity of nation-states to shape autonomously their own social and economic policies, while others are more sceptical. The popular view is that the international mobility of capital propels governments into competition with each other for investment. They are thus constrained to follow policies of low inflation, low taxation, low public spending, flexible labour markets and privatization – that is, to minimize their economic and social involvement, except where it facilitates capital accumulation. Mishra sums up this view very well:

> Put simply, by providing capital with an 'exit' option, globalisation has strengthened the bargaining power of capital very considerably against government as well as labour.... Thus money and investment capital can vote with their feet if they do not like government policies.... Indeed globalisation virtually sounds the death-knell of the classical social democratic strategy of full employment, high levels of public expenditure and progressive taxation. (Mishra 1999: 6)

If Mishra and others are right, the consequences for disabled people of such constraints on the welfare state are profound. Whilst the nature of state welfare for disabled people has often taken oppressive forms (Oliver and Barnes 1998), the provision of support services funded on the basis of collective social responsibility and risk pooling is a prerequisite for the equal participation of disabled people in society. Also more recently, because of the intervention of disabled people and other social care service users and their creation of new forms of support and new ways of organizing and controlling it, further prospects for achieving equality through collective provision have emerged. The removal of disabling social barriers necessitates that society must have goals other than simply profit maximization. However, many writers have pointed out that multinational corporations (MNCs) are seeking more than simply low taxes and cheap labour when taking decisions to invest. They may also seek developed infrastructure, skilled labour or simply new markets for their goods. The fact that most FDI flows to advanced capitalist countries undermines the belief that firms primarily seek cheap labour when investing abroad. Furthermore, competition between nation-states can be regulated where there is the political will to do so through multilateral agreements.

In any case, many writers have pointed out that different welfare states respond very differently in meeting the challenges of globalization (Esping-Andersen 1996a, 1996b; Keohane and Milner 1996: 14; Held et al. 1999: 13). Esping-Andersen, for example, argues that 'One of the most powerful conclusions in comparative research is that political and institutional mechanisms of interest representation and political consensus building matter tremendously in terms of managing welfare, employment and growth objectives' (1996a: 6). Thus, while post-war Western welfare states addressed similar objectives, they differed in terms of how they pursued these. Similarly, as these same welfare states seek to adapt to the changing conditions associated with globalization, they do so very differently. As Esping-Andersen points out, 'Each of these welfare state responses combines benefits and costs in a way which is hardly Pareto optimal' (1996b: 258).

However, even Esping-Andersen (1996b) argues that the costs imposed upon welfare states by globalization point towards a particular set of policy options, or 'positive sum solutions in a world of trade-offs'. These positive-sum solutions involve an emphasis on education as the preferred social policy weapon. This is because the social policies consistent with higher levels of employment, it is argued, are those which promote the flexibility of labour. Policies which offer greater protection to those who are already employed, on the other hand, tend to reduce the net number of jobs and create a division between those 'inside' paid employment and those outside it. Yet, when combined with education policies premissed upon skill acquisition and 'lifelong learning', flexible labour markets can also promote equality of opportunity, eliminating the surplus of unskilled workers and ensuring that inferior, low-paid jobs do not become life-cycle traps, but merely stopgaps or first-entry jobs. This is consistent with New Labour's policies, which are premissed upon increasing labour market participation rates and increasing skill levels through educational reforms (Holden 1999). These policies have in turn been influenced by the ideas of Reich (1991), who argues that workers in countries like the USA and the UK must compete with each other to attract internationally mobile investment. Only by competing on the basis of high skills, rather than low wages, can workers in such countries hope to maintain their standard of living. Labour market participation is also seen by New Labour as a means of combating social exclusion, hence the various types of 'new deal' on offer. New Labour's policies of increasing labour market participation thus dovetail with its educational policies to increase labour supply, aggregate skill levels and therefore labour market efficiency.

Such policies do have their critics. Jordan (1998) has pointed out how a new emphasis on attaching obligations to rights (or 'reciprocity') has been linked to this elevation of labour markets, involving a drive to increase participation in them through the placing of conditionality on benefits. Jordan develops a sustained critique of the new 'Clinton/Blair orthodoxy' on the basis that it provides neither efficiency nor social justice. He argues that the emphasis on education can only be part of the solution, since an increasing proportion of work in modern industrialized economies must take the form of 'low-productivity tasks for social reproduction' (Jordan 1998: 67). Such work, he argues, is not susceptible to technological change or enhanced efficiency. Placing the work ethic at the centre of social policy may be counter-productive if it leads to a 'blaming attitude' towards those who can no longer find work in traditional industries, or to costly social divisions, punitive policies and a breakdown of trust and co-operation. Such policies lead in the direction of forced labour and 'the barbarity of the workhouse' (Jordan 1998: 67).

The implications of this for disabled people are many. The emphasis on education has yet to be matched by full recognition of the need for disabled people's full and equal inclusion in education. Inclusive education for all disabled children and equal access to further and higher education for disabled adults continue to be distant goals. New Labour's emphasis on increasing the opportunities for employment has been welcomed by many disabled people, who have consistently expressed their desire to work, have campaigned for equality in the labour market, and conceived of employment as a right to be guaranteed and safeguarded (Oliver and Barnes 1998). The exclusion of disabled people from the labour market has been one of the principal sources of their oppression. As argued above, the development of industrial capitalism tended to exclude disabled people from the world of work, and therefore from equal participation in society. Disabled people have one of the highest rates of unemployment in Western societies like the UK. Mental health service users tend to have the highest rate among disabled people (Bird 1999; Mind/BBC 2000).

Yet, when in work, disabled people have often been consigned to the lowest-paying jobs (Oliver and Barnes 1998). There is evidence that the growth of those claiming incapacity/invalidity benefit has resulted from the expulsion of many disabled people from the labour market following the growth of unemployment after 1980. According to Berthoud (1998: 12): 'As the supply of labour has expanded faster than demand, employers may have become more selective in their choice of staff, excluding

marginal workers, such as disabled people.' New Labour policies effectively increase the labour supply still further. This may be efficient for
employers, who have a wider pool of labour to draw on. However, if
more disabled people are to enter the labour market, especially if they are
not simply to be pushed into the lowest-paying jobs, comprehensive
support policies will need to be put in place which exceed those which
have been offered by New Labour. Furthermore, the perception that they
will be inappropriately forced into employment is a source of great
anxiety for many disabled people. New Labour's reform of the 'all
work test' (the passing of which is a condition for claiming incapacity
benefit) to focus on what disabled people can do, as well as what they
cannot do (DSS 1998), has been welcomed by many. Yet disabled people
have pointed out that offering support to find work should be separated
from benefit assessment if it is to be effective and equitable. The narrow
spin placed on work by a 'hyperglobalizing' approach to globalization
converts the liberatory ideal of the disabled people's movement into an
oppressive and controlling obligation. The UK government slogan,
'Work for those who can, security for those who can't', over-simplifies
and ignores the reality that many disabled people face. The truth is that
many service users want both – work *and* support. Thus the inclusive
rhetoric of welfare to work is experienced by many disabled people as a
policy of *assimilation*, based on pressure to conform within a deregulated
labour market.

Policies premissed upon globalization and the need for increased com-
petitiveness thus have a number of important ramifications for disabled
people. Yet, as we have argued, the perception that globalization forces
governments to adopt certain kinds of policies is open to question. In this
context, 'globalization' may be seen as a powerful legitimating idea.
As Moran and Wood put it: 'Constructing external constraints ... allows
particular national elites to present their policy preferences as the more
or less unavoidable consequences of forces over which nationally organised institutions can have little or no control' (1996: 140). The disabled
people's movement, however, has shown that established ideas can be
challenged, and, through taking political action, has demonstrated that
the rights and needs of people can be brought centre stage, despite the
argument that 'there is no alternative' (Beresford and Holden 2000).
Furthermore, disabled people have organized on an international, as
well as a national, basis. In this they have mirrored the mobilizations of
anti-capitalist protesters at meetings of the World Trade Organization,
the International Monetary Fund and the World Bank. These mobilizations have brought together a diverse and often incoherent alliance of
interests. They have nevertheless succeeded in creating a public debate

about globalization, and the policies of the world's most powerful governments towards the world economy.

Globalization, social care and disabled people

We argued above that the state is not withdrawing as such, but that the form of its intervention may be changing in some areas. The elevation of education as a social and economic policy is one example of this. However, the provision of social care, and its underpinning ideology, is one area in the UK where the form of state intervention has changed dramatically over the last two decades. There have also been corresponding shifts in other EU countries. In the UK this has primarily been the result of the shift towards private provision in the 1980s, following the increased availability of social security funding for long-term care places (Bradshaw 1988; Harrington and Pollock 1998). This was compounded by the Conservative government's insistence that 85 per cent of the 'special transitional grant', which funded the community care reforms after 1993, be spent in the independent sector (Edwards and Kenny 1997). However, the move away from state provision did not mark the end of state intervention; rather, the form of state involvement shifted to subsidy and regulation. In recent years this shift towards state-funded and regulated private provision has promoted internationalization, as the provision of social care in the private sector has become more concentrated.

By 1998, the independent sector provided 88 per cent of all residential and nursing care home places (DoH 1998a). There were 347,400 residential places in 24,800 residential homes (including small homes) and 193,900 places in 5,800 nursing care homes. The majority of these were for older people, but many were for other adults with learning difficulties, physical impairments or psychiatric diagnoses. Corporate penetration is greater in nursing than in residential care, partly because homes are typically larger than in residential care. They therefore afford some economies of scale in delivering the service, which large corporate providers can add to their economies of scale in purchasing supplies. Between 1988, when the market analysts Laing and Buisson started maintaining records, and 1997, major providers more than doubled their share of the for-profit care home market (Laing and Buisson 1997: A186). Laing and Buisson's definition of 'major provider' includes all organizations with three or more homes. Yet there has clearly been a process of consolidation in the care home sector. For the first time in 1996 the number of for-profit major providers fell slightly. More significantly, the number of UK stock market-quoted companies fell sharply as the result of a series of mergers and acquisitions (M&As) during 1996 and 1997, reflecting increasing concentration (Laing and Buisson 1997: A186). At the end of 1998, there were 288 for-profit major providers (*CCMN*, March 1999). However, the ten largest operators owned or leased 13.8 per cent of total UK for-profit capacity, whilst the three largest owned or leased 7.9 per cent (Laing and Buisson 1999–2000: 176). Having facilitated the rise to dominance of independent provision during the 1980s through open-ended social security funding and the conditions attached to the special transitional grant, governments have subsequently facilitated concentration within the market through restricting local authority budgets. This is because it is the larger firms which can best withstand the current tight financial climate, by utilizing their substantial economies of scale.

Smaller homes therefore experience by far the most severe financial problems. For example, Andrews and Phillips (1998: 10) found that in Devon, where their study was focused, 70 per cent of the homes operating at or below their margins of profitability in 1994 were registered for fifteen beds or fewer. Many proprietors were disillusioned with working in the residential sector, and over one-third of home-owners stated they would sell their business if it were possible. Smaller homes are not necessarily owned by small companies, but on the whole this is the case, partly because large companies have engaged in some new building in order to take advantage of economies of scale. According to Bartlett and Burnip (1999: 10), in the process of improving quality in care homes, 'the loss of good smaller homes along the way seems inevitable'. As Andrews and Phillips (1998: 10) point out: 'Ironically, it is the smaller homes, being less "institutional", which sit best with the philosophy of care in the community.'

The shift towards private provision has facilitated internationalization because, as Porter (1990: 247) puts it, 'With rare exceptions, government-owned service organisations do not compete globally'. Foreign direct investment (FDI) in services has increased even more rapidly than in manufacturing in recent years (Hirst and Thompson 1999; Stopford and Strange 1991: 87). This reflects both the increased importance of services in advanced capitalist economies such as Britain (Daniels 1993), as well as the preference of service firms for FDI rather than trade when expanding abroad. Cross-border sales of services often have to take the form of FDI, since many services require physical proximity to the consumer, because they are consumed as they are produced (Hoekman and Primo Braga 1997: 286). So, for example, when a doctor travels abroad to carry out an operation, this may be regarded as trade, but when a health care company wishes to deliver its services abroad on a more regular basis, it must invest in setting up and running its own hospital. Multinationals have moved into the British health care market since the 1970s, when it was first opened up (Mohan 1991). Many of these multinational health care corporations were American, reflecting the longer tradition of private provision in that country and the greater expertise which such firms have consequently acquired.

This has been reflected in recent years within the British social care market, where American firms have taken advantage of opportunities for their expansion. Thus the second largest long-term care operator in the UK, Ashbourne, is owned by the American Sun Healthcare, which also has operations in Germany, Spain and Australia. Sun Healthcare consistently expanded its international operations in the second half of the 1990s. By the end of 1998, it operated 186 facilities with more than 11,700 beds outside the USA, an increase of 12 per cent over 1997 (Sun Healthcare 1998: 12). In February 1999 the company had 80,720 full-time and part-time employees worldwide (Sun Healthcare 1998: form 10k, 5). Calculations show that, of these 10,532 were based outside the USA. The company's annual reports (Sun Healthcare 1996: 11) pin-point 'favourable market conditions and regulatory environments' abroad as incentives for exploring opportunities outside the USA. Sun Healthcare entered the UK market in 1994, buying up the British firms Exceler, Apta and Ashbourne, and merging them into the country's second-largest provider. However, Sun Healthcare has experienced substantial problems arising from its borrowing to fund its expansion and from changes to the US system of state reimbursement for health care, and in 1999 entered 'chapter 11 protection', the US equivalent of receivership (Sun Healthcare Group press release 26 October 1999).

Other US firms have also entered the British market. The American National Medical Enterprises (NME, later Tenet Healthcare Corporation), for example, had a majority shareholding in Westminster Health Care (WHC) from early in its existence, before withdrawing in 1996. WHC has also built alliances with US companies in retirement home management and in health care real estate. WHC's most recent owners, Canterbury, were backed by the American investment bank Goldman Sachs and the American private equity firm Welsh, Carson, Anderson and Stowe (*CCMN*, March 1999). Canterbury's chief executive, Chai Patel, told *Community Care Market News* (May 1999) that the group was actively considering a number of propositions regarding expansion into Europe, including 'a number of potential opportunities for the group across all its activities in Germany, France and Spain'. Idun Healthcare, which acquired the UK firm Tamaris after its failure in 1999 (*CCMN*,

November 1999, March 2000), is a subsidiary of the American-based real estate investment trust (REIT) Omega Worldwide.

However, British firms have also begun to internationalize. The largest provider of long-term care in the UK, the British United Provident Association (BUPA), has significantly expanded both its insurance and its directly provided services abroad in recent years. BUPA claims to insure four million people from 115 different nationalities who live in around 190 countries (http://www.bupa-intl.com/about2.html). The majority of these are British, living at home or abroad, but BUPA claims that one million of its members live outside the UK. By 1997, BUPA had direct operations in seven countries other than the UK (BUPA 1997: 3), including Spain, Ireland, Thailand, Hong Kong and Saudi Arabia. Its *Annual Review* (BUPA 1997: 8) indicated that in 1997 the organization had met its 'ambitious target for international development', and had become 'a more comprehensive international healthcare business'. In 1999, the organization opened a primary care and diagnostic clinic in India. Its Spanish arm, Santitas, has recently moved into care home operation (*CCMN*, July 2000).

BUPA's status as a provident society means that, technically, it is non-profit making. However, it can be regarded as operating within the market as any for-profit firm would: it must compete with other businesses, must do this in a cost-effective way, and has attempted to expand and gain market share throughout its existence (Maynard and Williams 1984: 107). The doubling of its advertising budget between 1979 and 1981 has been taken as 'evidence of a more expansionary, marketing-oriented strategy' (Griffith and Rayner 1985: 15), a trend which has continued. The increasing arrival of for-profit organizations in the British health care market after 1979 had intensified competition (Papadakis and Taylor-Gooby 1987: 68), compelling BUPA to adopt the strategic thinking of its for-profit competitors. From the late 1980s, competition in health insurance increased, as banks, building societies and insurance companies entered the market. By 1996, BUPA's share of that market had fallen to 46 per cent (Laing and Buisson 1996). Whilst Private Patients Plan (PPP) decided to demutualize to raise the capital necessary to compete (May and Brunsdon 1999: 285), BUPA has increasingly expanded into other areas of health care. However, the dominance of the NHS in acute hospital care has influenced BUPA's move into social care, as well as its expansion abroad. Like other long-term care providers, BUPA has borrowed substantial sums in order to fund the expansion of its care home operations (*CCMN*, February 2000), although its provident status means it is not under pressure from shareholders to demonstrate short-term profit gain.

Furthermore, these developments are taking place in a context where in the UK, for example, the nature of voluntary or charitable organizations in the contemporary economy increasingly mirrors that of other large organizations. This relates partly to the way in which voluntary organizations are increasingly being used by government to pursue its own agenda. Funding to voluntary organizations often comes primarily from governments and official bodies. Voluntary organizations are often the favoured providers of government and its agencies, since they can implement government policy, but carry more legitimacy than government bodies among the public. This increasingly semi-official status of some voluntary organizations also exists at the supranational level, where organizations like the World Bank and IMF have accorded international non-governmental organizations (INGOs) unprecedented influence (*Economist* 1999). Thus the role of the IMF and World Bank in effectively dictating the economic and social policies of developing countries has sometimes in practice been complemented, rather than challenged, by large INGOs. This is linked to the increased professionalization and managerialization of such voluntary organizations, including those which may be large-scale 'care' providers. An example in the UK is Leonard Cheshire, which has 10,000 plus domestic service users of domiciliary, day care and residential services, as well as parallel operations internationally. Like BUPA, such organizations increasingly operate on a similar basis to for-profit firms, but, rather than being listed on the Stock Exchange, reinvest their 'surplus' in the organization, notably in its infrastructural, lobbying and profile-raising activities. The increasing competition and innovation introduced by internationalized for-profit firms can only extend such tendencies, as voluntary organizations struggle to retain and expand their market share, both individually and as a service supply sector.

Mohan (1991: 864) points out that, when considered from the standpoint of overall market share, the impact of multinationals in health care may appear to be limited, and this is also the case for social care. However, internationalization is likely to increase in the social care sector as the continued restriction of state funding and the higher costs imposed by forthcoming changes to the regulatory system (DoH 1998b, 1999a, 1999b) continue to squeeze out smaller providers. By the end of 2000, there were signs that the over-capacity in the sector was reversing in some areas, as small providers took advantage of the rise in property prices to get out of the business before the new regulatory changes were implemented (*CCMN*, October 2000). Furthermore, as is demonstrated by the transformation of BUPA into a multinational health care business, the qualitative effects of multinational involvement in the market are at least as important as the extent of that involvement. As Mohan (1991) argues, multinationals are leaders in terms of innovation in marketing and budgeting techniques, as well as in work organization. As such, they are often more cost-efficient (though not necessarily more effective at meeting need) than domestic providers, and increase the level of competition in the market overall. This has an effect on all providers, be they for-profit firms, provident associations or charities, as they must increasingly operate according to the criteria of for-profit firms if they are to capture and retain market share.

The implications of this for users of these services are many. First, the merger and acquisition process, which is a feature of the concentration of provision and the entry of foreign firms, may severely disrupt the lives of residents. Changes of ownership may lead to changes of regime within the company's care homes, to accelerated turnover of staff, and in some cases to the closure of some homes and the physical transfer of the residents. All of these tend to have a negative effect on the rights, health and well-being of residents, especially the very old, in the worst cases leading to fatalities. The better providers may consult residents about changes to the services they receive, but residents have no control over changes in ownership. Secondly, large companies approach issues of quality on the basis of branding and standardization. Their goal is to be seen to deliver high-quality services of the same standard across all their homes, wherever they may be located. Quality is thus controlled through process standards, which stipulate the tasks to be completed by workers. The individual judgement of the worker is thus subordinated to a more 'Taylorist' system of work control. This may produce high-quality care in one sense, but it also standardizes that care. Internationalized firms may also be able to draw on a greater pool of expertise in creating their quality systems. However, some disabled writers (Oliver and Barnes 1998) have criticized the very notion of 'care' as part of a paternalistic ideology which underpins the dependent status which disabled people are often forced into. Furthermore, increasing provision by large companies may reduce the degree of choice available to purchasing agencies, especially if local monopolies emerge as a result of the concentration process. This simply serves to highlight the contentious nature of much 'community' and social 'care' provision, and intensifies the debate about what kind of services should be made available to disabled people, young or old.

Conclusion

The increasing integration of the world economy clearly raises a number of important issues for social policy and for disabled people. The idea that the world market, and the internationalized companies which operate within it, constitute an irresistible force which no government can withstand has been used as a powerful weapon in justifying welfare budget restraint. It has also influenced the development of specific government policies and spending priorities, most notably the emphasis on labour market efficiency and education. The government's concern with increasing labour supply by widening participation in work is promoting an ideology of 'inclusion' in work for disabled people. This is in contrast to the earlier phase of capitalism which Finkelstein (1981) and others identified as effectively expelling disabled people from the labour force and socially marginalizing them. Yet, without adequate support, disabled people will continue to be disproportionately pushed into low-paid routine jobs, especially as an increase in labour supply will increase competition for jobs. Furthermore, the government's persistent emphasis on paid employment risks further marginalizing those left on benefits (Riddell 2001).

However, globalization may have implications for disabled people at levels other than simply policy formation. Thus, the internationalization of social care providers has reflected the increasing internationalization of other services, and of the world economy more generally. One of the ironies of globalization may be that as it reinforces disability through its damaging and disrupting effects, it also gives rise to an internationalized social care industry to meet the needs which it helps generate. All these developments increase, rather than reduce, the importance of governments and other domestic actors, including the political movements of disabled people and others. They highlight the continuing need for disabled people and their movements to develop their demands and their strategies for achieving them in relation to governments. But they also point to the increasing importance of acting internationally, as well as nationally, and of addressing and developing strategies for action and change in relation to multinational corporations.

New relationships are developing between governments and these MNCs. Complex and new relationships between politicians, civil servants and MNC executives are emerging, associated with significant interchange of, and links between, personnel. These pose new and difficult questions about accountability for disabled people and other social care service users. There are worrying questions about whether increasing economic pressure will lead to increased warehousing of disabled people in standardized low-grade residential institutions instead of them being ensured adequate and appropriate personal assistance to live independently. The emphasis on employment for disabled people within the framework of a discriminatory and oppressive labour market also raises big questions about whether disabled people will increasingly be categorized on the basis of those who can and those who can't work, with the former deemed 'acceptable' and capable of 'inclusion' and the latter stereotyped as 'dependent' and 'socially excluded'. Such economic pressures, combined with advances in, and the renewal of interest in, gene technology and the perception of new possibilities for genetic forecasting and engineering, may come to constitute a fundamental assault on the human and civil rights of disabled people included in the second category. We may expect to see an increasing polarization of attitudes towards disabled people, in line with the government slogan 'Work for those who can, security for those who can't'. This may be translated into greater 'tolerance' of those who can be fitted into a globalized labour market and increased intolerance of those who it is perceived cannot. Organizations of disabled people and mental health service users/survivors are worried that there may be an increased emphasis on genetic solutions to reduce, if not eradicate, this latter group.

This makes it all the more important for disabled people and their organizations to develop their own critiques of globalization as a basis for both taking forward their understandings of disability and developing new strategies to deal with its contemporary expressions. Globalization is not a force beyond human control (although some governments encourage this assumption); rather, it is part of the development of a pattern of human relations which all of us have a stake in shaping.

REFERENCES

Abberley, P. 1996: Utopia and impairment. In L. Barton (ed.), *Disability and Society: Emerging Issues and Insights*. London: Longmans, 61–79.

Abberley, P. 1997: The limits of classical social theory in the analysis and transformation of disablement (Can this really be the end; to be stuck inside of Mobile with the Memphis blues again?). In L. Barton and M. Oliver (eds), *Disability Studies: Past, Present and Future*. Leeds: Disability Press, 25–44.

Andrews, G. and Phillips, D. 1998: Markets and private residential homes: promoting efficiency or chaos. *Generations Review* 8 (3), 9–11.

Bartlett, H. and Burnip, S. 1999: Improving care in nursing and residential homes. *Generations Review*, 9 (1), 8–10.

Beresford, P. 1996: Poverty and disabled people: challenging dominant debates and policies. *Disability and Society*, 11 (4), 553–67.

Beresford, P. and Holden, C. 2000: We have choices: globalisation and welfare user movements. *Disability and Society*, 15 (7), 973–89.

Berthoud, R. 1998: *Disability Benefits: A Review of the Issues and Options for Reform*. York: Joseph Rowntree Foundation.

Bird, L. 1999: *The Fundamental Facts...All the Latest Facts and Figures on Mental Illness.* London: Mental Health Foundation.

Bradshaw, J. 1988: Financing private care for the elderly. In S. Baldwin, G. Parker, and R. Waller (eds), *Social Security and Community Care.* Aldershot: Avebury Press.

BUPA 1997: *BUPA Annual Review.* London: BUPA.

CCMN (*Community Care Market News*).

Coleridge, P. 1993: *Disability, Liberation and Development.* Oxford: Oxfam.

Daniels, P. W. 1993: *Service Industries in the World Economy.* Oxford: Blackwell.

Disability Awareness in Action 1995: Employment special. *Disability Awareness in Action Newsletter,* 27 May.

DoH (Department of Health) 1998a: *Community Care Statistics: Residential Personal Social Services for Adults, England.* London: Government Statistical Service.

DoH (Department of Health) 1998b: *Modernising Social Services.* London: DoH.

DoH (Department of Health) 1999a: *Fit for the Future? National Required Standards for Residential and Nursing Homes for Older People Consultation Document* (including regulatory impact statement). London: DoH.

DoH (Department of Health) 1999b: *Regulatory Impact Appraisal – Modernising Social Services.* London: DoH.

DSS (Department of Social Security) 1998: *A New Contract for Welfare: Support for Disabled People.* London: Stationery Office.

Economist 1999: The non-governmental order. *Economist,* 11 December, 22–4.

Edwards, P. and Kenny, D. 1997: *Community Care Trends 1997: The Impact of Funding on Local Authorities.* London: Local Government Management Board.

Esping-Andersen, G. 1996a: After the golden age. In G. Esping-Andersen (ed.) *Welfare States in Transition: National Adaptations in Global Economies* London: Sage, 1–31.

Esping-Andersen, G. 1996b: Positive-sum solutions in a world of trade-offs? In G. Esping-Andersen (ed.) *Welfare States in Transition: National Adaptations in Global Economies.* London: Sage, 256–67.

Finkelstein, V. 1981: Disability and the helper/helped relationship: an historical view. In A. Brechin et al. (eds), *Handicap in a Social World,* London: Hodder and Stoughton, 59–63.

Griffith, B. and Rayner, G. 1985: *Commercial Medicine in London.* London: Greater London Council Industry and Employment Branch.

Harrington, C. and Pollock, A. M. 1998: Decentralisation and privatisation of long-term care in UK and USA. *Lancet,* 351 (13 June), 1805–8.

Held, D., McGrew, A., Goldblatt, D. and Perraton, J. 1999: *Global Transformations: Politics, Economics and Culture.* Cambridge: Polity.

Hirst, P. and Thompson, G. 1999: *Globalisation in Question,* 2nd edn. Cambridge: Polity.

Hoekman, B. and Primo Braga, C. A. 1997: Protection and trade in services: a survey. *Open Economies Review* 8(3), 285–308.

Holden, C. 1999: Globalization, social exclusion and Labour's new work ethic. *Critical Social Policy* 19(4), 529–38.

Ingstad, B. and Reynolds-Whyte, S. (eds) 1996: *Disability and Culture*. Berkeley, University of California Press.

Jordan, B. 1998: *The New Politics of Welfare: Social Justice in a Global Context*. London: Sage.

Kaupinen, L. 1995: Statement on behalf of the World Federation of the Deaf, the World Blind Union, the International League of Societies for Persons with Mental Handicap, Rehabilitation International and Disabled People's International. *Disability Awareness in Action Newsletter* 25 March, 2.

Keohane, R. O. and Milner, H. V. (eds) 1996: *Internationalization and Domestic Politics* Cambridge: Cambridge University Press.

Laing and Buisson 1996: *Review of Private Healthcare*. London: Laing and Buisson.

Laing and Buisson 1997: *Review of Private Healthcare*. London: Laing and Buisson.

Laing and Buisson 1999–2000: *Healthcare Market Review*. London: Laing and Buisson.

May, A. and Brunsdon, E. 1999: Commercial and occupational welfare. In M. Page and R. Silburn (eds), *British Social Welfare in the Twentieth Century*. Basingstoke: Macmillan, 271–98.

Maynard, A. and Williams, A. 1984: Privatisation and the National Health Service. In J. Le Grand and R. Robinson, (eds), *Privatisation and the Welfare State*. London: George Allen & Unwin.

Mind / BBC 2000: *Mental Health Factfile*, January, London, Mind.

Mishra, R. 1999: *Globalization and the Welfare State*. Cheltenham: Edward Elgar.

Mohan, J. 1991: The internationalization and commercialization of health care in Britain. *Environment and Planning A*, 23: 853–67.

Moran, M. and Wood, B. 1996: The globalization of health care policy. In P. Gummet (ed.), *Globalization and Public Policy*, Cheltenham: Edward Elgar.

Ohmae, K. 1990: *The Borderless World*. New York: Harper Collins.

Oliver, M. 1996: *Understanding Disability: From Theory to Practice*. Basingstoke: Macmillan.

Oliver, M. and Barnes, C. 1998: *Disabled People and Social Policy: From Exclusion to Inclusion*. London: Longman.

Papadakis, E. and Taylor-Gooby, P. 1987: *The Private Provision of Public Welfare: State, Market and Community*. Brighton: Wheatsheaf.

Porter, M. 1990: *The Competitive Advantage of Nations*. London: Macmillan.

Reich, R. B. 1991: *The Work of Nations*. London: Simon and Schuster.

Riddell, S. (2001): Disabled people's rights. *SPA News, Newsletter of the Social Policy Association*, May / June, 29.

Ruigrok, W. and Tulder, R. van 1995: *The Logic of International Restructuring*. London: Routledge.

Stone, E. (ed.) 1999: *Disability and Development: Learning from Action and Research on Disability in the Majority World.* Leeds: Disability Press.
Stopford, S. and Strange, S. 1991: *Rival States, Rival Firms: Competition for World Market Shares.* Cambridge: Cambridge University Press.
Sun Healthcare 1996: *Sun Healthcare Group Inc. Annual Report.* Albuquerque, NM: Sun Healthcare.
Sun Healthcare 1998: *Sun Healthcare Group Inc. Annual Report.* Albuquerque, NM: Sun Healthcare.

11

Disability, Citizenship and Rights in a Changing World

Marcia H. Rioux

The best reparation for the suffering of victims and communities – and the highest recognition of their efforts – is the transformation of our society into one that makes a living reality of the human rights for which they struggled.

Nelson Mandela, *Civilization Magazine*, June 1999

It then occurred to me that the right to be the same ... and the right to be different ... were not opposed to each other. On the contrary, the right to be the same in terms of fundamental civil, political, legal, economic and social rights provided the foundation for the expression of difference through choice in the sphere of culture, life-style and personal priorities. In other words, provided that difference was not used to maintain inequality, subordination, injustice and marginalisation.

Albie Sachs, *Human Rights in the Twenty-First Century*

In 1996 the Supreme Court of Canada ruled that no one could be lawfully sterilized without personally consenting, unless it is a matter of medical necessity. There is no legislation in Canada that permits a third party (including parents, next-of-kin, the public trustee or the administrator of a facility) to consent to a non-therapeutic sterilization on behalf of a person with a disability.

This case was the first in a line of cases that together make it possible to tease out the legal and social parameters of what human rights and equality mean for disabled people. Similar cases in other countries provide contrasting views of disability, and also build a picture of what human rights mean in practice, and how pervasively the notions of charity and disentitlement attach to disability. These cases draw a line in the sand as to where rights can be exercised by disabled people and where the usual rules, norms, standards and customs do not require that disabled people be treated to the same benefits of citizenship as do others. These are not cases about substantive issues – sterilization, sign language interpretation and so on. Rather, they are case studies of the interplay between law, social theory and disability. The tension between promoting rights, enabling citizenship and paternalistic protection underlie these legal cases (Rioux 1990).

The court in the *Eve* case limited the *parens patriae* power, a beneficent, paternalistic area of responsibility, and argued that the right to procreate or the privilege to give birth is fundamental, thereby circumscribing the power of the state to restrict fundamental rights based on disability or on the duty of the state to protect vulnerable people. In England, at the same time, the House of Lords rejected the findings of *Eve*, and applied the best interests test to a similar situation, a seventeen-year-old girl with an intellectual disability. They determined that the procedure was in her best interests, and upheld the trial judge's granting of the application for wardship and gave permission for the operation to be performed. The court made a finding that the right to reproduce is valuable only if the individual can exercise autonomy. In their view such a right would be irrelevant to the girl concerned, and even harmful in the particular case, and it was the prerogative of the court to determine when that would be the case. They viewed intellectual disability as such a case.

Lord Hailsham, LC, stated that while the history within the Canadian court's decision of the *parens patriae* jurisdiction was 'extremely helpful' to him, he found that

> his [Mr Justice LaForest writing on behalf of the Canadian Supreme Court] conclusion that the procedure of the sterilization should never be authorized for non-therapeutic purposes [is] totally unconvincing and in startling contradiction to the welfare principle which should be the first and paramount consideration in wardship cases.... To talk of the 'basic right' to reproduce of an individual who is not capable of knowing the causal connection between intercourse and childbirth, the nature of pregnancy, what is involved in delivery, unable to form maternal instincts or to care for a child appears to me wholly to part company with reality. (*Re B* 1987).

Mr Justice LaForest wrote for the Canadian court:

The grave intrusion on a person's rights and the certain physical damage that ensues from non-therapeutic sterilization without consent, when compared to the highly questionable advantages that can result from it, have persuaded me that it can never safely be determined that such a procedure is for the benefit of that person. Accordingly, the procedure should never be authorized for non-therapeutic purposes under the *parens patriae* jurisdiction.

Lord Bridge, while not disputing the *Eve* decision on the facts, was critical of the nature of rights that was proposed by the Canadian court. His criticism was categorical and revealing.

This sweeping generalization seems to me, with respect, to be entirely unhelpful. To say that the court can never authorize sterilization of a ward as being in her best interests would be patently wrong. To say that it can only do so if the operation is 'therapeutic' as opposed to 'non-therapeutic' is to divert attention from the true issue, which is whether the operation is in the ward's best interest, and [turn it into a] debate as to where the line is to be drawn between 'therapeutic and 'non-therapeutic'.

He rejected the Canadian Supreme Court's rights analysis, and focused on the insignificance of rights in this context and the potential harm that could result. He dismissed the argument by stating that:

The Supreme Court of Canada in *Re Eve (Eve, 1986)* at 5, refers...to 'the great privilege of giving birth'. The sad fact in...[this] case is that the mental and physical handicaps under which the ward suffers effectively render her incapable of ever exercising that right or enjoying that privilege...I find it difficult to understand how anyone examining the facts humanely, compassionately and objectively could reach any other conclusion.

Lord Oliver interpreted the *Eve* decision as having challenged the notion that the best interests of the female involved were the primary concern. He wrote:

His (Mr Justice LaForest's) conclusion was that sterilization should never be authorized for non-therapeutic purposes under the *parens patriae* jurisdiction. If in that conclusion the expression 'non-therapeutic' was intended to exclude measures taken for the necessary protection from future harm of the person over whom the jurisdiction is exercisable then I respectfully ... disagree with it for it seems to me to contradict what is the sole and paramount criteria for the exercise of the jurisdiction, viz the welfare and the benefit of the ward.

The critique of the Canadian case by the House of Lords is important to understanding what is meant by rights and citizenship when they attach to disability. The two courts addressed the question from very distinct perspectives which led them to quite different determinations. The Canadian court approached it from the perspective of rights and equality, while the British court conceptualized it as a welfare issue and found resolution in the legal concept of 'best interests' as a legitimate determination of the court and a basis for granting wardship.

The right which the Canadian court argued was being protected was the natural right to bear children. This right took precedence in the court's decision over the right to enable sterilization to be performed without the individual's consent. Their argument was framed in terms of the non-therapeutic nature of the medical procedure itself. This is consistent with the usual legal discourse about non-therapeutic medical treatment. The British court, on the other hand, put that right itself in question. They claimed it as a limited right, dependent on the ability to exercise it. If, as they claim, the right is limited only to those who can make a legitimate case for being able to exercise it, then they can rightly argue that it can be removed by whatever authority is put in a position to determine who can fulfil the prerequisite on which the right is based.

The Canadian court recognized the context of the sterilization decision. That it is a question of values was written into the decision:

> There are other reasons for approaching an application for sterilization of a mentally incompetent [sic] person with the utmost caution. To begin with, the decision involves values in an area where our social history clouds our vision and encourages many to perceive the mentally handicapped [sic] as somewhat less than human. This attitude has been aided and abetted by now discredited eugenic theories whose influence was felt in this country as well as the United States.

They thereby put in question the concept that a right is dependent on the ability of those who have to exercise it – a condition that is not otherwise conventionally accepted. But even if it were just to make a right dependent on the ability to exercise it, it would not be so from a rights perspective in the case where the limitation of the right is based on an assumption that there is a *prima facie* class of people who will be unlikely to be able to exercise the right. In this case, it is the class of women who have learning difficulties. It would also not be just in the case where other citizens were not similarly expected to be able to show that they could exercise the right according to the presumed or set criteria. There is no requirement that females who are not disabled understand 'the causal connection between intercourse and childbirth, the nature of pregnancy, what is involved in delivery, and [able] to form maternal instincts or to care for a child'.

The welfare principle that is the 'welfare and benefit of the ward' and 'the best interests of the woman' was the principle that the Canadian court found contentious. The court made the argument that the 'best interests of the woman' ought to be framed in terms of her right to bear children and the preservation of that right over the right of the state to interfere within the parameters of the *parens patriae* power. The claim by the English court that the 'best interests' test could be substituted for the more stringent consent procedures required for medical treatment that was non-therapeutic emasculated the long history of legal jurisprudence in medical law and enabled the label of learning difficulty to override traditional legal protections for individuals in medical treatment.

In many nations, custom and laws have been in place to protect those too infirm or too incapable to protest their fundamental deprivation. But in the process of 'protecting', such laws and customs sometimes put people in the position of having to prove that they are entitled to goods and services and opportunities that are considered the rights of the non-disabled population. The result is that for many disabled people, rights become privileges to be earned. This model of law, which bestows rights as 'charitable privilege' (Rioux 1993, 1994) emphasizes benevolence and pity, and puts in practice control exercised through expert and professional decision making. The rationale for denying rights is usually argued from the perspective of the best interests of the individual concerned. This raises some fundamental questions about the basis for rights entitlements, and gives the authority in law to experts to decide who ought to be able to exercise their rights and the criteria one has to meet to be given the option to exercise those rights. For the disabled individual, the decision may fall to the knowledge of the 'expert' about a particular disability.

Law and jurisprudence relating to disability, by their character, set up a framework for the consideration of social facts, including the recognition of past discriminatory and differential responses to disabled persons. So legal cases and their arguments – for example, the contrasting cases of *Eve* and *B* – help to focus on clarifying the meaning and reality of human rights and citizenship for disabled people. They suggest that there is, at least in some places and in some legal circles, an attempt to move beyond impairment as the sole criterion for the exercise of rights.

The courts and legislatures in other countries are also struggling with how to put rights into practice, and with what human rights and citizenship mean when disability becomes part of the consideration. It is telling that the resolution of these issues for non-disabled or non-identified disabled people is not an issue in the same manner. This is where the questions at the margins become central to the exercise of human rights and citizenship and the places where it becomes clear how rights are infringed and the exercise of citizenship restricted on the basis of disability.

In a similar case in Australia (*Marion*, 1992), the court acknowledged that sterilization was not about medical issues *per se*, but rather gender issues and disability discrimination (Brady et al. 2001). The court decided in *Marion* that the scope of parental authority did not extend to special medical procedures, and that sterilization of children requires a judicial or quasi-judicial authority in all cases.

While it clearly articulated the need for heightened accountability in this type of decision making, it expressed the issues as the balancing of the right of bodily integrity of the child with the family interests and with the child welfare approach, using the 'best interests of the child' as the paramount principle for decision making. The balance of the social and moral issues in this case can be distinguished from both the English and the Canadian decision.

The result has been an individualized case-by-case approach to determining when sterilization is justifiable. The requirement of court authorization 'ensures a hearing from those experienced in different ways in the care of those with [an] intellectual disability and from those with experience of the long term social and psychological effects of sterilization' (*Marion*, 1992 at 259).

The High Court prescribed guiding principles, which are the guidelines to be followed by the court authorizing the procedure. The guiding principles are:

- The issue for the court in considering whether to consent to a sterilization procedure is whether in all the circumstances of the particular child the procedure is in the child's best interests (*Marion*, 1992 at 259).
- Sterilization procedures should never be authorized unless 'some compelling justification is identified and demonstrated' (*Marion*, 1992 at 268).
- To come to the view that a sterilization procedure is in a child's best interests, the court has to be satisfied that sterilization is a step of 'last resort', or in other words that 'alternative and less invasive procedures have all failed or it is certain that no other procedure or treatment will work' (*Marion*, 1992 at 259–60).

Significantly, the court recognized the policy inherent in past discriminatory practices related to disability and put sterilization in its broader context, including the history of the eugenics movement of the early part of the twentieth century. The fundamental principle of bodily integrity was acknowledged as having equal importance for disabled persons as it has for others, thereby inherently recognizing their equal value and entitlement as citizens. The court, to preserve the conventional notion of family privacy and autonomy, balanced the child's right to bodily integrity with the interests of the family.

The court, however, still held the child's best interests to be the overriding principle for decision making. 'Some commentators see [this] as endorsing an approach to decision making in these matters based on fundamental human rights, whereas others see it as endorsing a paternalistic child welfare approach' (Brady et al. 2001: 7). There is general agreement that this has the potential for discrepancies in outcomes for children.

Citizenship

These cases provide a way in to understanding how concepts of citizenship and the consequent rights have been applied in the case of disabled people. Citizenship determines the conditions for full membership and inclusion in a society. The meaning of citizenship touches on the definition of the community and the conditions of inclusion and exclusion – that is, who belongs and under what conditions. Claims for citizenship then can be seen as claims for membership, for determining who is in and who is out. Setting the boundaries of citizenship frames the rights and responsibilities of citizens and the elements of both state and individual responsibility. The boundaries of citizenship have historically determined the relationship among individuals who share a relationship with a state and between the individual and the state (Jensen and Papillon 2000). There is no universally agreed-upon notion of citizenship, although the many definitions share commonalities. A useful definition for our purposes is one that presents it as a dynamic relationship along three complementary dimensions: rights and responsibilities, access and belonging (Jensen and Phillips 1996). Kymlinka and Norman (1995: 283) used a two-dimensional approach, rights and belonging. Marshall (1963) introduced the notion that in addition to civil rights (freedom of speech, mobility, religion and association; the right to enter contracts; and the right to due process of law) and political rights (the right to vote and to participate in elections) conferred on individuals, citizenship also conferred a status on an individual that entitles them to social and economic security. 'Social citizenship was presented as a status that recognized the individual's rights to be included in the institutions of society, to have basic needs met, to be cared for when needed, to develop capacities and to make contributions to society' (Roeher 1993). Social rights included such rights as the right to education, access to housing and health services, and income security.

Citizenship presumes equality between citizens, as well as equality in the way in which the state operates in relation to individuals. Citizens are presumed to be equal in rights. Thus, the state guarantees equality by making rights and responsibilities equally available to all citizens. To ensure social rights, then, requires more than formal equality (equal treatment); it requires equality in practice – that is, equality of results (Rioux 1994). Rights and responsibility as elements of citizenship entail that there be some way of guaranteeing that they can be realized, if they are not to be hollow rights. The institutions of society, both the political institutions and social institutions such as schools, the labour market, and health care have to be able to guarantee the realization of those rights.

A citizen also has to have both the right and the capacity to participate. Disabled people tend to lack both. They lack the right as a consequence of legal structures that assume an inherent incapacity and use legal notions of paternalism to safeguard them. They trade rights for charity (Herr 1977; Rioux 1993). The capacity to participate is restricted by legal, social and physical barriers to participation that result from institutional design and the lack of support provided by the state and community to those with disabilities.

The third element of citizenship, the element of belonging, usually refers to being

> part of a specific political community, to participate in its economic and social life and to enjoy its support in case of need. Citizenship defines the boundaries of belonging, giving specific recognition and status to the ones entitled to participate and benefit from the political community. From the time of ancient Greece, the status of citizen identified those who were part of the community, distinguishing them from those excluded from it, whether because they were strangers or because they were not deemed deserving. (Jensen and Papillon 2000: 11)

The disabled status has almost universally been a condition that has been used as a rationale for disentitling people from citizenship based on an ethical argument of who is deserving. Claims to protection from harm from self or others and to services have been more widely available to disabled people than has a claim to citizenship. This is certainly the case in the Western industrialized states, where the status of 'worthy poor' led to some entitlements but not to the exercise of citizenship status. In many cases, there are still rights to services, but not rights to citizenship. The court in England in its finding in *Re B* was following this reasoning, in particular when it argued that there was no need to consider the right of an intellectually disabled woman *not* to be sterilized, because the issue is about protecting a woman in whose best interests the action is being taken.

Inclusion, as it is used here, does not suggest homogenization of the population, but recognizes differential rights and that difference has to be accommodated for citizenship and rights to be achieved (Minow 1990; Sachs 1996). The sterilization cases suggest ways in which citizenship and the consequent rights have been circumscribed for disabled people. First, economic globalization has had an impact on limiting citizenship and its attached rights. Second, rights are made dependent on normative standards and on customary practice. In this second case, a new legal status has been substituted that either does not carry citizenship or carries a restricted form of citizenship. This happens when rights are dependent on formal equality or equal treatment or where an individual is expected to show some threshold capacity to 'responsibly' exercise the right before being entitled to it.

Globalization

There is a growing literature that argues that the social bond of citizenship and the effective exercise of rights are being challenged as a result of globalization. As states are becoming increasingly less autonomous and self-governing, as a result of structural readjustment (Esping-Andersen 1985; Kaul et al. 1999), international monetary systems and global trading policies, the relationship of the individual to the state is much less clear. The boundaries of citizenship and the incumbent rights are no longer seen as necessarily within the influence of the state, as national policies become less central to economic development and democratic development.

As economic effectiveness and efficiency and monetary crises become state priorities, there has been widespread acceptance of privatizing the impacts of poverty, lack of education, isolation and neglect of those who are unable to contribute economically. This has had a significant impact on those with disabilities. Increasingly in this context, there is evidence that disability is being privatized (Rioux and Zubrow 2001). The shrinking public domain excludes those who are in need or who require institutional restructuring to participate in the social, economic and political life of the state and to exercise citizenship and rights. The economic rationale for privatizing the issue of disability has become both politically and functionally useful for the globalization of capital and for governments that are downsizing, decentralizing and dealing with imposed debt restructuring and liberalization.

While 'the public domain has been reoriented to incorporate market machinery into its activities; it has also undergone a change in goals which are no longer committed to a socio-political perspective that covers the values of equity and social justice' (Arora 2001: 23; Kuttner 1984). The narrower perspectives of efficiency and profitability have replaced these goals. States have then arbitrarily disowned their responsibility towards meeting the basic needs of citizens. Deficit reduction is argued to be a greater social good than social justice and basic rights (Kuttner 1984). Individual self-sufficiency triumphs in this scheme as a valued economic and cultural commodity. Consequently, social well-being has effectively shifted from a public good to a private good, and social activities – health, education, housing, jobs, job security, etc. – are privatized and run with a profit motive as the norm. Efforts towards legitimating these changes continue to be made through policy aimed at replacing the discourse of basic rights with that of efficiency and profitability, often used interchangeably. Social concerns, from this vantage point, are not supposed to interfere with economic processes of the market or the state.

> This is meant to increase efficiency. The question of access to this efficiency is not considered important. Access comes to be defined as an individual problem not a social concern . . . many social problems are simply dismissed as individual problems, calling for individual solutions. Unemployment becomes a problem of acquiring skills, insecurity in jobs a matter of upgrading skills, health and education more a subject of consciousness raising. Structural content of problems facing the society is thereby de-linked from everything except market opportunities. Markets themselves become an important social concern when redefinition of issues creates legitimacy for them. They are expected to answer social problems but through their own definition of issues, through individualization, so to say. (Arora 2001: 29)

> Health is not simply turned into a business with growing access on market orientation; implicit in this process is its loss of status as a right. It is this denial of meaning of citizenship through a denial of even basic rights that is the most disturbing implication of liberalization. (Arora 2001: 32)

The failure of the economic liberalization and reforms programme of the 1990s (Drache 2001) to take an integrated view of economic and social policy accounts for the trend towards redefinition of many problems as individual problems rather than social concerns, thereby denying the responsibility of state to even address them. This has had a significant impact on the exercise of rights and citizenship for disabled people, who have a history of exclusion that is being further entrenched by the supremacy of economic policy.

Non-rights-bearing citizens

Rights and citizenship have often been restricted for disabled persons by the argument that rights are extended to people only to the extent to which they can show a capacity to exercise them. United Nations instruments created specifically for disabled people in the 1970s had clauses that limited the full exercise of rights by incorporating clauses that limited rights 'to the extent possible'. The clause covered both the capacity of the individual to exercise the rights and the capacity of the state to provide support for their exercise. See specifically the Declaration on the Rights of Mentally Retarded Persons (1971) and the UN Declaration on the Rights of Disabled Persons (1975). This is precisely the argument of the English court in *Re B*. When disability is seen as a permanent status in which the impairment is the locus of the disability, then there is a strong argument for such restriction. When disability is recognized as a social construct, the functional incapacity resulting not from individual impairment but as a consequence of social relationship, the argument for restricting citizenship and rights is not sustainable.

> Equality requires that focus not only be directed at 'illness' or 'impairment' but also at activity and participation. Unless [disabled people] are treated with dignity and respect, there is little hope that the structural features of society will be re-moulded to incorporate accommodations to include them. (Jones and Marks 2000: 153)

The history of this type of exclusion of individuals in receipt of relief can be found, for example, under the English Poor Laws, which excluded those who were poor from citizenship.

> The Poor Law treated the claims of the poor, not as an integral part of the rights of the citizen, but as an alternative to them – as claims, which could be met only if the claimants ceased to be citizens in any true sense of the word. For paupers forfeited in practice the civil right of personal liberty, by internment in the workhouse, and they forfeited by law any political rights they might possess. (Marshall 1963: 88)

Full citizenship required the capacity to be self-supporting and fully responsible. While there has been a shift from the 'poor relief' of the English Poor Laws and their pretenders in other nations, such as Canada and the United States, welfare laws and disability benefits in many countries still require that disabled people prove that they are permanently incapable of working (limiting the right to work) and require that people live in designated housing and receive social programmes through the agency that filters the state benefits as a condition of receiving them (limiting the right to choice of personal life-style or self-determination). Means testing as a method of determining disability benefits is not uncommon, and it limits entitlement to own property and other benefits of citizenship. The social rights of citizenship have consequently been restricted for disabled people by the context in which disability is viewed.

The provision of public services such as education, health care, housing and income support is rarely seen in terms of promoting human rights. While the idea of a national minimum standard of living as a right of citizenship has been an important underpinning of the welfare state in industrialized democracies since World War II, disabled people, precisely because of their disabled status, have not had access to these services as they are provided to others (with parallel systems of services being established for those with disabilities) or to the same level of services. They have not been included within the planning of services and support of generic services, but have been provided for, if at all, outside the parameters of the legitimate boundaries of the rights-bearing citizens. Services for disabled persons have, then, been provided as charitable benefits, not as part of the state mandate to provide for its citizens. Claims of out-of-control expenditures that threaten economic growth have been used by governments as a basis for re-evaluating the provision of services and for, in some cases, redefining what is a disability. The inability of governments to support their current levels of public expenditure on such services has therefore been used as an argument for downsizing.

The notion of social citizenship, one that incorporates an element of entitlement, has been argued by the 'cost-cutters' (Mendelson 1993), and those trying to limit the role of the state, to encourage citizens to take but not give, to disengage from the labour force, and to be willing to live off social assistance. The 'cost-cutters' argue that it is necessary to reintroduce the notion of responsibility into citizenship. This has led to the increasing privatization of social disadvantage. This is the argument underlying the reasoning of both the English and the Australian courts with respect to sterilization and the mechanism for transforming disabled people into non-rights-bearing citizens.

There has been increasing recognition, however, that economic exclusion and poverty affect the capacity of the individual to exercise citizenship. In some countries, policies have been enacted that require tax expenditures to provide the support that disabled people need to exercise their citizenship. For example, the Americans with Disabilities Act (1990) mandates expenditures on making the society accessible. Human rights legislation in a number of countries also makes provision for the redress of those who have been disadvantaged and for decisions that require expenditure to enable citizens to participate in their societies. These developments enhance both the ability to exercise citizenship rights and to take on social responsibilities.

Recent reflections on the importance of social policy in citizenship can be seen in a statement such as the following in Britain's Prime Minister Tony Blair's *New Britain: My Vision of a Young Country* (1996: 1): 'People are not separate economic actors competing in the marketplace of life. They are citizens of a community. We are social beings. We develop the moral power of personal responsibility for each other and ourselves.' The consequences of exclusion and poverty for access to the full rights of citizenship are at least recognized in theory, even if they are not yet fully ameliorated for the most marginalized groups, including disabled persons.

The fiction of the rights of citizenship is exposed when there are social, legal and political mechanisms for enabling people to be declared non-citizens in relation to the exercise of some rights. The fiction is also exposed when meaningful access limits the level of participation, whether due to economic or other reasons, for a particular group. Both these circumstances have faced disabled people expecting to exercise their citizenship.

Globalizing social rights

Both the trend toward globalization and the legal-social recognition of a class of non-rights-bearing citizens have had an impact on the exercise of citizenship for disabled people. The result for disabled people has been the denial of their citizenship and the rights that would normally be accorded to others. This has occurred both through benign neglect and through the systemic denial of any attempts to carry out structural adjustment to enable their participation and through the ongoing, normative and legal assumptions of incapacity that have led to charitable support.

An alternative to these limiting approaches to citizenship is to introduce notions about the extent and degree of rights violations that can be documented and the implications that this has for social and economic development. The crisis is not then an economic crisis, but a crisis of social justice, a crisis of equality and a crisis of fairness. This leads to questions about why some people have so much and some so little; why power rests in the hands of only a few; why jobs depend on colour, race and able-bodiedness; why learning is limited to subjects that measure people as economic entities or contributors and so on. The importance of parity of social sustainability with issues of economic and environmental sustainability becomes evident when these questions are raised.

The incorporation of social rights within the parameters of human rights in the Universal Declaration on Human Rights, enacted by the United Nations in 1948, was a significant development. Michael Ignatieff in *The Rights Revolution* (2000) held that the declaration

> altered the balance between national sovereignty and individual rights. With the declaration, the rights of individuals were supposed to prevail over the rights of states when those states engaged in abominable practices. This might be the most revolutionary of all the changes that have taken place .... With each passing year, we get closer to a new dispensation in which the sovereign rights of states are conditional upon there being adequate protections for the basic human rights of citizens. (Ignatieff 2000: 49)

The declaration provided a starting point for recognizing the globalization of social rights – the rights of every individual to a basic minimum standard of living commensurate with human dignity and a sense of inclusion in the community (Mishra 2001). It is arguably a global social charter despite the fact that its system of ratification and implementation is voluntary, which focuses national social policy on a set of international norms and standards, initiatives and developments, aimed at establishing social rights. This recognizes the potential of social and economic policy as social investment to contribute to the spurring of human capital and therefore to economic growth.

Two major covenants of the United Nations, the International Covenant on Civil and Political Rights (ICCPR) and the International Covenant of Economic, Social, and Political Rights (ICESPR) have established the framework for the advancement of human rights worldwide, aimed at the institutionalization of a set of universal norms within each nation-state. These two covenants were adopted by the United Nations in 1966. It took another ten years for them to receive the minimum of thirty-five ratifications to come into force. By 1999 about three-quarters (141 out of 185) of the member states of the UN had ratified the ICESPR. It was in the late 1980s that a system of supervising compliance with the covenant was put in place. The concept of global social rights is premissed on the notion that there are certain fundamental basic needs which an individual ought to be entitled to have met as a human being.

The ICESPR begins to move towards the entrenchment of social rights on a global scale. Its implementation, however, involves a consideration of a nation's material wealth. The universal validity of the covenant is subject to the economic constraints of the individual nation-state. Thus the covenant acknowledges that states are expected to achieve the rights enumerated 'progressively' and to the 'maximum of available resources'. While this acknowledges the significant disparity between the economic developments of individual nations, it provides no mechanism to determine how such a calculation is to be made.

The expert committee appointed by the Economic and Social Council (ECOSOC) oversees compliance with the covenant. In General Comment no. 5 (1994), the committee specified core obligations under the covenant to 'ensure the satisfaction of, at the very least, minimum essential levels of each of the rights', which it is incumbent on the states to ensure. These core obligations include essential foodstuffs, essential primary health care, basic shelter and housing, and basic forms of education. What 'essential' and 'basic' mean in the general comment is not made clear. The formula for calculating what a country can reasonably invest in even these minimal core obligations has not been worked out; nor has the formula for deciding the degree of available resources and expenditure that would be required by economically advantaged nations. Which types of 'resource constraints' would entitle a lesser standard of enforcement of the covenant is also left unanswered.

Despite these limitations, these instruments put social rights on a par with the traditional liberal rights of civil and political liberties, and set a normative standard that all nations honour their commitment to these substantive rights, without distinction based on category, including disability. They subject the social policy of nation-states, at least nominally, to international norms and monitoring. In the case of disability, this has a particular consequence, because the conventional assumptions about disability as a restrictive condition attributable singularly to the inherent biological or medical condition of the person individualize the discrimination, including the restrictions on rights and citizenship. This is a cross-national phenomenon. The social policy of particular states is generally based on notions of disability as an individual pathology (Oliver 1990; Rioux 1997; Barnes 1999), and is legitimized by scientific rationalization of incapacity. The significance of bilateral and multilateral aid as well as international NGO aid work in the field of disability has resulted in entrenching conventional notions of disability in the types of programmes that have been funded in developing countries. In some cases, this has supported notions of limited citizenship and social rights by developing services and facilities based on charity and social development models, rather than rights models. Consequently, to promote human rights and citizenship for disabled people requires the support of international norms.

The entrenched globalization of science and economics that have supported limiting rights and citizenship of disabled people underscores the claim for globalizing social rights. Some argue that this anticipates the beginning of a global citizenship based not on nationhood but on personhood (Jensen and Papillon 2000). For disabled people who have been caught in a definition of their status as static, unchanging, individual and biomedically based, and on the strength of such scientific notions have had governments claim that it costs too much in the current economic climate to entrench their rights and citizenship, this has important implications. It does not follow from this that it is necessary for the individual to appeal only to global rights, and not to the benefits of citizenship found in the state apparatus. If science is global, then so too should there be the institutionalization of a set of human rights, enforceable at the national level. It is an argument for the acceptance of international norms and for international monitoring of those norms and standards. If economic and scientific globalization disproportionately disadvantage some classes of people, then it is reasonable to argue that social rights ought also to be globalized and monitored.

The way governments allocate their resources is a reflection of their interpretation of citizenship and rights and the role of the state. The development and protection of social rights – that is, a minimum standard of life as an entitlement – is fundamental to social justice. Social globalization is not so much a new idea as one that needs to be pursued with renewed vigour and clarity in the face of economic globalization. Disabled people have never been included in the mainstream of social rights. Traditionally their issues have been relegated to social development, to charity, to dispensation or to the determination of their best interests. But economic liberalization and globalization have highlighted the extent to which some people are excluded through the denial of their liberties and the restriction of participation in society. Those fundamental freedoms that governments promise to their citizens in democracies must also be protected for those with disabilities.

REFERENCES

Arora, D. 2001: website. *Institute for Studies in Industrial Development*, Delhi and Robarts Centre for Canadian Studies, York University.

Blair, T. 1996: *New Britain: My Vision of a Young Country*. London: Fourth Estate.

Brady, S., Britton, J. and Grover, S. 2001: *A Report Commissioned by the Sex Discrimination Commissioner and the Disability Discrimination Commissioner at the Human Rights and Equal Opportunity Commission*. Sydney.

Drache, D. (ed.) 2001: *The Market and the Public Domain: Global Governance and the Asymmetry of Power*. London: Routledge.

Esping-Andersen, G. 1985: *Politics against Markets: The Social Democratic Road to Power*. Princeton: Princeton University Press.

Herr, S. 1977: Rights into action: implementing the human rights of the mentally handicapped. *Catholic University Law Review*, 26, 203–318.

Ignatieff, M. 2000: *The Rights Revolution*. Toronto: House of Anansi Press.

Jensen, J. and Papillon, M. 2000: website. *The Canadian Policy Research Networks*.

Jensen, J. and Phillips, S. D. 1996: Regime shift: new citizenship practices in Canada. *International Journal of Canadian Studies*, 14, 111–36.

Jones, M. and Basser Marks, L. 2000: Valuing people through law – whatever happened to Marion? In Marks (ed.), *Law in Context Special Issues: Explorations on Law and Disability in Australia*, Sydney: Federation Press, 147–80.

Kaul, I., Grunberg, I. and Stern, M. A. 1999: *Global Public Goods: International Co-operation in the 21st Century*. New York: United Nations Development Program.

Kuttner, R. 1984: *The Economic Illusion: False Choices between Prosperity and Social Justice*. Boston: Houghton Mifflin.

Kymlinka, W. and Norman, W. 1995: Return of the citizen: a survey of recent work on citizenship theory. In R. Beiner (ed.), *Theorizing Citizenship*, Albany, NY: State University of New York Press, 283–322.

Marshall, T. H. 1963: Citizenship and social class. In T. H. Marshall (ed.), *Sociology at the Crossroads and Other Essays*, London: Heinemann.

Mendelson, M. 1993: Social Policy in Real Time. In L. Bella (ed.) *Rethinking Social Welfare: People, Policy and Practice*. Newfoundland: Dicks and Company Ltd, 5–22.

Minow, M. 1990: *Making All the Difference: Inclusion, Exclusion and American Law*. Ithaca, NY: Cornell University Press.

Mishra, R. 2001: Globalizing social rights. Robarts Centre for Canadian Studies website.

Oliver, M. 1990: *The Politics of Disablement*. Basingstoke: Macmillan.

Rioux, M. H. 1990: Sterilization and mental handicap: a rights issue. *Journal of Leisurability*, 17, 3–11.

Rioux, M. H. 1993: Exchanging charity for rights: the challenge for the next decade. *British Institute of Learning Disabilities*, 89, 1–8.

Rioux, M. H. 1994: Towards a concept of equality of well-being: overcoming the social and legal construction of inequality. *Canadian Journal of Law and Jurisprudence*, 127–47.

Rioux, M. H. 1997: Disability: the place of judgement in a world of fact. *Journal of Intellectual Disability Research*, 41, 102-11.

Rioux, M. H. forthcoming: On second thoughts: constructing knowledge, law, disability and inequality. In S. S. Herr et al. (eds), *Different but Equal: The Rights of Persons with Intellectual Disability*, Oxford: Oxford University Press.

Rioux, M. H. and Zubrow, E. 2001: Social disability and the public good. In D. Drache (ed.), *The Market and the Public Domain: Global Governance and the Asymmetry of Power*, London: Routledge, 148–71.

Roeher, I. 1993: *Social Well-being: A Paradigm for Reform*. Toronto: Roeher Institute.

Sachs, A. 1996: Human rights in the twenty first century: real dichotomies, false antagonism. In *Human Rights in the 21st Century*, Ottawa: Canadian Institute for the Administration of Justice.

12

Emancipatory Disability Research

Geof Mercer

Introduction

The alternative conceptual framework for understanding disability that emerged in the 1960s and 1970s shifted attention to the ways in which a 'disabling society' rather than individual impairments contributed to the exclusion of disabled people from everyday social life. By the late 1980s, disabled people argued for an extension of the notion of social barriers to a critique of contemporary research on disability. This resulted in the generation of a new emancipatory research paradigm that complemented radical, socio-political models of disability.

This chapter will review key issues in the emergence of emancipatory disability research with particular reference to the British literature. The discussion begins by outlining competing paradigms of social inquiry, and highlights the formative influence of critical theorists on those writers appraising the defining features of a radical approach to doing disability research. The discussion then concentrates on the issues raised when moving from theorizing to understanding the products of disability research and the importance of attending to methodological as well as epistemological questions. It argues, against recently expressed pessimistic concerns, that 'good', openly partisan, emancipatory research is a 'realistic goal' that should not be weighed down with an 'impossible dream' of what can be achieved by research alone (Oliver 1997).

The parasite people

From the dominant perspective, disability was equated with 'undesirable difference' and individual functional limitations. Hence it located the 'solution' primarily in medical and allied professional rehabilitation. This orthodoxy underpinned a system that condemned disabled people to the status of second-class citizens, characterized by wide-ranging social exclusion from mainstream society and segregated living in residential institutions. Criticism of this established, individualized approach to disability 'took off' in Europe and North America in the 1960s. In Britain, the Union of the Physically Impaired Against Segregation (UPIAS 1976) was in the vanguard of those advocating an alternative sociopolitical analysis. This pin-pointed the impact of 'disabling' social and environmental barriers on people with impairments and, more specifically, the role of non-disabled 'experts' in controlling their lives.

The need to extend this critique to the activities of mainstream research experts was accentuated by the experiences of disabled residents at the Le Court Cheshire Home in the south of England during the 1960s. They had invited the Tavistock Institute to investigate living conditions at Le Court following a dispute with management. However, as Paul Hunt, a resident and key player in establishing UPIAS, bitterly records, it soon became clear that the research experts were 'definitely not on our side'. (1981: 39). Instead, they played the role of 'detached' and 'unbiased' social scientists (1981: 39) while pursuing a traditional, individual approach to disability. The researchers, Eric Miller and Geraldine Gwynne (1972), describe themselves as trapped between two irreconcilable interests. For their part, the disabled residents were at a loss to understand the researchers' failure to condemn an institutional regime that even they acknowledged was equivalent to 'social death' for inmates (Miller and Gwynne 1972: 8). Hunt (1981) categorized the researchers as 'parasite people', by siding with the oppressors, looking after their own professional and academic interests, and leaving the residents feeling exploited and betrayed. This conclusion is echoed in more recent critiques: 'Disabled people have come to see research as a violation of their experience, as irrelevant to their needs and as failing to improve their material circumstances and quality of life' (Oliver 1992: 105). Hunt also condemned the researchers' lack of scientific rigour, notably their refusal to engage in an 'objective evaluation' (1981: 40), by which he meant the failure to side with those experiencing social oppression. This general attack on traditional research as disablist has acted as a reference point to later writers exploring a new course for disability research.

Paradigm wars

In the 1980s, the literature on research within the social sciences empha-sized the deep divisions between competing perspectives (Blaikie 1993). This was captured in references to 'paradigm wars'. Thus, when a new approach to disability research was articulated in the early 1990s, it took as its reference point the contrasting ambitions and assumptions associ-ated with the main positivist, interpretive and critical theory accounts (Oliver 1992).

Positivism

Until the last decades of the twentieth century, *positivism* (or a revised *post-positivism*) dominated social research. Its foundations lay in nineteenth and early twentieth-century arguments that the social sciences should adopt a similar logic of inquiry to that of the natural sciences (Blaikie 1993; Smith 1998). This guided answers to central questions of ontology (what is the nature of reality?), epistemology (what is the relationship between the knower/researcher and knowledge?) and methodology (how does the knower/researcher go about obtaining knowledge about the social world?) (Guba and Lincoln 1994).

The early formulation of positivism attracted widespread criticism and underwent important revisions while also demonstrating 'internal' differences (Blaikie 1993; Guba and Lincoln 1994). Yet, at its ontological core is the assumption that the social and the natural worlds contain a single reality and discernible patterns and uniformities, although these vary over time and across cultures. This is generally (but not exclu-sively) linked with a quantifying approach (using numerical data and associated techniques and assumptions) to establish cause-and-effect re-lationships between social phenomena. In a hypothetico-deductive meth-odology, there is a distinctive sequence of stages: specify theory, derive hypotheses, operationalize concepts and develop measures, collect data, test hypotheses, and reassess theory. There is a further attachment to the criteria of validity, reliability and objectivity for judging the quality of knowledge generated (Smith 1998). Its epistemology is secured by a commitment to value neutrality and objectivity, even if these are difficult to achieve in practice (Hammersley 2000).

Interpretive approach

By contrast, the *interpretive* paradigm (including hermeneutics and phenomenology) stresses clear-cut differences between the natural and social sciences. Its unifying belief centres on the social construction of reality and the existence of multiple versions (ontological pluralism). It highlights everyday experiences and understandings. The theoretical and research orientation is shifted from establishing causal explanations to exploring the situation-specific interpretation of social action.

Particular weight is attached to the 'authenticity' of lay accounts. Knowledge is not so much 'discovered' as 'produced' and refined through interaction (consensus building) between researcher and research participants (Schwandt 1994). The accent is on interpretive (qualitative) data, with an inductive buildup of concepts, research questions and theories, rather than testing hypotheses; information expressed in feelings, attitudes and actions; and engaging researcher and researched as fellow participants in producing, generating and validating meanings about these phenomena (Lincoln and Guba 2000).

Critical social theory

A very different refutation of positivist social theory and research insisted that it had become so obsessed with objectivity that the critical potential of the 'sociological imagination' to expose entrenched power relations was downgraded (Mills 1959). A key contribution of critical social theory was that it reinterpreted many seemingly 'personal troubles' as more appropriately understood as 'public issues' that have their origins in wider social structures and processes. Moreover, successful knowledge claims were linked with dominant interests and social relations in specific social and historical contexts.

An early influence was Paolo Freire (1972), who sponsored participatory research in pursuit of 'education for liberation' among poor people in Latin America. He outlined a process of 'conscientization' or critical reflection on everyday realities and common-sense knowledge. This emphasized empowerment through self-understanding as the outcome of social investigation, education and political action (Reason 1988). It accentuated interactive or 'dialogic' methods, which went well beyond interpretive empathy for the subject and stressed the researcher's partisan involvement in emancipatory struggles.

This praxis orientation was epitomized by the researcher's participation in social movements as a means of 'raising their *capacity for historical action*' (Touraine 1981: 145). Taking the side of the socially excluded acted as a catalyst for investigating the interplay of theory, practice and action. In comparison with the positivist submission that partiality provided a source of contamination in research, critical theorists highlighted its capacity to generate theoretical insights and inform political practice. This also underscored feminist writings, such as Maria Mies's (1983) account of 'conscious partiality' in producing research knowledge.

Since the 1970s, critical theorists and researchers have begun to recognize the breadth of social oppression beyond social class to include, for example, social divisions around 'race' and gender. Again, the rebuttal of mainstream social theory also implicated research approaches for their role in 'silencing' these different forms of social inequality and domination (Kincheloe and McLaren 2000). In addition, the proliferation of contrasting theories of power and domination encouraged wide-ranging debates about the possibilities for emancipation and empowerment of oppressed groups. Major influences include Gramsci's discussion of hegemony and the generation of willing consent among subordinate groups to a Foucauldian emphasis on discourse and power/knowledge relations. Power is less about confrontation with an external force. It has become more diffuse and covert with the development of systems for public surveillance and self-regulation (Foucault 1984). This in turn has led to a reformulation of research into emancipation/empowerment as a long drawn-out process, with lulls and reversals as well as radical advances, and no fixed end state.

Most recently, the debates within critical theory have moved beyond the established trinity of research paradigms. Lincoln and Guba (2000) add poststructuralist/postmodern as well as participatory approaches. These offer different epistemologies (attending to previously ignored groups), novel ways of representation (in experience and text), and innovative styles of research (and ways of determining its 'quality' or authenticity).

Emancipatory research

In probably the most influential and widely cited contribution to establishing the credentials of the new paradigm for emancipatory disability research, Mike Oliver (1992) locates it firmly within critical theory precepts, including anti-imperialist/racist and feminist attacks on positivist and, to a lesser degree, interpretive research models, together with 'social model' theorizing of disability. He follows Jurgen Habermas (1974) in arguing that the historical shift in research approaches – from positivist to interpretive to critical-emancipatory – is underpinned by different kinds of reasoning for producing research knowledge – instrumental / technical, practical and critical / emancipatory. A further link is with distinctive forms of policy making: engineering / prediction (positivist), enlightenment (interpretive), and struggle (emancipatory). Finally, each is associated with a distinctive view of disability – individual, social and political – although in any specific historical conjuncture these may overlap. On this basis, traditional research is castigated for reinforcing a personal tragedy approach to disability that represents disabled people as victims of their individual pathology, largely passive to their circumstances, and as in need of 'care and protection' (Oliver 1992; Rioux and Bach 1994).

The emancipatory mode is geared to praxis-oriented research that exposes social oppression and facilitates political action to transform society (Humphries 1997). Echoing Paul Hunt's (1981) denunciation of the 'parasite people', a stark choice is outlined: 'Do researchers wish to join with disabled people and use their expertise and skills in their struggles against oppression or do they wish to continue to use these skills and expertise in ways in which disabled people find oppressive?' (Oliver 1992: 102). Support for emancipatory struggles then translates into a disability research model that stresses the following features:

- rejection of the individual model of disability and its replacement by a social model approach;
- concentration on a partisan research approach (so denying researcher objectivity and neutrality) in order to facilitate the political struggles of disabled people;
- reversal of the traditional researcher–researched hierarchy / social relations of research production, while also challenging the material relations of research production;
- pluralism in choice of methodologies and methods.

These points illustrate how the early writers on emancipatory disability research promoted it as a radical alternative to the positivist and interpretive paradigms, by stressing above all its commitment to political change and empowerment rooted in a social model approach. In comparison, methodological criteria were downplayed. Hence, the choice of methods was regarded as a subsidiary matter, and the support for pluralism did not reflect detailed consideration of the many difficult issues raised when translating these broad ambitions into everyday research practice (Stone and Priestley 1996). This contrasts unfavourably with the burgeoning literature on this subject by feminist researchers (e.g. Lather 1991; Stanley and Wise 1993; Maynard 1994): 'We who do empirical research in the name of emancipatory politics must discover ways to connect our research methodology to our theoretical concerns and political commitments' (Lather 1991: 172). Even a sympathetic review of disability research in the mid-1990s felt obliged to point out that 'none of the advocates of the paradigm have yet laid claim to the achievement of truly emancipatory research *within the context of a field study*' (Stone and Priestley 1996: 706).

Social model approach

The orthodoxy among British disability writers has been that 'the adoption of a social model of disability' provides 'the ontological and epistemological basis for research production' (Priestley 1997: 91). This confirms its clear separation from an individual or personal tragedy approach. It is graphically illustrated in the 'translation' of survey questions addressed to disabled people by government departments. One item from the Office of Populations, Censuses and Surveys (OPCS) asked: 'Does your health problem / disability affect your work in any way at present?' Its social model alternative reads, 'Do you have problems at work because of the physical environment or the attitudes of others?' (Oliver 1990: 7–8).

However, the revised questions also demonstrate the structuralist leanings of early social model accounts (Barnes et al. 1999). This has triggered criticism from disabled feminists that disability research must widen its ontological gaze to incorporate the feminist maxim that the 'personal is political' and include the experience of both impairment *and* disability (Morris 1992). The social model was also censored for ignoring or downplaying differences in the experience of oppression within the disabled population. As more disciplines and theoretical perspectives entered these debates, the parameters of disability research became even more disparate and contested. Most notably, poststructuralist accounts now offered a significant competing discourse around emancipation.

The early literature was inclined towards a 'standpoint' position in which disabled people's experiences and knowledge claims, at least where informed by a social model approach, were regarded as 'authentic'. However, the focus shifted increasingly to differences in the experience of oppression among disabled people, particularly on the basis of age, gender and 'race'. This effectively undermined the notion of a homogeneous category of 'privileged' knowers. The spotlight turned to competing discourses, voices and experiences within the disabled population (Corker 1999). This has been reinforced by the poststructuralist accent on listening to the range of disabled people's voices and hitherto silenced narratives. It also allowed for much more analytical space in considering the fluidity of identities and experiences. This has evident consequences for the conduct of disability research.

The social model has been further criticized for exaggerating the commonality of different impairment groups. Deaf people, people with learning difficulties and mental health system users/survivors have all questioned the inclusiveness of the social model. This has focused attention on contrasting epistemologies and on competing 'knowledge claims' within the disabled population. In their review of research with mental health system survivors, Peter Beresford and Jan Wallcraft (1997) illustrate not only variation between the accounts of 'survivors' and disability writers, but also the contrasting viewpoints articulated among those with direct experience of an oppressive psychiatric system. (An associated, but largely unexplored, issue is the choice of research strategy for disability research with 'able-bodied' people and their experiences of disabling others.)

Even so, arguments for the incorporation of the diversity of disability experiences into social model research remain highly contested. Vic Finkelstein, one of the main architects of the social barriers approach in Britain, argues against an obsession with experience, because of its overlap with impairment and individualistic concerns. Equally, subjective experience is not necessarily the same as critical awareness and understanding, and experiential studies too often ignore power relations and wider contextual factors. As a feminist critic has argued:

> [E]xperience is represented as unmediated: spoken words are placed directly on a page with no account given of how and where they came from, the power relations involved, the publishing deals signed, the editing and selection processes. Or researchers take as self-evident the identities of those whose experience is being documented... Our experience is part of a social, historical, cultural, economic, political process. (Skeggs 1995: 15)

Instead, Finkelstein ties the social model and disability research to a critical analysis of the 'inner workings of the disabling society' (1999: 861) that must avoid entrapment in professional and service provider agendas. This underscores his condemnation of those studies that pursue emancipatory aims within policy reforms of community care, but in so doing risk diluting the necessary research focus on social barriers.

On a different tack disability theorists have also been charged with slowness in acknowledging the validity of different national contexts and agendas in disability theorizing and practice. A particular instance is provided by assertions that social model-based research is inappropriate outside Western industrial capitalist societies. For example, Emma Stone (1997) reported considerable difficulties in doing emancipatory disability research field-work in China, because it was perceived as an instrument of Western imperialism and at odds with Chinese experience and culture. A stark choice beckoned for the researcher between championing the social model perspective and overriding disabled people's perceptions and experiences, or making compromises to salvage the research project.

The originators of the social model did not claim that it was a comprehensive theory of disability. However, recent theoretical debates have significant and wider implications for the conduct of disability research.

Partisanship and commitment to political change

Howard Becker's (1967) much-quoted question, 'Whose side are we on?', has been widely invoked to highlight the necessary partisanship of disability research. It is bolstered by a dismissal of the 'myth' of neutrality and objectivity stressed by positivists. At issue is whether academics too often cede their claimed independence in order to secure their own professional position, although this needs to be set against the institutional and structural constraints in which researchers work (Barnes 1996; Shakespeare 1996; Stone and Priestley 1996; Zarb 1997). The contrary position elaborated by mainstream researchers is that partisan approaches threaten a 'rampant subjectivity where one finds only what one is predisposed to look for' (Lather 1991: 52).

For emancipatory researchers, the 'conscious partiality' promoted by Maria Mies (1983) must resonate with disabled people's lived experience in an unequal society. The partisanship of disability directs it to 'explore and identify appropriate avenues for change' (Finkelstein 1999: 862), or 'gain' and empowerment (Oliver 1997). This elevates outcomes as a central issue in judging research. Indeed, Oliver downgrades research in which he was involved – *Walking into Darkness* (Oliver et al. 1988) – precisely because of its lack of tangible impact on service provision.

However, the reasons why local and national policy makers accept, ignore or reject research findings and recommendations are diverse and rarely within the control of the researchers, let alone the participants. Contributors to the feminist literature similarly dismiss statements that 'studies which cannot be directly linked to transformational politics are not feminist. It raises the question as to how far the researcher is in control of the extent and direction of any change which her research might bring about' (Maynard 1994: 17). Moreover, research may 'succeed' or 'fail' at different levels, or have an unintended impact, with any judgement liable to variation over time. In most instances, there can be no guaranteed 'outcomes', except perhaps an end-of-research report.

The same difficulties surround attempts to establish whether benefits have accrued to disabled participants or disabled people more widely. The criteria for judging disability research are not so much whether it facilitated the self-empowerment of disabled people in terms of 'individual self-assertion, upward mobility and the psychological experience of feeling powerful' (Lather 1991: 3). Nor is emancipatory research 'successful' only when it leads to all social barriers being overturned, so that people with impairments are liberated from the disabling society, perhaps waiting on a much longer-term evaluation of the impact, well 'after the event' (Oliver 1997: 25). Rather, empowerment and emancipation are used interchangeably and are defined in terms of revealing social barriers, changing perceptions of disability, and generating political action. Even then, empowerment / emancipation is not in the gift of the researcher: 'The issue then for emancipatory research is not how to empower people, but, once people have decided to empower themselves, precisely what research can then do to facilitate this process' (Oliver 1992: 111). By contrast, disability writers have been quick to argue that some (disabled and non-disabled) researchers have benefited professionally and materially from their involvement (as with those teaching and writing about disability studies). Indeed, the literature is replete with 'confessions' from disability researchers that they have been the chief beneficiaries of their work – what Finkelstein (1999: 863) has aptly labelled 'Oliver's gibe'. This has done little to stimulate innovative research practices.

One frequently mentioned exception is the project sponsored by the British Council of Organisations of Disabled People (BCODP) into the social exclusion of disabled people (Barnes 1991). Its emancipatory credentials rested on its commitment to political change within a social model approach and accountability to disabled people through an advisory group of representatives from organizations controlled by disabled people. A further emphasis was the wide-ranging dissemination of its findings to stimulate campaigns and legislative action. Indeed, the priority accorded to producing and disseminating materials in a variety of accessible formats has become a feature of emancipatory disability research.

The stress on political change and gain constructs a research 'balance sheet' in which oppressor and oppressed and their respective gains are easily identified. In concrete social contexts, such calculations are often disputed. Research is not necessarily a zero-sum contest with one 'winner' and 'loser', just as among the winners/losers some gain/lose more than others do. Moreover, oppressors and oppressed are not always easily distinguished, or stable categories across different social contexts. What benefits disabled people may not advance the interests of other oppressed groups. Participants are not always agreed on where their best interests lie. Nor does the failure to transform the lives of research participants necessarily preclude a lack of impact more widely. Furthermore, disabled people may be implicated in the oppression of each other, or espouse reactionary viewpoints – for example, on the basis of people's age, 'race' or gender.

What research can achieve also depends on the social and historical context. Researchers work within a range of organizational and structural constraints, and sometimes relatively minor changes assume significance. Certainly, if disability research is equated solely with grandiose political projects, it will miss many opportunities for a positive impact, including many potentially illuminating small-scale studies.

Social and material relations of research production

Early descriptions of emancipatory disability research targeted the ways in which researchers position themselves with respect to the social and material relations of research production (Oliver 1992; Zarb 1992). The 'material relations' of research production cover the reliance on external funding bodies, as well as organizations that undertake research, including universities (Lloyd et al. 1996; Oliver 1997). Typical expectations and constraints from funders reinforce traditional research hierarchies and values (Moore et al. 1998).

However, disability writers have concentrated on reversing entrenched social relationships. Indeed, the transformative potential of disability research is equated with disabled people being 'actively involved in determining the aims, methods and uses of the research' (Zarb 1997: 52). Hence, researchers must forgo their traditional autonomy and 'learn how to put their knowledge and skills at the disposal of their research subjects, for them to use in whatever way they choose' (Oliver 1992: 111). The aspiration to break down the traditional hierarchy and build researcher accountability to disabled participants raises questions about the nature of 'control' and how it is 'measured'.

1   Who controls what the research will be about and how it will be carried out?

2 How far have we come in involving disabled people in the research process?
3 What opportunities exist for disabled people to criticize the research and influence future directions?
4 What happens to the products of the research? (Zarb 1992: 128)

A continuum spanning 'weak' to 'strong' direction by disabled people may be identified. Instances of disabled participants assuming full control are rare, but this has been claimed in some research studies involving groups of mental health survivors (Chamberlain 1988). In other cases, the intention has been to eradicate the distinction between researcher and researched by an emphasis on 'co-researchers and co-subjects' (Reason 1988: 1). This indicates a reflective dialogue with neither side dominating the other (Lloyd et al. 1996). Some believe that participatory options are the most realistic in the present political and economic context (Ward 1997; Zarb 1997).

However, disability theorists in Britain demonstrate conflicting views of participatory research and whether it rests on less than full control by disabled people. Mike Oliver (1992) is particularly dismissive, and equates it with playing by the rules of the system and geared to improving organizational efficiency rather than challenging established values or structures. However, this ignores the several branches of participatory (action) research and the commitment of some variants to the 'vital link between knowledge generation, education, collective action and the empowerment of oppressed people' (Cocks and Cockram 1995: 31). This radical form draws on liberation theology, Third World community development programmes and neo-Marxist forms of critical theory (Woodiu 1992). It highlights the active, partisan support for disadvantaged groups in exposing power relations and developing emancipatory action (Kemmis and McTaggart 2000). From this perspective, what is needed is 'a workable "dialogue" between the research community and disabled people in order to facilitate the latter's empowerment' (Barnes 1992: 122).

In practice, participatory approaches include many instructive attempts to overcome the conceptual and practical difficulties in finding common ground between researchers (perhaps from different disciplinary and/or theoretical perspectives) and research participants (Kemmis and McTaggart 2000). These offer some ways forward to some of the key dilemmas confronting emancipatory disability research. For example, how are lay and academic concepts and theories integrated? What happens when disabled people insist on individualistic accounts of disability? (Barnes and Mercer 1997; Moore et al. 1998). Quite simply, the structural constraints and inequalities between researcher and researched are not easily eliminated, and building a trusting relationship is often problematic (Lloyd et al. 1996). The disability literature has also been very reticent to acknowledge power relations and hierarchies within research teams.

Not that all disabled people have the time or inclination, even if politically aware, to take control of research production. A graphic illustration is provided by John Swain's (1995) description of the difficulties he encountered in involving 14–18-year-olds in a newly opened college for students with 'special educational needs' in a disability research project. His experience details a more general experience of disabled participants tending to defer to the 'research experts', particularly in areas perceived as technical matters, such as devising research questions, collecting and analysing data, and disseminating research: 'there was much resistance to the idea that emancipatory research should involve a *reversal* of the social relations of research production' (Priestley 1997: 104). In Priestley's research, his categorization as an 'independent' expert was actually exploited by the disabled people's organization to collect views from service users, as well as in the research dissemination process. Disabled participants attached more weight to building a 'working partnership towards mutually beneficial outcomes' (1997: 104–5).

Participatory research was given a major boost by the intervention of the Joseph Rowntree Foundation (JRF), a major funder of disability research. It now requires that funded projects be located within a social model of disability, include significant and appropriate user involvement, and have a clear potential to improve disabled people's lives. Notable examples include Jenny Morris's (1993) study of community support for disabled people and a series of studies of direct payments building on Gerry Zarb and Pamela Nadash's (1994) influential work. Most recently, the National Lottery's Community Fund has become a major funder of disability research that gives priority to user-led initiatives. Even so, studies with service providers suggest that non-disabled professionals demonstrate considerable reluctance to include disabled people as co-researchers (Moore et al. 1998).

A further claim is that the pioneers of disability theory ignored the diversity of research contexts and participants. This has been raised extensively in studies undertaken with people with learning difficulties, where some of the most imaginative attempts to develop collaborative approaches have been implemented (Ward 1997; Chappell 2000). The absence of researchers with learning difficulties within academic institutions has also been an important factor. The spotlight has been on ways in which researchers (whether non-disabled or disabled) 'take the side' of people with learning difficulties (Goodley and Moore 2000). This has generated a number of inventive methodological approaches, often adopting 'advocacy' models, with people with learning difficulties acting as research advisers through to conducting their own research with some researcher support (People First 1994; Sample 1996; March et al. 1997; Ward 1997; Stalker 1998; Rodgers 1999).

The aim of emancipatory research is to enable participants to take more control of their lives, to a greater or lesser degree. Kirsten Stalker further confirms how research with people with learning difficulties has moved a considerable distance over the last decade towards recognizing them as reliable informants who hold 'valid opinions and have a right to express them' and are the 'best authority on their own lives, experiences, feelings and views' (1998: 5). Nevertheless, barriers to assuming full control remain. There is a tendency towards acquiescence among re-search participants whose lives are routinely controlled by others. This raises basic methodological and ethical questions as to whether all par-ticipants understand and agree to the 'rules of engagement' in the re-search process. Yet even this stage may not be reached, because external bodies such as public service agencies and medical ethics committees take decisions about research participation on behalf of client groups such as people with the label of learning difficulties (Rodgers 1999). Similar presumptions of incapacity have also applied in research with disabled children (Ward 1997).

Another important suggestion is that researchers need to allow for differing degrees of participation, both across issue areas and within specific groups. Jan Walmsley (2001) suggests that collaboration is easier to achieve where the focus is on improving services rather than data analysis or theory generation. A further concern is the importance of making research more accessible. While the use of Braille, large print and cassettes for people with sensory impairments has become more widespread, equivalent support for those with cognitive impairments has been far less widely recognized (Ward 1997; Goodley and Moore 2000).

There are additional barriers to overcome in the employment of dis-abled researchers (Oliver and Barnes 1997; Zarb 1997). The organiza-tion of the research must be more accommodating towards individual researcher support needs, within the context of an inaccessible built environment and transport system. The uncertain trajectory of some impairments adds a further challenge to project management. Funding bodies are not as sensitive as they might be to such constraints in allocating more time and resources for disability research.

The breadth of opinion on the role of the researcher in emancipatory research may be illustrated by two very contrasting standpoints. Tom Shakespeare argues, 'I don't really care' whether my work is rated as 'emancipatory research'. He professes to follow his own 'individual and ethical standards, rather than trying to conform to an orthodoxy' (1997: 185). While welcoming 'advice and feedback', he would not want 'to be accountable to anyone other than my publisher and my conscience' (1997: 186). In contrast, Vic Finkelstein (1999) warns against the emergence of a new breed of disability research 'expert' who will assume the mantle of other 'disabling' professionals unless radical changes are made to the social relations of research production.

Methodology and methods matter

In this discussion, 'methods' comprise the specific techniques for data collection, such as surveys or participant observation, and analysis, while 'methodology' refers to a theory of how research should be conducted (Harding 1987). Early elaboration of emancipatory disability research tended to conflate methods and methodology and to treat both as ancillary, technical matters. The contrary argument underlined here is that 'methodology matters' (Stanley 1997), and requires much more than a vague commitment to pluralism, whether of methodologies or methods.

The methodological criteria advanced for evaluating social research (as opposed to 'retreating' into relativism) vary significantly between paradigms. In positivism, the emphasis is on

> internal validity (isomorphism of findings with reality), external validity (generalisability), reliability (in the sense of stability), and objectivity (distanced and neutral observer)... (while those within the interpretive paradigm stress)... the trustworthiness criteria of credibility (paralleling internal validity), transferability (paralleling external validity), dependability (paralleling reliability), and confirmability (paralleling objectivity).
> (Guba and Lincoln 1994: 114)

More recently, the same authors have supplemented their account by noting the recent concern with achieving 'authenticity' in both interpretive and poststructuralist accounts (Lincoln and Guba 2000).

The broad intention is to make transparent how the research unfolds, from design through data collection, analysis and recommendations. The aim is a transparent and persuasive research narrative that makes the whole process more accountable and understandable to research participants and others (Mies 1983; Stanley and Wise 1993; Maynard 1994).

Nonetheless the application of formal tests of 'quality control' promoted by mainstream research has often hidden disablist assumptions that rarely acknowledge the specific circumstances of researching disability (Sample 1996; Stalker 1998).

For the most part, disability research has concentrated on participant validation: that is, the involvement of disabled people in identifying research questions, collecting data and disseminating findings. The notion of taking field-work data back to respondents for verification is widely regarded as a key marker, whereas collectivizing the whole process of data collection and analysis (except perhaps to a small advisory group) is infrequently practised. Not least, achieving full participation requires additional time and resources if it is to prove effective. Only two of the thirty key activists who provided in-depth interviews for Campbell and Oliver's (1996) study of disability politics took up the offer to 'validate' interview transcripts or read the draft manuscript. Oliver candidly admits that 'we neither had the time, energy or money to make it a wholly collective production' (Oliver 1997: 19). This option may result in substantial changes in the research agenda, and possibly its funding, something institutions are reluctant to sanction.

Another bench-mark has been feminist contentions that the validity of their methods is reflected in the quality of their relationship with participants. Friendliness, openness and general close rapport with participants have acquired a confirmatory status. Researchers record how their disabled participants expressed their appreciation that their views were taken seriously and they were encouraged to express their 'real' feelings (Barnes and Mercer 1997). However, such declarations are imprecise indicators of 'quality assurance'. There are also ethical issues in exploiting an individual's willingness to reveal 'private' thoughts or relationships in order to enhance the 'quality' of the research data. This suggests much greater sensitivity to how researchers directly and indirectly influence the research process (Lloyd et al. 1996; Davies 2000). In practice, the problems of balancing methodological and political goals surface infrequently in the disability literature.

Disability researchers have also demonstrated a willingness to incorporate new approaches to collecting, processing and analysing their data (Barnes and Mercer 1997), including innovative studies with disabled children and people with learning difficulties (Ward 1997). Qualitative disability researchers have particularly stressed the importance of choosing a disabled person as interviewer or the equivalent (Vernon 1997), but little discussion has taken place about how far this matching process should be extended to cover, for example, age, ethnicity, social class and type of impairment.

> Having an impairment does not automatically give someone an affinity
> with disabled people, nor an inclination to do disability research. The
> cultural gulf between researchers and researched has as much to do with
> social indicators like class, education, employment and general life experi-
> ences as with impairments. (Barnes 1992: 121–2)

Notwithstanding if the merits of employing non-disabled researchers are
disputed, it is rare for anyone to contend, like Humphrey (2000), that
research knowledge may be improved by their involvement (providing
they start from a social model baseline), because taken-for-granted ideas
and practices among disabled participants require detailed deconstruction.

There have also been few attempts to involve research participants,
beyond a small advisory committee, in collectivizing the processing and
analysis of data. The exceptions are mainly restricted to small-scale,
interview-based studies, but the enduring impression is that participants
defer to researcher expertise (Vernon 1997). More generally, disciplinary
and theoretical perspectives exacerbate the division between participants
and researchers by influencing what the researcher 'hears' and how it is
interpreted. This includes a decision about how far researchers will go in
re-presenting or 're-authoring' lay accounts by making inferences,
selecting, abstracting and reformulating what people said or 'really
meant' (Shakespeare et al. 1996; Vernon 1997; Corker 1999).

Initially, exponents of emancipatory disability research expressed uncertainty about the relative merits of different quantitative and qualitative research methods. 'I am not sure whether interviews, questionnaires,
participant observation, transcript analysis, etc., are compatible or incompatible with emancipatory research' (Oliver 1997: 21). Subsequently,
the majority has emulated the general trend in social research by utilizing
more qualitative procedures and data. This is justified on the grounds
that quantitative methods are inherently exploitative of research participants and produce less 'authentic' data, in comparison with the qualitative emphasis on inter-subjectivity and non-hierarchical relationships.
Even though there are some notable counter-examples, including Miller
and Gwynne's (1972) much-derided study of life in a residential home, a
generally dismissive attitude to the quantifying method won favour. It
was forcibly expressed by critics of the OPCS surveys, who charged that
reliance on postal questionnaires and structured interviews reinforced the
wide gulf between research expert and lay disabled respondent (Oliver
1990; Abberley 1992).

Nevertheless, mainstream quantitative research has been widely exploited by emancipatory researchers to expose the extent of disabling
barriers (Barnes 1991). Even within feminism, there have been growing

claims that experiential studies have done much less than quantitative studies to document women's social oppression (Oakley 2000). Equally the 'qualitative turn' has been charged with discouraging researchers from devising 'participant-centred' structured interviews and surveys that might facilitate resistance to disabling barriers and attitudes (Kelly et al. 1994; Maynard 1994). In addition, specific methodological issues such as sampling, data processing and constructing concepts and explanations have generated little debate.

As Michele Moore and her colleagues (1998) demonstrate, the process of doing disability research throws up many unexpected issues. One of the most significant is the degree to which presumptions of objectivity and detachment are still prevalent, while familiarity with the counter-assertions of emancipatory disability research remain unknown or contested. Again, disability debates demonstrate too little recognition of the very different sites and contexts in which research is carried out – from personal interviews with a small sample of disabled volunteers to a large-scale study with many organizations involving disabled and non-disabled participants.

Conclusion

The emancipatory paradigm has been adopted as a distinctive approach to doing disability research. This encompasses its ontological and epistemological location in a social model of disability, an associated commitment to a partisan approach in challenging the social exclusion of disabled people, and a broad accountability to disabled people and their organizations. However, these have each attracted criticism from the increasingly diverse theoretical traditions that now engage with disability, while associated issues have been raised about the ease of translating these broad principles into research practice.

There has been a particular silence within the disability research literature on methodological issues, including the appropriateness and merits of specific methods of data collection, processing and analysis. While disability research is full of disclaimers along the lines that 'In the final analysis I would not claim to have accomplished a truly "emancipatory" piece of work' (Priestley 1997: 105), parallel methodological confessions (or declarations) are a rarity.

A final thought on emancipatory disability research surrounds concerns that it is proving 'an impossible dream' (Oliver 1997). Disability research should be judged in terms of its capacity to facilitate the empowerment of disabled people. Certainly, it is not an easy option, with an agreed set of epistemological and methodological guidelines and standards. Equally, the disabling world of social barriers will not easily succumb to individual emancipatory projects. Yet such research has an important part to play in challenging disabling social barriers, particularly where it is unashamedly rigorous and transparent in its methodology and partisan in its objectives.

REFERENCES

Abberley, P. 1992: Counting us out: a discussion of the OPCS disability surveys. *Disability, Handicap and Society,* 7 (2), 139–56.

Barnes, C. 1991: *Disabled People in Britain and Discrimination.* London: Hurst and Co. in association with the British Council of Organisations of Disabled People.

Barnes, C. 1992: Qualitative research: valuable or irrelevant? *Disability, Handicap and Society,* 7 (2), 115–24.

Barnes, C. 1996: Disability and the myth of the independent researcher. *Disability and Society,* 11 (1), 107–10.

Barnes, C. and Mercer, G. (eds) 1997: *Doing Disability Research.* Leeds: Disability Press.

Barnes, C., Mercer, G. and Shakespeare, T. 1999: *Exploring Disability.* Cambridge: Polity.

Becker, H. 1967: Whose side are we on? *Social Problems,* 14, 239–47.

Beresford, P. and Wallcraft, J. 1997: Psychiatric system survivors and emancipatory research: issues, overlaps and differences. In C. Barnes and G. Mercer (eds), *Doing Disability Research,* Leeds: Disability Press, 67–87.

Blaikie, N. 1993: *Approaches to Social Enquiry.* Cambridge: Polity.

Campbell, J. and Oliver, M. 1996: *Disability Politics: Understanding Our Past, Changing Our Future.* London: Routledge.

Chamberlain, J. 1988: *On Our Own.* London: MIND.

Chappell, A. L. 2000: Emergence of participatory methodology in learning difficulty research: understanding the context. *British Journal of Learning Disabilities,* 28, 38–43.

Cocks, E. and Cockram, J. 1995: The participatory research paradigm and intellectual disability. *Mental Handicap Research,* 8, 25–37.

Corker, M. 1999: New disability discourse, the principle of optimisation and social change. In M. Corker and S. French (eds), *Disability Discourses,* Buckingham: Open University Press, 192–209.

Davies, J .M. 2000: Disability studies as ethnographic research and text: research strategies and roles for promoting change? *Disability and Society,* 15 (2), 191–206.

Finkelstein, V. 1999: Doing disability research. *Disability and Society,* 14 (6), 859–67.

Foucault, M. 1984: *The Foucault Reader,* (ed. P. Rabinow.) Harmondsworth: Penguin.

Freire, P. 1972: *Pedagogy of the Oppressed*. Harmondsworth: Penguin.

Goodley, D. and Moore, M. 2000: Doing disability research: activist lives and the academy. *Disability and Society*, 15 (6), 861–82.

Guba, E. G. and Lincoln, Y. S. 1994: Competing paradigms in qualitative research. In N. K. Denzin and Y. S. Lincoln (eds), *The Handbook of Qualitative Research*, Thousand Oaks, CA: Sage, 105–17.

Habermas, J. 1974: *Theory and Practice*, (tr. J. Viertel), London: Heinemann.

Hammersley, M. 2000: *Taking Sides in Social Research*. London: Routledge.

Harding, S. 1987: Introduction: is there a feminist method? In S. Harding (ed.), *Feminism and Methodology: Social Science Issues*, Milton Keynes: Open University Press, 1–14.

Humphrey, J. C. 2000: Researching disability politics, or some problems with the social model in practice. *Disability and Society*, 15 (1), 63–85.

Humphries, B. 1997: From critical thought to emancipatory action: contradictory research goals? *Sociological Research Online*, 2 (1). http :1 / www.socresonline.org.uk/ socresonline /2/ 1/3.html.

Hunt, P. 1981: Settling accounts with the parasite people: a critique of 'A Life Apart' by E. J. Miller and G. V. Gwynne. *Disability Challenge*, 1 (May), 37–50.

Kelly, L., Burton, S. and Regan L. 1994: Researching women's lives or studying women's oppression? Reflections on what constitutes feminist research. In M. Maynard and J. Purvis (eds), *Researching Women's Lives from a Feminist Perspective*, London: Taylor and Francis, 27–48.

Kemmis, S. and McTaggart, T. 2000: Participatory action research. In N. K. Denzin and Y. S. Lincoln (eds), *The Handbook of Qualitative Research*, 2nd edn, Thousand Oaks, CA: Sage, 567–605.

Kincheloe, J. L. and McLaren, P. 2000: Rethinking critical theory and qualitative research. In N. K. Denzin and Y. S. Lincoln (eds), *The Handbook of Qualitative Research*, 2nd edn., Thousand Oaks, CA: Sage, 279–313.

Lather, P. 1991: *Getting Smart: Feminist Research and Pedagogy with/in the Postmodern*. New York: Routledge.

Lincoln, Y. S. and Guba, E. G. 2000: Paradigmatic controversies, contradictions, and emerging confluences. In N. K. Denzin and Y. S. Lincoln (eds), *The Handbook of Qualitative Research*, 2nd edn, Thousand Oaks, CA: Sage, 163–88.

Lloyd, M., Preston-Shoot, M., Temple, B. and Wuu, R. 1996: Whose project is it anyway? Sharing and shaping the research and development agenda. *Disability and Society*, 11 (3), 301–15.

March, J., Steingold, B., Justice, S. and Mitchell, P. 1997: Follow the Yellow Brick Road! People with learning difficulties as co-researchers. *British Journal of Learning Difficulties*, 25, 77–80.

Maynard, M. 1994: Methods, practice and epistemology: the debate about feminism and research. In M. Maynard and J. Purvis (eds), *Researching Women's Lives from a Feminist Perspective*, London: Taylor and Francis, 10–26.

Mies, M. 1983: Towards a methodology for feminist research. In G. Bowles and R. D. Klein (eds), *Theories of Women's Studies*, London: Routledge & Kegan Paul, 117–39.

Miller, E. J. and Gwynne, G. V. 1972: *A Life Apart*. London: Tavistock.

Mills, C. W. 1959: *The Sociological Imagination*. New York: Oxford University Press.

Moore, M., Beazley, S. and Maelzer, J. 1998: *Researching Disability Issues*. Buckingham: Open University Press.

Morris, J. 1992: Personal and political: a feminist perspective on researching physical disability. *Disability, Handicap and Society*, 7 (2), 157–66.

Morris, J. 1993: *Independent Lives? Community Care and Disabled People*. Basingstoke: Macmillan.

Oakley, A. 2000: *Experiments in Knowing: Gender and Method in the Social Sciences*. Cambridge: Polity.

Oliver, M. 1990: *The Politics of Disablement*. Basingstoke: Macmillan.

Oliver, M. 1992: Changing the social relations of research production? *Disability, Handicap and Society*, 7(2), 101–14.

Oliver, M. 1997: Emancipatory research: realistic goal or impossible dream? In C. Barnes and G. Mercer (eds), *Doing Disability Research*, Leeds: Disability Press, 15–31.

Oliver, M. and Barnes, C. 1997: All we are saying is give disabled researchers a chance. *Disability and Society*, 12 (5), 811–13.

Oliver, M. et al. 1988: *Walking into Darkness*. Basingstoke: Macmillan.

People First 1994: *Outside Not Inside...Yet*. London: People First London Boroughs.

Priestley, M. 1997: Who's research? A personal audit. In C. Barnes and G. Mercer (eds), *Doing Disability Research*. Leeds: Disability Press, 88–107.

Reason, P. (ed.) 1988: *Human Inquiry in Action: Developments in New Paradigm Research*. London: Sage.

Rioux, M. and Bach, M. (eds) 1994: *Disability is not Measles: New Research Paradigms in Disability*. Ontario: Roeher Institute.

Rodgers, J. 1999: Trying to get it right: undertaking research involving people with learning difficulties. *Disability and Society*, 14 (4), 421–33.

Sample, P. L. 1996: Beginnings: participatory action research and adults with developmental disabilities. *Disability and Society*, 11 (3), 317–22.

Schwandt, T. A. 1994: Constructivist, interpretivist approaches to human inquiry. In N. K. Denzin and Y. S. Lincoln (eds), *The Handbook of Qualitative Research*, Thousand Oaks, CA: Sage, 118–37.

Shakespeare, T. 1996: Rules of engagement. *Disability and Society*, 11 (1), 115–20.

Shakespeare, T. 1997: Researching disabled sexuality. In C. Barnes and G. Mercer (eds), *Doing Disability Research*, Leeds: Disability Press, 177–89.

Shakespeare, T., Gillespie-Sells, K. and Davies, D. 1996: *The Sexual Politics of Disability: Untold Desires*. London: Cassell.

Skeggs, B. 1995: Introduction to B. Skeggs (ed.), *Feminist Cultural Theory: Process and Production*, Manchester: Manchester University Press, 1–29.

Smith, M. J. 1998: *Social Science in Question*. London: Sage / Open University.

Stalker, K. 1998: Some ethical and methodological issues in research with people with learning difficulties. *Disability and Society*, 13 (1), 5–19.

Stanley, L. 1997: Methodology matters! In V. Robinson and D. Richardson (eds), *Introducing Women's Studies*, London: Macmillan, 198–219.

Stanley, L. and Wise, S. 1993: *Breaking Out Again: Feminist Ontology and Epistemology*. London: Routledge.

Stone, E. 1997: From the research notes of a foreign devil: disability research in China. In C. Barnes and G. Mercer (eds), *Doing Disability Research*, Leeds: Disability Press, 207–27.

Stone, E. and Priestley, M. 1996: Parasites, pawns and partners: disability research and the role of non-disabled researchers. *British Journal of Sociology*, 47 (4), 699–716.

Swain, J. 1995: Constructing participatory research: in principle and in practice. In P. Clough and L. Barton (eds), *Making Difficulties: Research and the Construction of Special Educational Needs*, London: Paul Chapman Publishing Ltd, 75–93.

Touraine, A. 1981: *The Voice and the Eye: An Analysis of Social Movements*. Cambridge: Cambridge University Press.

UPIAS 1976: *Fundamental Principles of Disability*. London: Union of the Physically Impaired Against Segregation.

Vernon, A. 1997: Reflexivity: the dilemmas of researching from the inside. In C. Barnes and G. Mercer (eds), *Doing Disability Research*, Leeds: Disability Press, 158–76.

Walmsley, J. 2001: Normalisation, emancipatory research and inclusive research in learning disability. *Disability and Society*, 16 (2), 187–205.

Ward, L. 1997: Funding for change: translating emancipatory disability research from theory to practice. In C. Barnes and G. Mercer (eds), *Doing Disability Research*, Leeds: Disability Press, 32–48.

Woodill, G. 1992: *Independent Living and Participation in Research: A Critical Analysis*. Toronto: Centre for Independent Living in Toronto.

Zarb, G. 1992: On the road to Damascus: first steps towards changing the relations of research production. *Disability, Handicap and Society*, 7(2), 125–38.

Zarb, G. 1997: Researching disabling barriers. In C. Barnes and G. Mercer (eds), *Doing Disability Research*, Leeds: Disability Press, 49–66.

Zarb, G. and Nadash, P. 1994: *Cashing in on Independence*. Derby: British Council of Disabled People.

13

Disability, the Academy and the Inclusive Society

Colin Barnes, Mike Oliver and Len Barton

Introduction

In the introduction to this book we described the ways in which the protracted interface between the emergent disabled people's movement and the academy helped stimulate the development of disability studies in Britain and the United States in the last decades of the twentieth century. Subsequent chapters have provided a broad overview of the current state of knowledge within the context of this relatively new field of inquiry, with particular emphasis on sociological influences. In this concluding chapter we examine this relationship analytically, in order to explain how this particular form of knowledge production might continue to contribute to our understanding of disability and, in so doing, help work toward the further inclusion of disabled people in mainstream society.

Disability studies and the academy in the twenty-first century

When considering the relationship between political activism and the academy in the main, it is apparent that for most of its history the university has been a locus of quiet conservatism, rather than a force for radical social and political change. However, it is easy to forget that at certain times and under specific conditions, the academy has played a key role in the germination and nurturing of revolutionary social forces that, when unleashed, have the potential for radical political and cultural change. Examples include European universities and the revolutionary movements of the 1840s and 1960s, American campuses and the civil rights and anti-Vietnam War campaigns of the 1960s and 1970s. Finally, the academy played a key role in the Cultural Revolution in the People's Republic of China in the 1980s, culminating in the massacre at Tiananmen Square on 4 June 1989.

These examples notwithstanding, the fact remains that by and large the academy has been a reactionary, rather than a radical, political force for most of its history. However, as we have moved into the twenty-first century, it has been argued that we are seeing far-reaching changes not just in the role and organization of the university, but in the nature of knowledge production itself:

> What is occurring today in our post-industrial society is a crisis not only in the structure of authority and in the cognitive structures of society as was the case a few decades ago but in the very constitution of knowledge as a result of the extension of democracy into knowledge itself. (Delanty 2001: 2)

As several contributors to this volume have made clear, a central driving force in the development of disability studies has been the insistence by disabled people that their experiences be properly incorporated. This may be interpreted as an extension of democracy into the academic production of knowledge about disability. Accordingly, 'The university in the age of mass education has been a major site for the articulation of democratic and progressive values, for instance of racial equality, human rights, feminism and social democracy' (Delanty 2001: 9). Indeed, in the late twentieth century new social movements emerged, notably with reference to women, people from minority ethnic groups, gay men and lesbians and, latterly, disabled people, and their intellectual heart has often beaten, and continues to beat, within academic institutions.

Furthermore, many of those involved in the production of what at the time seemed new and radical ideas worked in universities and colleges. As we have seen throughout this book, this has certainly been the case with disability studies, where there has been a fusion between the everyday struggles of disabled people and the scholarly work produced by disabled and non-disabled academics. The outcome of this symbiotic relationship has been twofold. First, disability studies has developed as an academic discipline in its own right, based upon the direct experience of disablement. Second, the links between disabled people and disability studies have been maintained.

However, the precise nature of these links is becoming increasingly problematic, as both the movement grows in strength and disability studies becomes more popular as a legitimate field of inquiry. Again, Delanty makes this point in respect of knowledge production generally: 'With.... the coming of new politics, the university has become a major site of battles of cultural identity, confrontations which have had major repercussions for the very meaning of discipline-based knowledge as well as historically informed canon' (Delanty 2001: 4). Such conflicts have seen disability studies challenge the traditional disciplines of medicine, sociology and psychology with regard to the legitimacy of the knowledge they have produced about disability. Not only that, but the relationship between the disability movement, as the producer and transformer of a cohesive understanding of the collective experience of disability, and the academy, as the producer and arbiter of all forms of knowledge about impairment and disability, has also come under scrutiny. It is to this relationship that we now turn.

The disability movement and the academy

In conceptualizing the relationship between the academy and the disability movement, it is possible to identify three different approaches. The first, which we will call the 'inside-out' approach, derives from the women's movement, and is based upon the argument that the personal is political (Morris 1991). It argues that direct experience of a phenomenon is essential not only for facilitating an understanding of it, but also for developing an appropriate political response. In some of the more extreme versions it is suggested that only those with direct experience are entitled to speak about it: only women can speak about women's experiences; only black people can speak about the black experience; only disabled people about the disability experience, and so on.

Thus, we see within the British disabled people's movement that some groups are comprised solely of disabled people, both as individual members and as salaried employees. Others take slightly different positions in respect of non-disabled allies, as they have come to be called. Some will not admit non-disabled people as members, but will employ them as staff, and other groups will admit non-disabled people to all areas of the organization, as long as disabled people remain in control (Morgan et al. 2001a). In sum, there is no one universal position on how the relationship between experience and the movement should be constructed. The same is true of the way in which disability studies is taught and researched within the university. The relationship between experience and scholarship is constructed differently between different universities and the individuals and groups concerned (Pfeiffer and Yoshida 1995; Gordon and Rosenblum 2001; Albrecht et al. 2001).

There are a number of problems with the inside-out standpoint. To begin with, it can take a position of exclusivity that can result in the marginalization of the group concerned. Most groups recognize this, and while they may have a separatist element or wing, they none the less attempt to build relationships with the rest of the world. Additionally, as noted above, the inside-out approach ultimately reduces experience entirely to the individual level, rendering the prospect of producing meaningful analyses based on collective insights almost impossible. Finally, positions based exclusively on direct experience can often come across as special pleading – leading to the kind of experience-based work which has been characterized as the 'true confessions brigade': that of '[t]hose intent on writing about themselves rather than engaging in serious political analysis of a society that is inherently disabling' (Barnes 1998: 146).

Our second approach is the 'outside-in' position. This emerged from some groups of disabled people themselves, partly because of the way in which direct experience has sometimes been over-privileged, and even over-sentimentalized. It has recently been trenchantly restated by Vic Finkelstein:

> The political and cultural vision inspired by the new focus on dismantling the real disabling barriers 'out there' has been progressively eroded and turned inward into contemplative and abstract concerns about the subjective experiences of the disabling world. (Finkelstein 1996: 34)

This outside-in stance does not deny the importance of direct experience, but suggests that, by itself, it is not enough. In this context Finkelstein argues that while the direct experience of disabling barriers (inside) is important, it has to be wedded to a political analysis (outside) of why these barriers exist and how to eradicate them. This is precisely why the relationship between the academy and the disability movement is so important; whilst the movement can provide direct experience, the academy can provide a coherent, scholarly political analysis. Therefore, what is at stake is not whether such a relationship should be constituted, but how it should be constituted and maintained.

Again there are some difficulties with this approach. Carol Thomas (1999), for example, has recently argued that this perspective fails to take account of the achievements of groups like the women's movement, which has rooted the bulk of its activities in 'the personal is political' standpoint. Further, she suggests that it is structured upon an erroneous separation of the private and public spheres that is no longer tenable in the postmodern world of the twenty-first century. Finally, she suggests that the solution to this problem is to write oneself into the picture – that is, to be explicit about the relationship between subjective experience (inside) and objective action in the wider world (outside).

The third approach is that of 'outside-out', and is the one favoured by most accredited experts of all kinds, including academics. It has its origins in the nineteenth century and the development of positivism as a world-view. Central to this is the assertion that the social world can be properly understood only through the application of the principles of rational thought and the natural sciences (Giddens 2001), and not by building upon personal experience as the two previous positions discussed would suggest. The outside-out position is the one that has sustained the academy throughout its existence. As a consequence, most universities and colleges have constructed themselves as organizations devoted almost exclusively to the pursuit of objective knowledge. However, in recent years this approach has increasingly come under attack. In response, many academic institutions and subject disciplines are now trying to incorporate direct experience into their work (Truman et al. 2000).

Nevertheless, in many respects these attempts still seek to justify and sustain the position of the academy as ultimate arbiter of what counts as meaningful knowledge; trying to both have your cake and eat it, so to speak. A classic example is the recent work of Martin Hammersley (1995, 2000), who, while providing a detailed appraisal of research based upon the other two positions, suggests that, ultimately, it is the role of the academic researcher to produce knowledge through the operationalization of objective research procedures. A further example is Alan Dyson, who calls himself a professional intellectual, rather than a positivist. He has recently argued that the academy has a role to play as 'instigator and sustainer of rational debate' between the insider and outsider positions (Dyson 1999).

This outside-out perspective also gives rise to a number of difficulties: not least that this is precisely the position the academy has adopted for most of its history. This, as we have already suggested, is one of reaction and conservatism. In seeking, at this juncture, to take direct experience seriously, we would suggest that many academics and researchers are in serious danger of doing what they have always done – that is, colonize and reproduce in a less radical form the work, ideas and experience of others. For this reason we suggest that attempts to build meaningful working and fruitful relationships between the academy and disabled people and their organizations based on the outside-out position should be treated with the utmost caution.

Disability studies and the inclusive society

Based on the above analysis, it is possible to suggest that the orthodoxy of the outside-out position is no longer sustainable. There are several reasons for this. To begin with, in the postmodern world, knowledge is becoming much more diffused throughout society, and the university is no longer the only, or even the most important, producer of what counts as useful or meaningful knowledge (Castells 1996). Additionally, the conventional symbiosis between the state and the academy is breaking down. This is especially evident with the insidious encroachment of market forces into academic life. Lastly, with the rise of new social movements we have seen a gradual challenge to the right of the academy to decide what counts for knowledge. All this means that 'the central task of the university in the twenty first century is to become the key actor in the public sphere and thereby enhance the democratization of knowledge' (Delanty 2001: 9). Furthermore, 'In organized modernity the university was important in shaping social citizenship; today it has the additional task of cultivating technological and cultural forms of citizenship' (Delanty 2001: 10).

In light of the above, it may be argued from a disability rights perspective that, since the university has failed to shape social citizenship, we cannot be confident that it will perform adequately the extra task of nurturing technological and cultural citizenship. However, we do not accept this rather pessimistic view. As the contributors to this book have shown, our knowledge and understanding of the complexity of the experience of disability has been greatly enhanced by the symbiotic relationship between disabled people and the academy, whether that relationship has been constructed from an outside-in or an inside-out position. Equally, we remain optimistic that this relationship will flourish and grow under the changing conditions of postmodernity, especially given the relatively firm base upon which it now rests. As a consequence, we would expect the body of knowledge concerning the nature of disability to continue to grow and, in turn, help facilitate the further inclusion of disabled people into the mainstream of society. It goes without saying, of course, that the disability movement needs to grow in strength too.

The academy and postmodernity

There is little doubt that if the links between the academy and the disabled community are to continue to be mutually beneficial, then academics and researchers must be actively involved with disabled people and their organizations on a continuous basis. But the intensifying marketization of academic life means that establishing and maintaining protracted involvement with grass-roots organizations is increasingly difficult. Indeed, the increasing impact of economic rationality within the academy is a major cause for concern. Since the mid-1990s there has been a growing emphasis on issues of economic viability, fiscal relevance and competition that have their roots in business interests and thinking. There is little doubt that this has contributed to an increasing emphasis on assessment-led learning and the vocationalizing of scholarship. Forms of managerialism are also developing that have little interest in critical theory or political analysis. In a recent discussion of the impact of globalization and market priorities on academic activities, Simon (2001) maintains that such forces have brought into question the very nature of what constitutes critical thought in university life. The extent to which we can still speak about the transformative capacity of intellectual endeavour is one that needs to be urgently and seriously addressed.

This has particular significance in relation to disability studies in terms of the dangers of becoming incorporated into these burgeoning institutional processes and demands. We have already seen the deradicalization of much that now passes for sociology, and even the transformative potential of specific disciplines such as feminism and black studies is now being called into question (hooks 1984; Sheldon 1999). Accordingly, disability studies needs to be wary of incorporation, as it has already attracted its fair share of criticism from disability activists in the USA (Linton 1998) and in the UK (GMCDP 2000).

The combination of heightened teaching, research and administrative responsibilities within most universities and colleges means that, all too often, academics and researchers have little time to be actively involved in 'non-academic' activities such as attending local group meetings on a regular basis, for example. Furthermore, historically, academics generally have been seen as part of the problem rather than the solution within the disabled people's movement. Consequently, many organizations have neither the inclination nor the resources to pay for academic involvement. The situation is exacerbated further by the growing sense of 'research fatigue' amongst disabled people and their organizations, as a direct result of the increased attention paid to them by academics and researchers over recent years (Morgan et al. 2001b).

None the less, in our view, universities and colleges are likely to remain the seed-beds for tomorrow's politicians and policy makers. Therefore it is important that disabled people's perspectives be properly represented within the academy – notwithstanding that the more mainstream disability studies becomes, the more attention it is likely to attract from scholars of the 'outside-out' persuasion, many of whom, for a variety of reasons, see their primary role as problematizing what need not necessarily be problematic. Hence, exponents of disability studies are inevitably drawn into seemingly ever more complex and tedious debates that become in many ways almost unrecognizable to those without any kind of formal academic training. This is a problem for many disabled people, as they have only a limited access to education, and higher education in particular (Hurst 1998). As we have already argued, it is essential that the relationship between the disability movement and the academy continue to develop if we are to ensure that the disability studies agenda will reflect the issues and concerns of disabled people and their organizations.

However, whilst all of this may be viewed as 'healthy', since it heightens the level of scholarly debate and dialogue, both inside and outside the university, it poses particular problems for those of us trying to communicate effectively with both. As discussed by Geof Mercer in chapter 12, researchers have raised several important issues when trying to balance the demands of an 'emancipatory' disability research agenda with those of the academy. Besides compounding the distance between academics and the general public, these considerations can effectively neutralize the political implications of a disability studies perspective, in much the same way that feminism has been neutralized within British and American universities over the last couple of decades.

It is worth noting too that the status and income generally associated with university life has the added risk of seducing academics into thinking that their views are more important than they really are. Here, it is useful to remember that one definition of the word 'academic' is 'of theoretical interest only, with no practical application'. If this is what disability studies is to become, then there is no doubt in our minds that we have failed those who brought us here: disabled people and their organizations.

Personal reflections

Nevertheless, the extent to which we have been, or can continue to be, effective in building relationships between disabled people and the academy in our work is questionable. That work is often uneven in both quality and impact. Nor can we claim that 'emancipatory principles' are easily demonstrable in the work already produced. We see these as ideals towards which we are, and should be, aspiring, and which are, and should be, subject to change during the ongoing process of engagement.

However, the securing and maintenance of constructive dialogue with disabled people, both at the individual and the collective levels, presents ongoing problems. The extent to which interactions are founded on reciprocity, trust and respect demonstrates that much more needs to be done. Establishing mutually beneficial relationships with disabled scholars is one thing, achieving them with grass-roots disability activists or disabled people with little or no interest in disability issues and concerns is a far more onerous enterprise.

Indeed, one of our greatest difficulties concerns the growing dilemma emanating from the demands and tensions of writing for both an academic and a lay audience. It involves issues of accessibility, values and purpose of writing, and also the regulatory influence of the academic role. Our very positions, titles and the growing demands of satisfying peer reviewers, the results of which involve status and money at an individual, departmental and university level, means that we are legitimators of that which we seek to critique. Within the academic community this is a divisive process (see, e.g., Barnes 1996; Bury 1996; Shakespeare 1996). All of which can only serve to exacerbate the fragile relationship between representatives of the academic and non-academic communities.

Perhaps it is fitting that the final word on this subject comes from a disabled woman activist: Penny Germon, writing about activists and academics. She states:

> It would seem that thus far the academic and research agenda and how far it is useful to activists has been to a large degree left to chance and the personal integrity of the individuals concerned. Consequently channels of communication and accountability remain ambiguous and unexplored. There is a need to develop a meaningful structure for debate and analysis which brings together academics and activists, which reflects a wide range of perspectives and which is open and accountable to the wider movement. Inevitably this will involve us in discussions about *how* we facilitate debate which is encouraging and supportive whilst also providing opportunity to develop, to learn, to challenge and to disagree. This will mean creating different fora and using different media and engaging in sustained development work. (Germon 1998: 254)

We would argue that, to achieve this formidable but desirable goal, a disability studies perspective must continue to support and develop the outside-in approach to disability scholarship and research. Failure to do so will almost certainly result in the fracturing of the tenuous link between the disabled community and the academy. It is our firm belief that this would be a tragedy for all concerned.

Final comment

Whilst the primary focus of attention in this chapter has been on disability studies, the questions raised also have important implications for the status, purpose and outcomes of sociological inquiry in the postmodern world, as well as for the institutions in which it takes place. It is our conviction that addressing such challenges is essential if both disability studies and sociological analysis are to continue to play a significant and meaningful part in the realization of an all-inclusive society in which disabled people are able to participate fully, irrespective of the nature of their impairment, age, gender, ethnicity, social class or sexual persuasion.

References

Albrecht, G. L., Seelman, K. D. and Bury, M. 2001: *The Disability Studies Handbook*. London: Sage.
Barnes, C. 1996: Disability and the myth of the independent researcher. *Disability and Society*, 11 (1), 110–13.
Barnes, C. 1998: The rejected body: a review. *Disability and Society*, 13, 145–46.
Bury, M. 1996: Disability and the myth of the independent researcher: a reply. *Disability and Society* 13 (1), 145–6.
Castells, M. 1996: *The Information Age: Economy, Society and Culture*, vol. 1: *The Rise of the Network Society*. Malden, MA: Blackwell Publishers Inc.
Delanty, G. 2001: *Challenging Knowledge: The University in the Knowledge Society*. Buckingham: Open University Press.
Dyson, A. 1999: Professional intellectuals from powerful groups: wrong from the start? In P. Clough and L. Barton (eds), *Articulating with Difficulty: Research Voices in Inclusive Education*, London: Paul Chapman Publishing, 1–15.
Finkelstein, V. 1996: Outside 'inside out'. *Coalition*, April, 30–6.
Germon, P. 1998: Activists and academics: part of the same or a world apart? In T. Shakespeare (ed.), *The Disability Reader: Social Science Perspectives*, London: Cassell, 245–55.
Giddens, A. 2001: *Sociology*, 4th edn, Cambridge: Polity.
GMCDP 2000: *Coalition: Special Issue: Where Have all the Activists Gone?* Manchester: Greater Manchester Coalition of Disabled People, August.
Gordon, B. O. and Rosenblum, K. E. 2001: Bringing disability into the sociological frame: a comparison with disability, race, sex and sexual orientation statuses. *Disability and Society*, 16 (1), 5–19.
Hammersley, M. 1995: *The Politics of Social Research*. London: Sage.
Hammersley, M. 2000: *Taking Sides in Social Research*. London: Routledge.
hooks, b. 1984: *Feminist Theory: From Margin to Centre*, Boston: South End Press.

Hurst, A. 1998: *Higher Education and Disabilities: International Perspectives.* Aldershot: Avebury Press.

Linton, S. 1998: *Claiming Disability: Knowledge and Identity.* New York: New York University Press.

Morgan, H., Barnes, C. and Mercer, G. 2001a: *Creating Independent Futures: An Evaluation of Services led by Disabled People, Stage Two Report.* Leeds: Disability Press.

Morgan, H., Barnes, C. and Mercer, G. 2001b: *Creating Independent Futures: An Evaluation of Services led by Disabled People, Stage Three Report.* Leeds: Disability Press.

Morris, J. 1991: *Pride against Prejudice.* London: Women's Press.

Pfeiffer, D. and Yoshida, K. 1995: Teaching disability studies in Canada and the USA. *Disability and Society,* 10 (4), 475–500.

Shakespeare, T. 1996: Rules of engagement: doing disability research. *Disability and Society,* 11 (1), 115–19.

Sheldon, A. 1999: Personal and perplexing: feminist disability politics evaluated. *Disability and Society,* special issue: *Theory and Experience,* 14 (5), 643–58.

Simon, R. 2001: The university: a place to think. In H. Giroux and K. Myrsiades (eds), *Beyond the Corporate University,* Oxford: Roman and Littlefield, 45–56.

Thomas, C. 1999: *Female Forms.* Buckingham: Open University Press.

Truman, C., Mertens, D. M. and Humphries, B. (eds) 2000: *Research and Inequality.* London: UCL Press.

Index

Abberley, Paul: impairment 52;
industrialization 193;
Marxism 126–8;
occupational therapists 129;
Office of Populations, Censuses
and Surveys 244;
oppression 12, 68;
psychological adjustment 165;
work/inclusion 133
Abbott, Andrew 27
abnormality 62
abortion 135
Abu-Habib, L. 78
academy: activism 7, 250–1, 258;
disability movement 252–4, 258;
disability politics 147–8;
disability studies 5–8, 53,
250–1, 254; identity 252;
market forces 256; new social
movements 151;
postmodernism 255–7
accessibility 25, 71, 134, 222
accountability 238–9
activism: academy 7, 250–1, 258;
disability 4, 5; disability
movement 147;
disability politics 65–6, 139;
disability studies 2, 256
Adam, B. 66

ADAPT (Americans Disabled for
Accessible Public
Transportation) 79, 167–8
advocacy models 241
aesthetic judgements 70, 73, 125
age 53, 83, 156; see also elderly
Ahmad, W. I. V. 80–1
Albrecht, Gary L.: consumers 32;
disability awareness 18;
The Disability Business 31;
disability studies 1, 8, 19, 253;
identity 30; pragmatism 9;
quality of life ratings 176;
societal perspective 31; *The
Sociology of Physical Disability and
Rehabilitation* 4
Alcock, P. 77–8
alienation 71; see also exclusion
Altman, Barbara M. 19, 26
American Public Transit
Association 167–8
American Sociological Association 26
American Sociological Review 24
Americans with Disabilities Act
(1990) 152, 163, 171, 185;
accessibility 222; cohesion 30–1;
Hahn 13, 171; resistance to 13,
181; Zola 29
Anderson, J. 110

272 *Index*